PRAISE

"Turning Pink is an astounding story of faith, miracles, heartache and joy as God moves in the details of our lives. With brutal honesty, Sherrie Gavin addresses the challenges of womanhood, of motherhood and of the miracle of our families and the love which binds us together. Miracles still happen today! A must read!"

—Cory Jensen, author of *Understanding Your Endowment* and *Completing Your Endowment*

"Have a box of tissues close at hand when you read Sherrie Gavin's heartfelt memoir of fierce and thoughtful motherhood. If your life has ever been touched by adoption (and whose hasn't?), you're going to love this riveting chronicle of becoming parents by choice, through all the trials and the triumphs."

—Jana Riess, author of *Flunking Sainthood*; senior columnist for *Religion News Service*

"Sherrie Gavin's remarkable story of infertility and adoptive motherhood is both fragile and fierce; both holy and harrowing. Her instinctive goodness and humility radiate from every scene. If she weren't on the other side of the globe with her beloved spouse and girls, I would hug her to bits."

—Linda Hoffman Kimball, boardmember of *Dialogue* and *Segullah*

TURNING PINK

For information contact:

>By Common Consent Press
>4062 South Evelyn Drive
>Salt Lake City, UT
>84124-2250

Cover design: D. Christian Harrison
Book design: Braxtyn Birrell

bccpress.org

ISBN-13: 978-1-961471-27-6

10 9 8 7 6 5 4 3 2 1

SHERRIE GAVIN

TURNING PINK

An American & Australian Memoir

DEDICATION

For Bruce, Cheyenne, and Elizabeth. I love you more than words could ever say.

This is also for women. Women who have fought with their hearts in pursuit of dreams, including education, work, and family, and especially for those who knew when to say, "I am enough as I am."

Thank you to all who supported me and whom I have written about within these pages. It was with your love and encouragement that this book came to fruition, especially Piper Anderson, April Young Bennett, Alisa Bolander, Libby Potter Boss, Becky Brouwer, Emily Clyde Curtis, Leslie Drew, Mali Dunbar, Heather Moore-Farley, Loraine Hawthorne, Aimee Evans Hickman, Sariah Kell, Caroline Kline, Linda Hoffman Kimball, Deborah Kris, Sandra Lee, Kathryn Ann Olsen, Aggy Ozlanski, Emily Gilkey Palmer, Amy Parkin, Meghan Raynes-Matthews, Rachel Hunt Steenblik, Heather Sundahl, Georgia Beth Thompson, Zoia Tui, Mandy Watene, Heather Weller, Kathryn Wells, Brooke Williams, and the past and present women of *Exponent II*.

I am also deeply grateful to the glorious team at BCC Press, especially Heidi Naylor, the brilliant Emily Wheeler of *The Writer's Cache* and my Segullah sisters, Shari Crall and Lisa Meadows Garfield, beloved thanks for your sharp eyes. Lastly, my Chi Sigma Upsilon and Zeta Tau Alpha sisters who continue to teach me how to be a better person through their examples.

AUTHOR'S NOTE

Please understand that this book is based on my experience. With this in mind and for the privacy of the children, I have omitted many of the signs, markings, and retellings of abuse that were experienced by the children. They and others have the right to share information about their own minds and bodies and are explicitly in charge of any information that is shared about their bodies. Thus, the few experiences that included a fraction of the harm experienced by the children were done so with their explicit permission.

INTRODUCTION

It was a bright February morning in Brisbane, Australia. The end of summer painted my fruit trees with lemons, blood oranges, and key limes, creating a luscious burst of happy colours against the shamrock-green leaf-covered boughs. The scent of lemon myrtle from the trees that lined the side of the house made the air smell alive. I had walked the dog, washed the dishes, and was about to settle into the day's tasks when the phone rang.

"I shouldn't have called. But… Oh, no…" The voice at the other end was familiar, and I knew it was Robin. "But… I just… I shouldn't have called…" she continued speaking in her typical, breathy way, but with an edge of anxiety. For her to sound so rattled was uncommon, concerning me.

"But I just… I'm too old. I think. I don't know. I hoped…" she said, sighing.

"Are you okay?" I asked.

"Oh! Yes. But… Oh, I'm not sure I should have called…" Puzzled by her uneasiness, I remained quiet, not sure what to think or say. "I just know of this family," she finally explained. "And they are looking for a home for two girls. I think they are only little, about two and three years old."

My back stiffened and I instantly distanced myself. For the last decade, many of my sweet yet ignorant friends would tell me of rumours and miraculous stories they had "heard" about children being "put up" for adoption. I was very surprised that Robin, someone I had comisserated with about this, would call me with what sounded like the adoption version of a "get rich quick" scheme.

I took a breath. Bruce was away on a business trip, and it was nice to hear a friend's voice, so I reconsidered my "no thanks" reflex, and tabled my snarky, "we prefer to obey the state laws regarding adoption" responses. I finally said, "Of course we're interested, but the laws for adoption—"

"*I know,*" she interrupted, then firmly said, "I know." After a pause, she continued, "The Lord works miracles. I don't know how it will work. But He works miracles."

I hesitated, then threw my heart into the wind. "You're right. Can't hurt to think about it. Tell me more."

1

MATCHES MADE IN HEAVEN

At the time of Robin's phone call, Bruce and I were only a few weeks away from celebrating our tenth wedding anniversary. We met when I came to Australia for an internship that lasted three weeks. My supervisor suggested that I enjoy some free time in Australia, and because I was on a student budget, he arranged for me to stay with his friend, Bruce. Bruce had recently moved in with his parents to finish his degree, so they would be there, and I would have the guest room to myself. That suited me perfectly.

One of the first places Bruce took me in Australia was a petting zoo where I could hand feed kangaroos. *Check!* Vegemite? Pretty salty. I liked it. After I met Bruce, I added one more thing to my list: kiss an Australian guy. *Check!* I really enjoyed Bruce's company, and because I was only there temporarily, I was totally myself, fearing no social or future fertility pressure from admitting that I had been diabetic since I was a toddler.

In my experience, the topic of children came up quickly when dating Mormon men. Through my teens and twenties, I often recalled the words of one of my very wise Young Women leaders, spoken to me when I was seventeen and confessed that I was unlikely to ever be pregnant. Without hesitation she said, "You're lucky. When you marry, you will know he really loves you, not just because of your body." Her prophetic words liberated me from seeing my body as a non-sexual dating commodity. But in a church that socially and even doctrinally teaches that the highest potential for women is motherhood, a woman's ability to give physical birth can lay severe judgement upon women's bodies and perceived righteousness.

One man sincerely told me on the first date that he wanted twelve children, and he had five girls' names picked out already. As he began listing the names, I recalled homework I needed to attend to immediately. I was asked by another if I could have children, on the second date. I jokingly responded that I was "not currently having sex and I am not righteous enough for Immaculate Conception, so no, I can't have children at this second." He laughed at my redirection, but I quickly refused any further dates with him.

Another returned missionary told me that the most important thing to him, marriage-wise, was to "find someone who would be a good mother to my children." It was a righteous way to look at dating, and I was intrigued. "What if you needed to adopt?"

I tested him, hoping for something encouraging. "I think it would be okay to adopt, after I have some of my own children first," he responded with a shrug. Clearly biological children were preferential to him, yet I pressed on. "But what if your wife is infertile and can't have children?" He looked at me seriously. "I would give her a blessing," he said. "Then she could have children." I thought this response was laughable, but I held my tongue and moved on.

Over the years, I dated several quality Mormon men who were open to non-traditional parenthood. But more often than not, I sensed that they felt sorry for me. Pity is not romantic. I found solace in the temple. Embracing the blessings pronounced in the initiatory session, I felt whole: whole as a person, as a woman, as a daughter of God. It was through this that I grew to be grateful for my body and all of the mortal flaws that are mine to manage. I was invigorated with the symbolism of the temple and sought rich interpretations that might not match someone else's thoughts but worked for me. Profoundly, I found peace. In my rented white tent of a dress, I felt like I was a welcomed part of something that was greater than anything I could otherwise imagine.

By the time I met Bruce, I was nearing 30 years old and confident enough to be very picky with men. Bruce was different, in a good way. A very good way, and I liked him. I really liked him! In staying with him and his parents, I quickly learned that his older brother was married to a woman from China. Testing the waters, I said, "Oh? I've always wanted to adopt from China." Within seconds, we were talking about the future, family and more. "I think we should adopt from China," said Bruce. "They'll match the rest of the family." Shortly thereafter, we married. I designed our wedding rings, where I chose the Egyptian hieroglyphic symbol for *protection*. In Bruce, I finally felt protected. I knew he loved me for me. And for him, family was not limited to biology. I'd met my match. In every way.

Bruce and I settled in Sydney and quickly began to unravel the complications of adoption. He was working full time, and because I had difficulty finding work, I worked various part-time jobs and side hustles. We knew that creating a family when navigating infertility was expensive, so we scrimped and saved as much as we could. Some weeks, if we had not met our goal of saving the money we had hoped, I would abstain from breakfast and lunch every second day of the following week, keeping my fasting a secret from everyone around me, including Bruce. Like many other infertile women, I blamed myself for being unable to become pregnant. Bruce never seemed bothered by this part of me, but a hidden sense of worthlessness still haunted me, more than I liked to admit. Yet I was determined, so I always began and ended this self-imposed fasting with a prayer, which added an influx of spirituality to my daily life, even if partly starving myself was a little reckless.

As Australian residents, we needed to abide by Australian law. Because Australia and the United States do not have an adoption agreement, we would not be able to adopt from the U.S., so that was off the table. Australian adoption is entirely government-based and private adoption is illegal. With my love of history, I wanted to know why this was the case. I found that starting in the mid-1800s, colonial Australian governments set up infant asylums, where unmarried pregnant women could go, give birth, and leave the infant until the mother married or found work and ideally, but very rarely, returned to retrieve the child. Some infant asylums also enlisted a "basket system" wherein newborns were anonymously left in a basket, with the intention of being placed for adoption. And just as in England, mid-nineteenth century Australia had "baby farms." Impoverished parents placed their children and babies in these "baby farms" and were supposed to make regular payments for the temporary or permanent support of the child. These payments, even when made regularly, were usually insufficient to properly provide for a child, giving birth to stories of infanticide and abuse that were common enough to become plot devices in Charles Dickens' *Oliver Twist* and even Gilbert and Sullivan's musical, *HMS Pinafore*.

The first adoption legislation enacted in Australia was *The Adoption of Children Act 1896*, but it was heavily amended until finally being repealed. By the mid-20th century, an increase in unexpected pregnancies resulted in an era wherein unmarried, pregnant women were "forced, pressured or coerced to give up their children rather than bear the shame and social stigma of pregnancy and birth outside marriage."[1] With the concept of the birth mother's consent becoming the much-needed forefront, and the Australian 1969 decriminalisation of abortion, the voluntary placement of children for adoption became increasingly politically and socially unpopular, until private adoption became illegal and Australian Family Law moved to restrictive preferences in favour of the biological family.[2] In 1998, Australia became party to the Hague Convention, meaning that Australian state and federal governments would be the only vehicle for processing adoption. At that time, adoptions in Australia were statistically one per one million residents.

This was depressing news. But we ambitiously embraced the promise in Matthew 7:7–8: "Ask, and it shall be given you; seek, and ye shall find; knock, and it shall be opened unto you: For every one that asketh, receiveth; and he that seeketh, findeth; and to him that knocketh, it shall be opened." For me, that meant doing everything we possibly could–praying for help (asking), researching every possibility (seeking), and engaging in physical work (knocking), to make way for the miracle of parenthood. We registered at a dozen or so global adoption agencies, but as soon as they saw that we resided in Australia, my e-mails went unanswered. Feeling defeated about adoption, I began the tedious process of *in vitro* fertilisation (IVF).

I liked to joke that I was born with a "some assembly required" sticker on my back. I was diagnosed with diabetes just before my second birthday, but I was fifteen by the time I was diagnosed with Mayer-Rokitansky-Küster-Hauser (MRKH) Syndrome. This is a rare condition that in summary means I was born without a uterus. Though I have ovaries, I cannot carry a pregnancy. Gestational surrogacy was only legal in the Australian Capital Territory (ACT), at that time, and even then, we were looking at a half of a million dollars (at least) to pay for the legal and medical costs. Instead, a couple of extremely generous American friends offered to become gestational surrogates. We were trying everything, and life was very stressful, and I especially felt exposed with all of the extremely invasive medical history questions and verifications that were required for me to go through.

IVF was also hard on my diabetic body. The influx of chemicals can be hard on any woman's body, causing bloating, hot flashes and even painful discomfort until the liver and kidneys can flush away the synthetic hormones. Insulin is a hormone, so the increased doses of fertility hormones affected my insulin absorption, usually making my blood sugar run higher, but sometimes randomly causing me to suddenly crash low. One afternoon, I was spoiling myself at a hair salon when I could feel my blood sugar dropping alarmingly fast. I had some candy in my purse, but it wasn't enough. "Would you like a cuppa?" asked the hairdresser, meaning a "cuppa" tea, or coffee, which was always brewing in Australian spaces. She was blissfully unaware of my distress as she programmed her phone to the measure of time needed for the painted highlights in my hair to develop. Normally, I would say no, but this time, I said, "Yes, please, tea and six sugars." I was near panic when she brought the syrupy sweet brew, already feeling guilty, but also very grateful.

It felt like we had little privacy with all we were going through, so we told very few people what was going on, making this a very lonely period in our lives. At the time, I was able to find a job working for a furniture importer. This was a Lebanese business, and though the owners spoke English as well as Arabic, they hired me to write descriptions for the furniture in English and manage written online communication. I loved working for people who did not mind my American accent and enjoyed the creativity of the job. Mostly, I treasured their greeting me with a smile when I arrived at work, as well as learning about Islamic Lebanese culture, Islamic holidays, and tasting delicious Lebanese foods that their wives generously shared with me. It was truly a blessing to work with fellow immigrants.

At this time, I discovered that my new Australian ward was similar to my past American wards in that church socialisation was largely limited to family-centred gatherings. Probably because I was both an immigrant and childless, I was not invited to baby showers for fellow church members, nor had I been invited to the "Mum and Bub" play dates claimed to be open-invitation meetups in Relief Society. I once mentioned my slighted feelings to another woman in the Relief Society presidency. "Everyone is invited," she said, politely dismissing my feelings. "But the play date locations and times are not announced in Relief Society, and no one ever contacts me to attend," I responded. "Who am I supposed to call to find out when everyone is going?" As the words tumbled out, I began to tear up due to loneliness and possibly all of the IVF chemicals, and my fragile emotions embarrassed me. She looked surprised but offered no apology. She never spoke to me about it again, and I continued to be and feel left out.

My childlessness became more obvious the longer Bruce and I were married. Though I was working and considering postgraduate school, most of my fellow ward and stake members knew nothing about me, except to occasionally comment on my childlessness. They were sad for me, pitied me, or worse, made unkind and presumptive judgements on my worthiness. "I don't know why God hasn't blessed you…" said one, suggesting I was unworthy of "blessings." Others told me that "in the next life you'll get to be a mother. Right now, you can learn." This implied two things: first, I needed to be dead to become a mother, and second, I was too stupid to parent, so I was stuck in some kind of maternal educational purgatory. Another suggested that my "calling" was to "serve those who are called to be mothers in this life," which implied that I was a lesser person, stuck in the lowest level of a type of eternal fertility caste system.

My experience as an immigrant was also challenging. My in-laws seemed distrustful of this American Mormon that their son had married, and though they were polite and generous, I longed to feel the warmth that American culture can invite. At one of my first Australian jobs as a receptionist, some people said my accent was confusing and problematic, and not understanding the Australian sense of humour, I struggled to know when I was being playfully engaged with or heartily criticised. At church, I was accused of being "from Utah," usually when I made a comment in Sunday School or Relief Society that was deemed obtuse and inapplicable. It was a phrase that was used to describe someone totally out of touch with reality and intended to dismiss and sting. Soon, I stopped informing fellow parishioners that I was from New York and began to engage only when called on, doing my best to avoid even that.

With this cultural exclusion, I also seriously debated if I could remain an active member (or a member at all) in a church that primarily identified women as mothers. I thought that perhaps speaking with an LDS counsellor could be helpful and made an appointment. This academically trained counsellor, who was a mother of four, could not comprehend my feeling of exclusion at church. I expressed how every Sunday, in a Relief Society room of barely twenty women, I felt like a festering boil that everyone wanted to go away. This counsellor was sure that I was incorrect. "Who do you sit by in Relief Society lessons on Sundays?" she pressed.

"No one," I replied. She stared back at me with a baffled expression, so I tried to explain. "Last Sunday in Relief Society, I sat by a woman close to my age. She told me that the seat was saved for someone else. So I moved to another seat. The woman there *changed seats* just as the lesson started, so I sat between empty chairs for the entire class." The counsellor sat looking at me with a wide, gaping mouth. The silence was uncomfortable, so I queried, "When was the last time you sat with a childless woman and made sure she didn't feel lonely at church?" She paused as if she were thinking, then curtly responded that I was not allowed to ask her personal questions. I never went back, even after she wrote me a personal letter inviting me to return.

I decided I would not attend Relief Society lessons or activities, since the loneliness had bitterly burned away any spirit I might have felt anyway. In making this decision, I felt an immense, isolating weight lifted from me and instantly felt happier. To be clear, I missed *the idea* of Relief Society: a group of women who work to support each other. But at the time, it was a closed club for mothers and expectant mothers. Infertile immigrants were not welcome.

As a single woman, my infertility had been masked in the absence of a husband. But as a married Mormon woman, it was a trumpeting elephant, announcing me well before I could utter my name aloud. This was a hard truth to face, especially for a believing, faithful, Latter-day Saint. Motherhood is often claimed as equivalent to priesthood in Mormon social dogma; but this is false, as male priesthood is bestowed upon any man who is deemed "worthy," but childbirth is based on the physical rather than the spiritual ability of women. The male priesthood is spiritual, the female motherhood is physical. More recent ideologies seem to have sprouted from various sources, including from the childless Sheri Dew, who was the first unmarried woman to serve in the General Relief Society Presidency (1997–2002). In quoting a series of male leaders, she determined that motherhood is an innate spiritual gift given to women, not limited to the sphere of childbirth. But every time I quoted that talk to physical, child-bearing mothers *in the church*, I was dismissed. "Of course, *she* (meaning childless Dew) would say *that*. She doesn't have children so has to find a way to try to relate to motherhood," was an all-too-common remark, even on Mother's Day. Other childless and known Latter-day Saint women such as Barbara Thompson, Sharon Eubank, and Kristin Yee refrained from mentioning themselves as mothers, as Dew had done, perhaps expressing that they also did not feel the same as she did.

Moreover, I found that motherhood, in many Mormon circles, equated to female righteousness. After all, the perfect and sinless Mary would miraculously become mother to Christ. Without motherhood, it felt like I was deemed an unworthy soul.

I held out hope that the visiting teaching program would help me to build friendships, and I diligently contacted my companion every month to arrange to visit the sisters we were assigned. My companion tolerated me but was clearly focused on a young American mother who was in Australia on a two-year work visa with her husband. Unlike me, this woman was invited to the ward "Mums and Bubs" gatherings with her toddler and was able to join local mother's groups, where women with children of similar age met to share and swap parenting tips. I found that in most of our visiting teaching meetings, I was excluded from the conversation, only being addressed when it came time to deliver the obligatory message. It was painful. Finding friends at church was a bust.

I still believed that God knew me personally and that my Heavenly Parents were mindful of my joys, sadnesses, hopes, and fears. Personal prayer was a haven; scripture study was a refuge. My testimony was mine alone, not based on those around me, and I was grateful for it. I pushed forward, seeking to improve myself, my life, and my marriage. In doing so, I was able to find work as an English teacher for non-English speaking immigrants. The school I worked at also included an English-immersion program for primary school-aged children, and before I knew it, I was teaching a seasonal class comprised of young students between the ages of nine and eleven. Several of the children were exchange students in need of host families, so Bruce and I ended up looking after a nine-year-old Korean boy for a couple of months. As we brought our young guest to church, the women who had children of similar age began to actually speak with me. It was uncanny! I quickly discovered that having a child presented a social reason to engage in conversation! The women began asking about my life, how we ended up looking after such a young exchange student, and even about my work.

I also learned that this mystery was not limited to church. In chasing my dream of a postgraduate degree, I applied for and was accepted into a doctoral program. The administrator in the university's postgraduate office had a sour reputation among my fellow postgraduates. Even over the phone, Meghan seemed utterly annoyed with any query that came to her, and in person, she could be quite callous. Like my fellow postgraduates, I dreaded communicating with her.

At the time, I was classed with a permanent resident visa, so my candidature was managed administratively differently to students who had student visas or were citizens. Collating additional layers of federally-required paperwork, where I professed that I obtained my undergraduate degree from a recognised American university and proved that I could proficiently speak English, I found that I did not understand how to complete some of the immigration-related departmental funding forms. I felt so dumb! I knew that I had to ask for help.

I made an appointment with Meghan and arrived cumbered with every personal form of identification I had, plus all of my visa paperwork, and my official, watermarked, stamped, academic transcripts. As soon as I began asking questions, she rolled her eyes and began rifling through files to find the forms that I lacked and needed to complete. She snidely remarked that it was "all on the website," and under her breath, yet still quite aloud, questioned my intellectual ability to start a postgraduate degree. Trying to be patient and maybe create friendly banter, I noticed something playful on her desk. "I have a nine-year-old at home who would love that," I commented, referring to our exchange student.

"I have a nine-year-old, too," Meghan said suddenly and with a smile. I had never seen her smile before, and I smiled back. "Boy or girl?" she asked.

"Boy," I said, determined to never confess that he was not *my* nine-year-old.

"Mine too!" she said with a laugh. "It's a hard age, but we'll get through it!" I laughed and nodded as if I understood. Within minutes, my paperwork was complete, and every time thereafter, no matter how infrequent, she greeted me with kindness. In this interaction, I learned that motherhood was an equaliser, even outside of church.

After our sweet exchange student went home, I was asked to teach the teenagers' Sunday School class at church. I grew to enjoy it, still avoiding the Relief Society. Bruce and I would sneak out after Sunday School and grab lunch. We would eat while giggling and chatting in the car about some of the silliness at church, healing the wounds of infertility-aimed darts. Eventually, Bruce's armour weakened. His own feelings as a childless outsider were too much, and I found myself attending church alone more often than not.

I still taught the Sunday School class, and I began to love the students. Yet every Sunday after class, I would slip out with my chin down, soundlessly sneaking past the Relief Society room and out of the building. After two years of this, I began to notice that a woman named Trish had begun to stand at the Relief Society room door as I slid by. Once, as I was moving past, avoiding eye contact, someone asked Trish why she was standing there. She brightly replied, "I am waiting for Sherrie to come in, then I'll close the door." I was startled! Not wanting to actually speak, and unfamiliar with being noticed outside of my Sunday School class, I silently went in, taking a seat in an empty row. As I anxiously prepared to spend the hour alone, Trish came in and sat by me. God bless Trish!

I did not open up to her, or anyone, about the IVF, the silence from adoption waiting lists, or anything else. That was between me and Bruce and God. But I finally had someone to sit with at Relief Society lessons on Sundays. I continued and increased my personal scripture study, discovering a new love of the Virgin Mary (Galatians 4:4–5), who in Catholic infertility support groups was sometimes called a surrogate mother for God. My passion for Ruth increased, reading and re-reading of her decision to remain steadfast to both God and her beloved mother-in-law, Naomi, for the purpose of providing a son for Naomi to adopt (Ruth 4:17).

After seven years in Sydney, Bruce was offered a job in the state of Queensland. I immediately felt the move was right for us; we desperately needed to recoup our finances, which had been spent on failed fertility treatments, and the new job paid well enough that I no longer felt like I needed to skip meals for financial reasons. We both knew that a fresh start would be good, so I withdrew from university and quit my job. Within two weeks, we were on our new adventure.

Australians call Queensland the "Sunshine State" because it is renowned as a sunny and warm vacation destination, not unlike parts of California, complete with theme parks, mild weather, and fruit farms dotting the coast. But Central Queensland, where we moved, is very different. It is inland from the coast, making it a vast, desert area where cattle and mining are the primary industries that sustain a few tiny, distant towns on a vast and arid map.

We lived an hour from the nearest branch, which was located in a small town with about 14,000 residents and two stop lights. Where we lived had less than 1,000 residents and no stoplights. Bruce started work, and I started my own private tutoring business working with primary school-aged children who needed help with maths or reading and grew to love each of my students. Their parents did not seem to mind that I was not a mother and asked me for advice on how to help their children. This new life was a breath of fresh air!

On Sundays when the roads were not closed to seasonal monsoon flooding, Bruce and I drove to the church to share the entire three hour service with 20 other members. I found Robin's name in a printed church directory that included the fewer than 300 members for the entire region. Robin lived in the opposite direction from us, and in a different church branch that only consisted of her and her husband. Yet they were only a 45-minute drive from us, making them the physically closest church members to us.

I cold-called her and happily discovered that we were both Americans married to Australians! I liked her instantly, and we soon revealed that each of us were struggling to become parents. Robin and I both wanted children, so along with the mutual emotional scars of failed IVF, immigrant humour, and a common faith, we also shared heartbreak, shock, and angst in the face of Australian anti-adoption legislation.

Our friendship felt like a liberating, deep breath that oxygenated a bright, fruitful garden within my soul. My parched loneliness was hydrated in finally having someone to speak openly with about childlessness in the church, and it was invigorating to have someone to laugh with when recounting some of the more outrageous adoption and fertility advice we had been given. "This one sister, in the middle of the Relief Society birthday dinner, told me that I was too old to be a mother and I should not even try!" once shared Robin with exasperation. "And then, after I cleaned this woman's entire kitchen," I said, "she did not thank me and told me that I would fall pregnant if I started eating persimmons!" In sharing the ridiculous ways we had been spoken to by well-meaning Saints, we were able to erupt into the kind of laughter that soaks up years of weighty, hidden tears.

Over the next three years, we spent time in each other's homes, chatted regularly, and became close. Robin was adamant that she would mother someone, even if it was in a life-long fostering situation, which was common in Australia. Bruce and I had discussed fostering children, but I wanted something more permanent. Having found such peace in the temple, I desperately wanted to be sealed as family, which is an impossibility outside of legal adoption.

As is common in the mining industry, Robin relocated twice over those three years, finally moving to an area south of Sydney in New South Wales, which had slightly improved its foster-to-adopt laws since Bruce and I had left that state, primarily owing to the copious amounts of children in foster care. And following three years of remote living, Bruce was also offered a new job, so we also moved, but to a different part of Queensland.

Bruce's new job was a corporate position, which meant he was away nearly every week, visiting different work sites. Though we were in a ward in this new location, my childlessness and my self-protective, cold armour isolated me, and I felt lonelier than ever. Trying to gather hope after our fourth IVF failure, I decided to attend a public adoption information event on a weeknight, which meant I went alone. It was there that the presenters happily told a room of around 400 hopeful parents that the state had a goal of processing less than a handful of adoptions for the entire year. This is common in Australia, where adoption is rare and the echoes of the Stolen Generation, a phrase used to describe Australia's forced version of American Indian boarding schools, demanded significant government checks and intervention lest any malfeasance occur. Thus, for the state of Queensland, processing this many adoptions was momentous.

The crowd of hopeful adoptive parents disagreed. It felt like we were in an endless line to buy a lottery ticket. Audible groans and grumbling began to drown the speaker out before one strong, male, audience member's voice pointedly asked why there were not at least as many adoptions per annum as there were full-time employees in the state adoption office. "Oh, I dunno," the speaker breathily responded with a dismissive smile and a shrug. "It is a lot of work."

As I stood in the parking garage lift with fellow attendees at the end of the meeting, the air was thick with dispirited dreams. "It's hopeless," muttered one man to the floor. "They don't care about children," said another woman in a whisper, her voice trembling. No one was smiling, no one made eye contact, and the downtown business district where this was held seemed spookily deserted for a weeknight.

It was not difficult for me to conclude that I was fighting a losing battle. The last round of IVF resulted in my body swelling to an unrecognisable state. Though Bruce teased me about having "IVF cankles," my doctor was alarmed at the state of my kidneys after processing so many medications to try to make a viable zygote. My body and soul were breaking. It was time to stop trying to be a mother, lest I lose my life.

In his wisdom, Bruce arranged for us to have a getaway. We took a ferry to Tangalooma Island, where we sat at a quiet beach, without internet or phone. We mourned the loss of the dream of having a family and discussed what we wanted out of life, sans children. We closed the door on parenting, and we vowed that we would be happy; Bruce was going to research and book us in on a comedy cruise, and I would get my PhD.

But I still felt like I needed to decide if I could remain active in the Church of Jesus Christ of Latter-day Saints, or join my husband on the fringe until we silently disappeared. The church is all about families, so without children, we were already very out of place; fellow members seemed leery of our worthiness, having not been righteous enough to be rewarded with children like Sarah (Genesis 18:12), Hannah (1 Samuel 1:20), and Elizabeth (Luke 1:24). I knew Bruce would support my decision to stay or leave the church, so I contemplated both formal and informal resignation. We knew less than a handful of other childless couples and saw how they were ostracised at church. Staying would be painful, and we had already been through so much.

Early one morning, I took a walk along the empty beach, alone. I spoke out loud to God, who I was sure had not heard our prayers. But this morning, I was too angry for prayer. "I get it," I shouted as loudly as I could at the surf as if yelling ensured God would finally hear. "*I* think I should be a mother. *You* think I shouldn't." Then I screamed, "We are going to agree to disagree!" I felt liberated yelling at God so defiantly. I was tired of quiet prayers, silent faith and contrition. As I bellowed until my throat and lungs burned, I felt an intense sense of peace come over me. The waves softened around me, lapping gently at my knees; it wasn't until then that I realised I had walked directly into the ocean, that my jeans were soaked. But in that moment, I felt like God accepted me and all of my offerings. I made my decision. "I am not leaving the Church," I said loudly, though no longer shouting. "Even if the Church doesn't want me because I don't have children. I won't leave. I might never go to Relief Society, but I will not deny Christ and His atonement are real. *We agree to disagree about motherhood, and I will not deny Christ.*"

I was not asking God with piety. I was telling God with defiance who I was. I was quite positive that God did like not me. And yet, somewhere I had a sense that maybe God loved me? I yearned to know, confused at God's withholding. I concluded that it was *not* a sin for me to *not* be a mother, even when LDS church culture demanded it. It also was not a sin for me to *stop* trying to be a mother. For me, womanhood never was about motherhood. Womanhood would always be defined by my relationship with God the Father, God the Mother, and Jesus Christ. Nothing else.

I looked at the clear sky. It was beautiful. In gazing at the morning horizon, I felt as though my sacrifice had been accepted. "Mormon culture be damned," I muttered. With a small spray from the sea, I suddenly felt loved. Deeply loved. Loved by God. Sloppy, messy, imperfect, stubborn me. God loved me. I stood in the water for a moment, taking it all in. I accepted and embraced my childless life in full, feeling spiritually re-baptised in the gentle surf of Morton Bay.

Three weeks later, Robin called.

CHAPTER NOTES

1.   State of Victoria Government Website, "History and Timeline of Forced Adoptions in Victoria," https://www.vic.gov.au/forced-adoption-history

2.   Baird, Barbara. (2017) Decriminalization and Women's Access to Abortion in Australia, Health and Human Rights Journal, 19(1): 197–208. https://www.ncbi.nlm.nih.gov/pmc/articles/PMC5473049

SHERRIE GAVIN

2

CONNECTING

At the time of Robin's call, she and her husband were fostering a special-needs toddler. In addition to medical appointments and foster care check-ins, Robin's time was often spent on long drives to take the child to visit her half-dozen siblings of different parentage in their various foster homes, in addition to travelling to visit each of the child's birth parents. Robin seemed to be in the car more often than not, which made this daytime, landline phone call unusual.

She told me what little she knew about the girls. She had met the family through church, and though Robin had moved since then, she remained in contact with Michelle, the mother of the family. Michelle and her husband, Trent had four biological children, plus the two girls that Robin believed were somehow related to the family. Familiar with Robin's interest in adoption, as well as her mixed nationality marriage, Michelle asked if Robin was interested in taking the girls, possibly adopting them.

Robin told me that she had an immediate spiritual impression that she was not the right person to adopt the girls. But she thought of me. As an American, a fellow church member, and childless, I might be a fit. The details of how the girls came to Michelle and Trent and where the birth parents were located were unknown to Robin. Michelle had only said that there was "no way for the girls to go back to the U.S.," implying that the girls were U.S. citizens.

Hearing these scanty details, I was surprised that Robin would even discuss this with me. The situation sounded very sketchy. But it was Robin. She knew as well as I did of the improbability of adopting in Australia and the impossibility of an adoption between Australia and the U.S. *But it was Robin.* I conceded to her sending me whatever information she had in regard to the girls. Later that day, she sent me an e-mail with the subject line "Angels from heaven."

"Honestly," she wrote, "I don't know how this can happen because private adoption is illegal in Australia as far as I know... But, the Lord can do anything, can't He?!" The message included images of the girls, explaining that "it looks like the youngest cut her own hair, because it looks shaved." She also added that "I think they look like they could be yours," meaning that the girls looked like

Bruce and me. Her words were hopeful and excited on our behalf. But in closing her e-mail, she added, "proceed with caution with Michelle."

I looked at the photos of the girls, allowing myself to imagine them as my own for a moment. The girls in this photo were beautiful. Too beautiful. They were two of the cutest children I had ever seen in my life. The older child had dark blond hair, while her sister's bald head was sharing no secrets. Though I could not decipher their eye colours, it didn't matter. The children were simply *too perfect* for someone to place for adoption. I immediately concluded that the whole thing was the result of Michelle being an exhausted mother who was speaking purely out of fatigue. I was positive it could not result in my becoming a mother, and I was not in the mood for a fool's errand, especially one that involved children.

And yet ... I could not help myself. I closed my eyes, smiled and imagined myself as a mother, just for a moment. Thinking better of it, I sharply closed the e-mail and moved on with my day.

I only casually mentioned it to Bruce when he called that night to check in. "Do it," said Bruce with firmness. "If it gets us a family, then do it."

"I don't know," I said warily. "It sounds too good to be true. I have the feeling it will cost a lot of money—"

"We have to check it out," he said, resolutely. "We've done everything else. If they have kids they want to give away, then we *have* to at least check it out."

"But what about Chile?" I asked. Bruce was going to Chile for a work conference, and I had hoped to tag along, though I guessed going with him was a long shot.

"Since this is my first overseas work assignment, I don't think it's good for you to go with me," he said. "Plus, what do you want more, a trip to Chile or a family?"

"Family," I responded instantly.

It was after 9PM when Michelle called me, after speaking with Robin and being given my phone number. I was hungry to hear about the girls, their situation, and the legality of everything, but I also wanted to be respectful of Michelle's privacy. She told me a little about the girls, but talked more about herself, her interests, and her background. She suggested that because the girls were American, she knew how to circumvent Australian adoption laws for us to eventually adopt them. I quite frankly did not believe she knew any special adoption loopholes, but I *wanted* to believe.

Over the next two weeks, I spoke with Michelle a few more times. We exchanged our addresses, e-mail, and became friends on Facebook, all while Bruce and I prayed about the situation. Neither Bruce nor I felt any specific spiritual prompting, but things seemed to fall into place for me to go to Sydney. Our friend, Mandy, and her toddler daughter were staying with us for a couple of weeks, waiting for their rental house to be prepared. They could look after the house while Bruce went to Chile and I went to Sydney. Bruce's parents were away, so I could stay at their house in Sydney without needing to explain my independent visit. I could go, meet Michelle, and if she liked me, she would consider allowing me to take the girls "for a trial visit."

It is only an hour flight from Brisbane to Sydney, so I could have flown there and back within a day, not even staying overnight. But the whole adoption thing was so ridiculously far-fetched that for self-preservation, I needed another reason or reasons to go to Sydney. I surmised that if I drove, I could listen to audiobooks and then have the freedom to visit the Sydney Temple as a treat. I also planned to window shop for some indulgent kitchenware at Victoria's Basement and even check out the American food options at the Sydney Costco, since Brisbane still didn't have one. As I had just enrolled in another doctoral program, I could also do some research at the state library or do some undistracted writing.

With plenty to fill my time, my heart, and my mind, when I came home childless, there would be only the tiniest of stings and it would not last for more than a moment. I was determined to come home happy.

I breathed a sigh of relief as I pulled into the driveway at my in-laws' house, ending the twelve-hour drive. Quickly settling in, I texted Michelle to confirm our meeting for the following day and checked my laptop for e-mails. I found myself opening Robin's e-mail, fixating on the photos of the girls. The girls didn't seem to be smiling in any of the photos. In one, the youngest had a bandanna tied around her head, and in another, her head was shaved. The older girl had darker hair that seemed wavy, the top tuft of hair pulled uncomfortably tight into a tiny plume. I thought they were perfectly darling, even if their appearance was a bit quirky.

"I am just heart-broken over the whole thing but just don't feel like I can do it anymore," Michelle wrote in an e-mail that Robin forwarded to me. "It's not having six kids that's an issue—between the kids it's just not working," Michelle explained, claiming that her children blamed the interloping girls for creating every problem the family encountered.

"I also think the truth is," wrote Robin to me, "that it is too much for Michelle and Trent. Michelle focuses on her own children more, and she thinks she can handle it, but I don't think she can." Robin added that Michelle could be after money and concluded her e-mail by reminding me to be very careful.

Robin was wise to be worried for me. If this turned out to be a scam, it would not be the first time that someone from church implied or stated that since we were childless, we were much better off financially and should hand our cash out to families with children. However, it would be the first time that someone teased us with adoption for a handout, so I tried to make sense of the situation. *Michelle is an overwhelmed mother*, I thought to myself. *I'll watch her children, clean her house, maybe even buy some groceries, then cut her off,* I told myself. Though I tended to stay away from these kinds of situations, I decided to trust Robin and be Christlike to the best of my ability. I was too tired to think too much about it, and within moments of closing my laptop, I fell into a deep, deep sleep.

SHERRIE GAVIN

3

TEDDY BEARS

I told Michelle that Costco was the reason I wanted to drive rather than fly to Sydney, so she agreed to meet me there. Anxious to be punctual, I arrived almost an entire hour early and peered inside the store, trying to make a mental shopping list. Just inside the entrance was a giant, steel-rimmed stand, filled with adult-sized teddy bears. They were incredibly soft and inviting. I smiled, thinking that if the girls came, I would buy them each a teddy bear. As soon as the thought came, I dismissed it, frustrated with myself. In time, a text came from Michelle, informing me that she and a friend had arrived. "Heavenly Father, please help me," I silently prayed, and began looking around.

Michelle and I had connected on social media, so I knew what she looked like. She was pretty, with curly hair that perfectly framed her face. I was surprised to find that her friend looked familiar. "I know you!" she said as soon as she saw me. "I'm Nora's daughter, Angela!" Seeing Angela put me immediately at ease; her mother and I met when we were both briefly in the same ward. Years earlier, Nora and I spent a morning buying fruits and vegetables in bulk at the Sydney seaside markets, and on driving home, Nora delivered some of the produce to Angela. That first meeting was brief, but warm, friendly, and filled with sun-ripened peaches.

After a quick catch-up, the three of us decided to wander inside Costco to shop and chat. Angela did most of the talking, adding a distinct element of cheer. Her friendliness relaxed me and possibly Michelle, making it easy to speak about our spouses, favorite American foods, and even Michelle's children. "This feels good," Michelle said every few minutes. I didn't know what that meant to her, and I didn't dare guess. Luckily I did not need to respond as Angela spoke about everything from tattoos to dill pickles, but said nothing about the girls.

She left that to Michelle, who occasionally offered up small bits of information. I gathered that the girls were American, and from her husband's side of the family. They were two and three years old, and had been living in Australia for about a year. "Where are the birth parents?" I ventured.

"Jail," said Michelle plainly. Then with firmness, "And the girls can't go back to them. I was given permanent custody." Stunned silent, I realised how naïve my previous thinking had been. I had presumed a television adoption scenario: I had imagined that there was a teenage birth mother who was weary of the reality of parenthood or possibly escaping a deadbeat birth father and had finally decided to place children for adoption. I had not considered a situation involving prison. "Wow" was all I could think to say.

Soon it was time for Michelle to go so she could collect her children from school. I felt the distinct impression *not* to pay for her groceries, so we paid for ourselves. As I walked with them to Angela's car, Michelle said she felt positive about meeting me. Angela hugged me goodbye, and I waved as they drove off.

Impetuously, I walked back to the shop entrance and looked at the teddy bears. They were totally delightful and fluffy. I would have loved having one of them as a child. I impulsively bought two, quickly reasoning that our house was big enough that I could hide them from Bruce until I sold them on eBay in the probability that the girls did not come home with me. It wasn't because I thought Bruce would be unhappy with the purchase. It was because I wanted to hide the evidence of hope, maybe even from myself. Hope is always a risky thing with infertility, and feeling hopeful scared me.

Returning to my in-laws' empty house with the giant bears stuffed into the boot of my car, I found the house too quiet for my comfort. I longed to speak with Bruce and wondered what time it was in Chile. Not having someone to talk to made me feel lonely and a little anxious. All of the things that I had planned to make this trip about were totally uninteresting to me. I only wanted to meet the girls. Pondering this, I decided to send a text to Michelle and offer to drop off lunch tomorrow. I reasoned that as well as being a typical Relief Society thing to do—drop off a meal to a family in need—I would also be able to meet the girls. Michelle immediately accepted the offer, and I decided to try and sleep to hide from my loneliness.

The next day, I rose and checked the blogger e-mail group for the *Exponent II*. I found the *Exponent II* blog sometime in 2006 when I was covering for a Relief Society lesson. Though I only attended Relief Society intermittently, I found the lesson plans there were more thoughtful, inclusive, inspirational, and suited to my way of thinking than the standard lesson materials. In the blog, I found a gold mine of like-minded thinkers: women who were inclusive of all Mormon women, regardless of marital status, parental status, or sexual orientation, and who savoured analyzing scripture outside of traditional, one-dimensional thought. I devoured every post. I began commenting and even sent in a guest post. Within a few months, I was welcomed into the perma-blogger fold. This blogger space was even more of a haven for me. It was a welcoming sanctuary where I felt safe. In addition to blog business, these saint-like women of diverse economic and political backgrounds shared hurts, wisdom, fears, and goals. They fasted and prayed for me when my husband and I were doing IVF. They cried with me every time I came home childless.

These trusted women were a source of positive reinforcement where I knew I would not be judged for being crazy enough to meet with Michelle, try IVF again, or decide that parenting was not for me.

Feeling alone and unsure of what crazy trip this might run into, I needed a dose of unconditional love. I sent a quick message describing my situation to the group, asking for support. A handful of the bloggers responded, offering words of love and support. It was exactly what I needed.

That morning, I bought two car DVD players and one children's DVD, just in case I ended up with children in my car. It was another impulsive purchase, but this time I tucked the receipt in my wallet so I could easily return them. I then went and bought two giant pizzas and drove to Michelle's house. Angela was there again, but the girls were not. "My brother and his wife offered to care for them for a while," Michelle explained, adding that they had been away for a week. "They are causing problems here with my children, so I try to get them away as much as I can." I felt slighted and was disappointed, but what could I do besides make small talk? The house appeared disorganised, more so than the average home with children. But again, I knew that this was a mother in distress, so I decided to try to not to judge or focus on the mess. The dining table was engulfed in a massive pile of unfolded clean clothes, which Michelle pushed aside to make a place for the pizza to be served. I went to wash my hands at the sink, but could not find soap or a towel. As I rinsed my hands in water, and dried them on my pants, I reminded myself, "Stiff upper lip. Just like camping."

Soon we were chatting between slices of the pizza. I learned that the house was a rental and that the landlords, also fellow church members, were working to evict her. Michelle stated that she owed the landlords money, but that she had reasons for not paying them. "They asked us to move!" she expressed with exasperation. "Even the Stake Relief Society President tried to get us to leave," said Michelle. "Just because we weren't paying." My questions were mounting, but I chose to listen and accept. I glanced at Angela for a reaction, but her eyes were focused downward as she texted on her phone or worked to fold the clean laundry.

The impending move must be why the house is out of sorts, I mused to myself, but I remained mostly silent, trying to process everything, internally praying for direction that I *could not discern*. I decided that the best thing to do was to just listen to Michelle with my full attention. She said that she loved the girls and was not sure if she could part with them, in a matter-of-fact way. She was adamant that the birth mother was wrong in every way, and angrily cautioned me to have no contact with her whatsoever, for "safety." Michelle lamented that her problems were the result of others in her life: her bishop refusing financial support, the landlords who were evicting her for nonpayment, and the girls for taking time and money away from her biological children. As words continued to spin from Michelle's mouth, I began to feel more and more targeted for money rather than possible child placement. I was not surprised. I wasn't even disappointed. I stifled a sigh and silently chided myself for hoping this could be something different.

Michelle shared little of herself other than of being in desperate financial need. Even my attempt to redirect the conversation by asking if she had a church calling was ignored. She began to lament about how she had won four tickets to a live stage show of *How to Train Your Dragon*. She desperately wanted to purchase one more ticket, "so our whole family could go together." The show was for children over the age of three, so I quickly did the math and presumed that Michelle wanted to take her three older children, plus the older girl, while her husband stayed home with the babies under two years old. This softened me, so I began to consider purchasing a ticket for her. "How many more tickets would you need?" I wanted to confirm before offering. "One more. Me and my three can go, and I'll get a sitter for the youngest. I need a ticket for my husband."

"What about the girls?" I asked, confused.

"*No.*" she said with distinct animosity, snapping me to alertness. "The girls are not here, and they can't come anyway. The prize is for *our* family. *Not them.*"

It was not the first time that her words seemed contradictory to me. In one breath, she stated that she loved her nieces, who called her "mummy." In the next, she said they were absolutely *not* a part of her family, and most definitely were *not* invited to this show, or—it seemed—most other family outings. Michelle stopped speaking to take a phone call from a real estate rental agent, while I stared at the kitchen window, trying to clear my mind and find some kind of peace through the light of the sun.

Michelle finished the call and announced that there was a rental house available for inspection and the agent could show it to her that afternoon. Angela said she needed to leave to pick up her own children from school, and Michelle invited me to go with her and her youngest child to look at this house. Within moments, I found myself seated in Michelle's car, silently processing, wondering what my purpose was in this whole mess. As Michelle drove, I continued to listen. She spoke of everything that disgusted her about her previous rentals, which were numerous, and then what she hoped to find in this possibility.

The house was only about a 15 minute drive away, so we arrived and parked, waiting for the agent. The house was a cute red brick place; I guessed that it had been built in the 1960s. It was on a cul-de-sac that circled a grassy inner island nestling a children's jungle gym. As the agent's car pulled up, I noted aloud that it would be easy to see the children playing on the swings from the house. "No," Michelle angrily shot at me. "I won't allow my children to play on that. Public play equipment is dangerous and infested with disease." Her reprimand felt intended to inform me of how unprepared I was to parent, and it stung.

Michelle unstrapped her two-year-old from his car seat, and after short introductions, I silently followed along through the vacant house. It was clean and sturdy, with a dated but functional kitchen, four small bedrooms, and a classic back porch. As we looked, I began to imagine which of the family bedrooms I thought would suit the children, thinking that the larger bedroom would comfortably fit Michelle's daughter and the two girls, and the two smaller bedrooms would suit Michelle's three sons. Michelle broke through my thoughts by telling me that the larger bedroom would be for her youngest sons, and her older children would have their own rooms. "Um … the girls?" I queried without thinking.

"Oh, they can stay in bunks in here, if they have to," she said flippantly, not identifying a room. Michelle's verbal disdain for the girls was becoming apparent and began to wear on me. I was positive that all she wanted was money, but her negative speech of the girls made me resolute to never give her a penny.

Michelle said she wanted to rent the house, so I excused myself to give her and the agent privacy to work out the details. Standing on the front porch, I stared at the playground. It was only about twenty paces away, on a quiet street, with no visual obstructions and no traffic. I saw nothing wrong with it, other than the grass needing mowing. "I'd smack the kids if they went there," Michelle said when she saw me. "They know better than that."

It was not the first time Michelle spoke of "smacking" her children and the girls; she spoke about it often. It was clear that she ruled her children with an iron fist, and each time she mentioned it, I felt prickly. I was squarely against the physical reprimand of children, but I already knew better than to say anything in opposition to Michelle. Oblivious to my discomfort, Michelle continued to talk as we drove back. "They will not be allowed out front to play, only in the back," she said, clearly happy with the house, jabbering about how she would set it up.

She seemed to think that running the household with strictness and corporal punishment was the sign of a good parent, almost bragging that she shaved the head of the youngest girl, Reesey. I suddenly recalled the photo Robin sent of the girls, where she mused that the youngest may have cut her own hair. But this was not the case. "She was pulling her own hair and eyelashes out," Michelle prattled as she drove. "So the doctor told me to shave her head. That'll teach her for doing that." To my knowledge, pulling hair out was one way that children processed high amounts of stress; it was a silent call for help. This was not the first time

Michelle mentioned that a "doctor" was giving this kind of advice, and I was grateful that Michelle's gaze was fixed on the road so she could not see my grimace. I was convinced that she was not being wholly honest and I just wanted to get back to my car and leave.

"I need to get my kids from school," she announced, to which I simply replied, "Okay." Michelle's phone rang as she pulled into the school pick up area, and she began busily chatting as if I were not there, for which I was grateful. Within moments, Michelle's two-year-old began crying. She remained completely engaged on her phone, so I looked back at him and began cooing, trying to soothe and distract him. "Just ignore him," Michelle shot at me, hardly breaking from her phone conversation. "If you coddle them, they'll never stop crying. *Ignore him*," she commanded.

I was stunned. Praying silently to get away from this situation, I began to take deep, silent yoga breaths in counts of four, breathing in through my nose and filling my lungs, then silently "whooshing" the air out of my slightly parted lips. Michelle's jabbering continued, and the baby's cries increased. It was getting to be all too much for me: Michelle's talk of not paying rent, her talk of "smacking" the children, her back-handed digs aimed at labelling me as inferior to her, and now her screaming baby. I didn't care how this all ended, I just wanted to get away.

In a sea of exiting students, Michelle's older three children suddenly appeared and jumped in the car. Michelle ended her phone call and began driving as the siblings soothed their baby brother. Gratefully, the positive energy of the children gifted the car with a tender mercy of Michelle's no longer speaking negatively. As we arrived back at Michelle's current house, I immediately excused myself, saying that I didn't want to "disrupt the after-school routine." I said quick goodbyes to all, and within moments, I was making my way back to my in-laws' home. As I processed the afternoon, I realised how unsafe I felt in Michelle's company. She never spoke well of the girls; she only said that she had taken custody of them because "no one else would." She spoke of how much of a trial they were, and yet that it would take a long time for her to "let them go." I was beginning to believe that saying this was her way of communicating that it would take a lot of money for her to let them go. She also bemoaned her landlords, her extended family, and even her bishop. Though I tried to push everything out of my mind, excusing it as move-related stress, I could not help but be worried about all of the children involved.

Arriving at my in-laws' empty house, I was able to shake off the day, unwind, shower, and even watch a little TV before slipping into bed, trying to shelve all of the negativity I had experienced that afternoon. As I reached to turn off the lights, a sudden barrage of text messages began coming from

Michelle. At first, she said she felt good about giving the girls to me for a trial. I responded that there was no hurry, but I was happy to help. She then said she did not feel good about the decision and felt like her family was being torn apart. "I am not a home-wrecker," I replied. "You are not obligated to me for anything," I added, sensing maybe she wanted me to fight for the girls? I did not know but liked the idea of no longer interacting with Michelle. Things just seemed all too stressful and I did not know how, or if, I should help.

Within seconds, she texted that she owed her brother money, and he would not give the girls back to her unless she paid him. "That's weird," I replied, suspecting this was a possible grifting technique. She texted again and again, increasing her hints for money, until she was almost demanding it. "I need to go to bed," I finally texted, increasingly uncomfortable with her continued asking and tired of politely refusing. "Goodnight."

I was emotionally exhausted, but I knew I would not sleep. I checked the time in Chile, and within minutes, Bruce and I were able to connect for a brief video call. I was so glad to see his face and hear his voice! I shared a brief summary of my day, hoping to see if he felt like I should keep engaging Michelle in case we could end up with the girls. Bruce said that he felt that it was my choice; I was closer to the situation, and though the occasional mention of Michelle giving the girls to us was probably a way of stringing us along for money,

I was in a better position to discern than he was. He had to leave for a meeting, closing by assuring me that he loved me and supported whatever I chose.

The call felt way too short, and I still wanted to process things with someone else. It was way too late to call anyone, so I decided to e-mail my friend, Kimberly. Kimberly was also an American Mormon married to an Australian. She and I became pen pals, having met virtually through the *Exponent II*, happily discovering our similarities. I trusted her and knew she would give wise, loving, and when needed, hard advice.

> *I am not sure about this whole thing. I am feeling more and more like I need to just report this to Children's Services and get out. Australia is terrible for adoption, so we would never have the girls placed with us through the Australian system—and because of the anti-adoption laws it is likely the girls will live the rest of their lives in foster care. It's sort of like I am turning my back on the situation, but the whole thing is much more complicated than I was led to believe. And maybe I'm wrong and this is all just moving stress for them. It must be crazy hard to move with kids.*

> *The dirty truth is, I am not sure I want to be a parent anymore, and this—what feels like game-playing—is too much for me. So I am going home on Friday, with or without the*

girls. I am over trying to have a family so have no patience with the government games mixed in with people manipulating children just to get money. I am concerned for all the children involved, so I think at this point it is best for me to report the situation and get out. I feel bad for the girls, but good about me.

Typing the e-mail relieved me and within moments of clicking "send," I was asleep. By morning, I had a response from Kimberly, written in her calming and fun style, which was just what I needed:

You can always take the portable DVD players back. If you want a giant teddy bear, keep it. Bruce might object to you sleeping with it, but that's your thing.

But what I am hearing here—and feel free to disagree with me—is that this is not something you want. There is nothing wrong with feeling that way. It is not your job to save all the children who need parents. Give yourself permission to let go of this if this isn't right for you. And then decide if there is anything you can do, and by that I also mean taking into account what you need right now. Maybe calling The Department of Children's Services is what this family needs?

*You don't have to make yourself sick to become
a mother. Nobody expects that of you. You have
already done so much more—so much more—
than most. It is enough. Nobody will think less
of you because of it. Heavenly Father certainly
won't. These girls are not your responsibility.
Good luck figuring it all out.*

Kimberly's words were just what I needed to make
a plan. I did not want to get stuck in Michelle's
car, and I did not want to give her any money. So
I decided I would offer to Michelle to pick up the
girls from her brother, and if needed, pay him
whatever money Michelle owed. Then I would drive
Michelle and the girls back to Sydney and leave
without getting out of the car. The next day, I would
drive home with a giant teddy bear seatbelted next
to me.

I prayed and, feeling at peace, called Bruce to
tell him what I had decided. "I think all they want
is money, and it just feels negative," I explained. "I
want to serve and get out."

"Maybe call the police as well," he agreed.
"The whole situation with the kids sounds dangerous.
Be careful." Resolving to report everything to the
local police afterwards, I texted Michelle with my
offer. She accepted instantly and told me when I
should pick her up.

4

WHEELS IN MOTION

I decided to spoil myself by getting a pedicure to help me relax for the day ahead. As I sat in the salon, feet soaking in a warm bubbling bath, I began to read in the *Doctrine and Covenants* as a part of my almost daily personal scripture reading. As I read, several verses struck me: "…I give unto you a new commandment, that you may understand my will concerning you…I give unto you directions how you may act before me…I, the Lord, am bound when ye do what I say; but when ye do not what I say, ye have no promise…" (82:8–10).

What was God commanding me? I wondered, quickly considering what God's will in this situation also might be. As I pondered this in my mind, I felt strongly that I was to protect these children. That I should not turn my back on them. I read on: "I give unto you this commandment, that ye bind yourselves by this covenant…" (82:15). I mused over this, wondering what commandment or covenant could be applied in my current situation, but as the sweetly scented foot spa bubbles began to tickle my toes, I relaxed. I had done enough. This trip was about service, not about adoption. "Trim and shape?" asked the nail technician, as she pulled the plug to the basin and nodded to my toes. "Yes," I said, moving my scriptures to find the nail polish I had chosen. I began to read again.

"...Orphans shall be provided for..." This was in Doctrine and Covenants section 83, verse 6, but this phrase seemed to jump from the page. *These children are orphans*, I thought. *Perhaps there is something we should provide for them?* I wasn't sure what I was supposed to learn, but I did feel the Spirit. I chuckled to myself about Section 83 and the part about wives and children being reliant on fathers for sustenance. Bruce and I had decided that in case we became parents, I would stay at home with the children. But those plans felt like a silly, youthful fantasy, the kind of thing that gave way to the smile of the older and wiser individual I had become.

Soon, my toes sparkled, and I felt rejuvenated.

Within the hour, I was standing in Michelle's living room. Her house was in commotion. Her children were running here and there as she and Trent barked out orders. After spending longer than I planned watching the chaos, Michelle finally decided that it was time to go. She carried more tension than the day before, but I presumed it was related to her impending move, in which I had no interest. "I have these great CDs," I said, trying to soften the mood. I wasn't looking forward to listening to Michelle for hours in the car, so I made sure I had something else. "They're by a church guy named John Bytheway. I thought you might like them."

Bytheway was a popular church speaker for teens because his talks were simple and entertaining. I appreciated his fun take on scriptures but was very weary of and disagreed with his traditional retelling of the place of women only as mothers. Still, because I had listened to these CDs previously, I was happy for the calm of a familiar and engaging faith speaker to accompany us on what might be an uneasy drive. As the road moved under us, Michelle said she liked what we were listening to, occasionally tearing up and looking longingly out the window. She mentioned giving the girls to me, but I wasn't biting. I was there to pay her debt and provide a lift. Nothing more.

In a little more than two hours' time, we arrived at her brother's house. It was a small beautiful house in a remote town, complete with water views. We went inside, where Michelle introduced me to her extended family, and they explained that the girls were having a shower. Within seconds, I spied the youngest one out of the corner of my eye, wrapped in a towel. She saw me, but ignored me, and began dancing, then flashing the adult male in the family, saying "I'm naked!" as if it were a joke, but to me, it seemed sexual and made me uneasy. I was already on edge

and surprised at the number of adults in the home.
I gripped my keys, ready to leave. Swallowing my
discomfort, I reminded myself that this would all be
for the police report.

Towel dance aside, this toddler was beautiful!
Even though her head was shaved, her bright,
smiling, blue eyes struck me. She was simply the
most beautiful child I had ever seen in my life!
Her sister was behind her, draped in a towel, and
she also began dancing in a manner that made me
uncomfortable. One of the women I had just been
introduced to picked up the older sister and began
to explain how she had cut and tried to style the
girl's hair. I wasn't impressed with the haircut, but
the bone structure of the girl's face and the beauty
of her sea-blue eyes were breathtaking. *No one gives
children this gorgeous away,* I thought. *No one.*

I was beginning to feel nauseous. Anxiety
filled me, and I craved the company of the Spirit,
which seemed very far away. I steadied myself
against a wall and someone offered me a glass of
water, inviting me to the kitchen. Sitting down, I
smiled and thanked them and soon found myself
alone. I did not mind being excluded; it gave me
a moment to offer a prayer, begging for protection.
They're going to ask me for money. Lots of money, I
thought. I was positive that this was a scheme. It
would not be the first time that church members
treated me as intellectually and spiritually inferior

because I was infertile. *The joke's on stupid, infertile me. Ha ha*, I silently berated myself. *I get it. Stupid Sherrie.*

Any lingering hope that the girls might be going home with me was well and truly gone in seeing these cherubs in person! I rolled my eyes, thinking about what a fool I had been to consider for a moment that anyone would ever give children this perfect away. I was angry at myself and desperately wanted to leave. I just wanted to get the girls, drive back, go to the police, then go home alone.

Over the next forty minutes, I sat alone in the empty kitchen, waiting and feeling like a lurker. Though my ongoing silent prayers brought a degree of peace, I remained on guard, occasionally listening to Michelle's muffled voice as she dressed the girls and discussed moving house with her extended family.

I was becoming impatient and looked at my watch creeping close to 7PM. It was at least a two-hour drive back to Michelle's, and from there, I had a forty minute drive to my in-laws'. It was Thursday night, and I wanted to make the twelve hour drive back to Brisbane on Friday. *This will all be over soon,* I reminded myself, still praying for release from this house that increasingly felt like a cage. Michelle finally called out that "we really need to get on the road," and within a few minutes, the pyjama-clad girls were secured in the car seats Michelle had strapped in. The John Bytheway CD began automatically playing when I started the car, but I turned the volume down to a whisper, allowing a hush to fill the space. I noticed that well before we made it to the highway onramp, the girls had already fallen asleep.

No one had asked me for money, and a swirl of relief washed over me. Taking a deep breath, I offered another silent prayer of thanks, begging God to remain with me. I was still anxious and afraid. As we drove, through sometimes teary eyes, Michelle occasionally muttered that she could not give the girls away. I said nothing, and reminded myself of my plan: *Drive back, go to the police. Drive back, go to the police. Drive back, go to the police.*

The autumn sunset was a spectacular escort, making for a glorious coastal drive, where I could not ignore the absolutely creative beauty of God's good Earth. Mesmerised, my thoughtful admiration was interrupted when Michelle's phone rang. I paused John Bytheway to allow her to better hear her phone, hoping to not wake the girls.

I tuned out of Michelle's conversation as best as I could, but she began clashing with whoever she was speaking with. She ended, answered, and made more calls, each time increasing in agitation until she was shouting. With my eyes glued to the road, I listened. I gathered that there had been a physical fight between students at the school of Michelle's oldest daughter, and the victim was a girl that Michelle's family knew through church. It seemed that Michelle's daughter fed false information to an aggressor, and those words caused the church girl to be physically assaulted. Michelle's heated speech in defence of her daughter woke the sleeping toddlers, yet they were silent, seemingly used to listening and watching the woman they called "Mummy" as she angrily bellowed into her phone. The calm of the sunset and Bytheway's words were gone, and my anxiety returned.

We eventually pulled in at Michelle's house, finding the most chaotic scene I'd ever experienced. The children were running in and out of the house with boxes and bags for moving, many of which were strewn across the front porch, yard, and driveway. Trent was out front, disjointedly directing the children as well as making and receiving calls regarding the trouble at school. It was after nine, and all four children between the ages of two and thirteen were wide awake, running in and out of the house.

Michelle exited my car without a word to me and began speaking with Trent about Peyton's involvement in the fight. Trent was angry about the situation but seemed even angrier with the other parents, the school, and church leaders, who all became involved in the situation. I released the girls from their car seats, speaking very little and only to the girls, and slowly, everyone moved into the house. I stood uncomfortably in the living room, anxious to leave, not sure how to excuse myself.

I was tired. Physically tired from all the driving, emotionally drained from listening to Michelle and even a bit frustrated with Robin for connecting me to this situation. It had been an intense week, and I just wanted to go home. *Perhaps I won't go to the police*, my exhausted mind reasoned. *Moving is hard. Maybe this is just a big house-moving mess and I'm reading everything wrong.*

It seemed that Michelle wanted to have a family talk about the situation with Peyton, and my heart softened toward her for moving to create a space for the family to communicate. But Trent sternly shut down Michelle's attempts at a family meeting, angrily reading aloud a curt, remorseless, and threatening text message he'd written in response to the Peyton situation, ending with "do not tell us how to parent our own child." As soon as he finished reading, he looked directly at Michelle with fire in his eyes and furiously pressed the send button.

Michelle paused, then shrugged.

She appeared utterly defeated, and I felt keenly sorry for her, even afraid for her. I slumped into a seat, taken aback by the interaction and wildly unsure of what to do. Within seconds, Michelle's three-year-old son climbed on my lap. He seemed to know that his smile could diffuse unease when needed, and he smiled charmingly, almost bewitchingly at me, distracting me for a moment from the utter turmoil surrounding us. Moving house is always stressful, but the level of tension at

Michelle's place was palpable, even sickening. I was tired of being surrounded and even felt like I was absorbing this feeling of turmoil. I felt like I was on a gyrating, unbalanced, emotional carousel that pulsed sour music, rotating in an uncomfortably dizzy spin.

The three-year-old boy was called away, and I excused myself to use the restroom, where I splashed cool water on my face. When I came out, everyone was gone! *What next?* Looking around, it appeared that everyone was in the driveway, piling up bags. I realised that by being outside, especially in the driveway where I was parked, I was physically closer to being able to leave and get out of this whole situation. I smiled as I quickly sailed towards my car. I intended to wish everyone well and tell them "keep in touch," among other polite lies, then slip into my car and *go.*

I stopped suddenly when I saw how intensely Michelle was looking at me. "I don't want them," she said. Her voice was empty of emotion. I froze. Was she saying what I thought she was saying? I was not prepared for whatever was next, and fear overcame me. *What is going on?* She turned toward her children. "Everyone say goodbye to Cheyenne and Reesey." The children obediently gathered around, hugging and saying goodbye.

At that moment, I fully believe that time stopped. It felt like the zenith performance of an intensely and perfectly trained ballerina: after a lifetime of fervent swirls and passion, she was crystallised in pure muscular elongation on a single toe. This moment could not last for more than a breath. I needed to decide exactly and immediately if I would take the girls home; then the moment would be gone, never to happen again. I was in shock, and instinctively began to form the word no, frantically wishing I knew where the closest police station was. But my mouth was suddenly paralyzed. I heard a voice that was audible to me, but I knew no one else could hear it. The words were deliberate, casting a sharp light through the confusion and anarchy.

"*I have put this in place for you to be a mother, if you desire. It is your choice.*"

I knew it was the voice of God. In my heart, I hastily, powerfully, and gratefully responded with a resounding, Yes! I want to be a mother. And instantly, time started its fervent dancing again.

Michelle's husband was holding Cheyenne, the three-year-old. "We're really sorry," he said to me, as he and his wife shared knowing smiles and nods. Michelle began pushing the child's head from side to side, revealing a beautiful, square-shaped face. Michelle continued, "her head is shaped so weird. I tried cutting her hair, but it's fine and naturally wavy and she has a widow's peak." I was confused, my sense of vanity taking over. I have a square face shape, my hair is fine and naturally wavy and I have a widow's peak. Was she trying to insult me?

Trent agreed. "The colour is ugly, too," he said… "not brown, and not blonde…" I've been called dishwater blonde, mousey blonde, wannabe blonde—all of the names! But that never bothered me. I loved the colour of her hair—it was the same as mine! I was totally confused, trying to make sense of the spiritual and emotional pandemonium I was experiencing.

Like lightning, revelation struck me. They were apologising to me for giving me what they believed was an ugly child! I was sickened and outraged as they continued to hurl insults at this celestial being, yet my mouth was clamped shut. I feared speaking the wrong thing and losing the miracle, and could only observe the halo around the gorgeous child in their arms. She remained silent as they spit out the kinds of words that would have brought anyone to tears. She seemed to retain a kind of inner glow that reflected that she wanted to believe what they were saying was wrong. Yet she cast her face down, putting her hands over her eyes, trying to hide.

Trent handed the magnificently gorgeous girl to their eldest son and directed him to put her in my car. It was then that I realised that they had been shoving garbage bags into my car. The bags were filled with the girls' things! Michelle picked up the two-year-old, Reesey. "Maybe we should keep her," she said to her bald husband. "She looks more like us." Microscopic hair regrowth seemed to be peeking out with a light blonde sheen and her blue eyes made her look like a classic cherub.

Thunder rolled into my ears only: "*No. They remain together.*" In that instant, I knew that these sisters were not to be separated, at any cost. If they chose to give only the eldest child to me, I would have to decline. I knew that these sisters were bound in ways that reached beyond mortality, beyond anything I could ever imagine. I desperately wanted them, but I knew immediately that God had commanded me to keep them together. With complete faith, I took a deep breath and prepared to refuse both as a means of keeping them together.

"Naw," said Trent, his southern drawl piercing through the spirit that had surrounded me. "They both go," he said dryly.

The next thing I remember, I was driving in silence to my in-laws' house. I glanced back at the girls, who had instantly fallen asleep in the car seats still secured in the back. It was pitch black out, and as I began to listen to the rhythm of my tires on the road, I recognised that adrenaline was still pumping through me. I felt terrified, like I was in a complete state of shock.

5

THE LONG DRIVE HOME

The girls woke when I pulled in at my in-laws' house. Within seconds, the girls were racing around the house, opening every cupboard and door they could reach. I was tired, surprised, and confused! In my years of teaching and babysitting, I had never seen children so boldly take over! As they moved around the house, I tried to tidy up after them— but they were much too fast for me!

My mother-in-law collected fragile Lladro figurines, and I was terrified of an expensive disaster. After I corralled the girls away from the breakables, they ran to the kitchen where they promptly emptied everything from the refrigerator in mere seconds. Thankfully, there was very little in the fridge. As I began to put the few items back, the girls raced to my father-in-law's computer and printer! Here they helped themselves to paper and pencils in a mad dash to scribble as many drawings as they possibly could, as I silently thanked God that they had not drawn on the walls!

I miraculously persuaded the girls to go to the car and help me bring in some of the garbage bags that had their belongings. They watched as I carried and dragged some of the bags into the house and dumped them on a table, hoping to find some kind of toy or something that could help settle them. I also searched for clean underwear. Michelle told me that they were both potty-trained, but the youngest already had a tiny accident, and I was wary. I couldn't find clean or dirty underwear, but before I could worry about that, the girls grabbed all of the entertainment system remote controls and began aggressively pushing every button. Swiping the remotes away, I said, "This is not working!"

"Broken?" said one of the girls, referring to the remote. If only! I was too tired to process and respond, so instead, I suggested we have a night-time prayer and go to bed. *Poof!* That did the trick! They dutifully folded their arms and listened to me pray, thanking God for them. They chorused an "Amen" at the end. I was hopeful for rest.

I led the girls upstairs to one of the ready-for-visiting-grandchildren bedrooms with twin beds. I put each of them in a bed and tried to settle them. No luck. We moved to a neighbouring room with a queen-sized bed, where I hoped they might fall asleep together. Nope. Not even close. This time, they began loudly crying and wailing as if I was torturing them! This was not going well. The girls seemed to instantaneously tear the covers off each bed, creating a chaos that I did not have the wherewithal to deal with. Fearing they would go in and destroy my in-laws' bedroom, I finally took them to the room I had been staying in.

"Third time's a charm, right?" I spoke aloud, desperately trying to remain calm. This room was built into the back of the garage and removed from the rest of the house. It had a queen bed, a private bathroom, and my small suitcase. Because the room was accessed through the garage, the door had a deadbolt, well out of reach from little hands. I slid the bolt shut, locking us all in the room. At least the rest of the house would be protected.

As the girls opened, shut, and reopened the closet and every drawer in the room and bathroom, I decided to open my laptop and send Bruce a short e-mail explaining to him that I had the girls. I looked around to see that this room had also become a jumbled mess, but as it was creeping close to midnight, I did not care. I turned the bathroom light on but turned off all the other lights, virtually ignoring the girls. At last, I slipped off my shoes and crawled into bed. I was exhausted. Even if they didn't sleep and still found things to destroy and play with, I needed rest. Within seconds of placing my head on a pillow, the girls came and joined me in bed, giggling themselves silly. I was asleep in seconds.

Around 2AM, I awoke. The girls were both soundly asleep on either side of me, and I became worried that they might fall out of the bed. I slithered out from between them, then moved them closer to the centre of the bed. Slightly awakened, yet with a new panic, I crept out of the room to send frantic e-mails to Kimberly and the *Exponent II* women asking for suggestions for handling children on road trips. With the grand time zone differences, I prayed I would have responses by daylight. I soon crawled into one of the upstairs beds and crashed hard, only waking when my alarm went off at 5AM.

Bruce suggested that I stay at my in-laws' and on his return from Chile, he would fly to Sydney and we could drive back together. But I was too acutely aware of everything breakable in the house to dare stay a second longer than necessary. Besides, my in-laws had a pool. Though the pool was encased by a security gate, I had discovered that these wee girls were climbers, and I was concerned about their safety. Mostly, I felt prompted to just go home.

I silently checked e-mails, praying that advice about road trips with children had arrived. Kimberly responded and recommended that I not have the girls sit side-by-side in the car, and reminded me that kids' DVDs would make the drive significantly better. She also suggested stopping regularly at play parks to encourage the girls to burn some energy. In a twelve-hour drive, that would be a lot of play parks! The *Exponent II* women responded with various tips and tricks in working with children, mostly offering congratulations, love, and support. Importantly, they uniformly recommended getting the girls into a routine as soon as we arrived "home." These women kindly knew that although I had experience with other people's children in teaching and child-minding, I had no real experience with caring for toddlers in a long-term arrangement.

Most charitably, no one mentioned how crazy it was to do a twelve-hour road trip in a single day with toddlers.

I heard a tiny brushing noise, directing me away from the e-mails I was furiously reading. I saw a small head peek around the edge of the door to the room where I was sitting. It was Cheyenne, standing behind the door she had pushed open enough to reveal her smiling shyly, yet trying to hide. "Good morning, beautiful," I said to her, grinning. I was still disturbed about the way Michelle and Trent had spoken about Cheyenne's appearance, so I decided to call both girls "beautiful" as often as I could.

"What are you doing?" she asked, then covered her mouth with her hand as if to hide that she had spoken aloud.

"I'm getting ready to drive to Queensland!"

"Where's that?"

"North. A long drive. We'll go today—all three of us."

"Even Reesey?"

"Even Reesey."

Cheyenne went and woke Reesey, and within minutes, they were each doing tiny jobs to load things into the car for our trip. They chose fresh clothes from their bags and slowly dressed themselves. My in-laws had dry breakfast cereal, but no milk, and I was too weary to try going into a grocery store with them. I found some bread in the freezer and made toast with margarine and a side of seasonally fresh strawberries. They shyly ate a few bites of the toast and gobbled down the strawberries. It was still early, just after six, but I hoped to be on the road soon.

There was a ringing on my computer–it was Bruce on a video call. "That's Bruce!" I said to the girls. Cheyenne and Reesey flanked me, sometimes standing behind me to hide, other times pointing and touching the computer screen.

"Hi," said Bruce in a soft, loving, and excited voice. His speech was gentle and caring, a tone I had only heard him use sparingly in the past. The girls chattered at him while Bruce sat smiling. I could see tears in his eyes. He was in love. I was in love, too. Even though the behaviour of the girls was difficult for me to comprehend, all I really felt was love. I loved their little hands. I loved their noses. I loved the slapping sound their tiny feet made as they ran across the tile floor. I loved the scribbled drawings they made on stacks of paper. I loved their voices. I loved hearing them laugh. I was in love.

Bruce was working to get a flight home as soon as possible. From Chile, that would still take some time. "It's really okay if you stay at Mum and Dad's," he assured me. "They'll be back from their trip soon and can help out." I was hesitant to be honest with Bruce about how poorly behaved the girls had been the night before, and about my fear of them breaking … everything. In a way, I already felt like I was failing at parenthood, because I was not confident to take them into a store, fearing they would run amok. The only thing I confessed to him was what a *terrible* state his parents' house was in. "Don't worry about it," he laughed. "They've had kids. They get it."

"No," I said to Bruce. "I really feel like I need to get home as soon as possible."

"Okay," he said. "But you don't need to drive the whole way today. You could take two or three days and just stay at motels along the way." As soon as he said it, I dismissed it, fearing what havoc the girls might cause at a motel. But I didn't want to scare Bruce, so I said nothing. Mostly, I felt even more impressed to get the girls to my home.

"I'll see how I go," I responded to Bruce, eyeing a pair of tiny hands as they began again to start grabbing at items in the kitchen, sure to be strewn about the house. "Your parents' house is a mess. Like bad. Really bad," I said, worried about damaging my relationship with Bruce's parents.

71

"They won't mind," Bruce replied. I wasn't so sure. Every room the girls went into turned into a disaster! How did they do that so fast? As our call concluded, Bruce and I told each other we loved each other. But this time, it seemed more intense. His obvious, immediate devotion towards the girls reflected a faith in God that we would be parents; it was a faith that I had buried on that Tangalooma beach some months before. His faith—rather than my own—inspired me.

I rolled the giant teddy bears into the foot wells of the back seat, creating footrests so the girls' legs wouldn't dangle for the drive. As I packed their things into the car, I tried to focus on clothes rather than the broken and miscellaneous toys that looked mostly like garbage. The unopened car DVD players sat on the front passenger seat because I thought we would be fine without them. I still had not found any clean underwear for the girls but trusted that somehow everything would work out.

It was 7:30AM by the time I scrawled a note of apology to my in-laws for the terrible mess I left in their home and began the drive, with the girls securely strapped in their car seats, side by side, against Kimberly's recommendation. *They might be afraid*, I reasoned to myself. *They should stay together.*

I soon discovered how formidable my naïveté truly was. After forty minutes, we stopped because one of the girls needed to use the toilet. We stopped about ten minutes after that because the other one felt she needed the toilet. Each time we stopped, it took a colossal amount of time to get in and out of the car and in and out of the bathroom. I quickly learned to insist that they both use the toilet every time one said they needed to go. I also learned that it was typical for two- and three-year-olds to take longer to get in and out of the car, but having limited experience with children of that age, everything was new to me. I was on a steep learning curve. I stopped two more times because of squabbling between the girls.

"How is the driving going?" texted Michelle at one of my stops.

"Good," I lied in reply, determined to remain positive. "I'll easily make it home tonight."

"Drive safe," she returned, then was silent.

We finally made it to a fast-food restaurant that normally only took me two hours to reach when driving on my own but had taken almost four hours to get there that morning. I guessed at some food choices for the girls and ordered for myself, choosing a table in the outside play area. I quickly ate while they zipped back and forth, playing on the slides and rocking horses. There were very few customers at this removed rest stop, and my car was parked next to the gated play area, so I knew the girls were secure and were within my line of sight. I decided to set up the car DVD players. It had been a very foolish idea to forgo installing them, and I hoped that with them, the girls would stop fighting with each other.

Cheyenne noticed immediately as I moved outside of the play area. "Where are you going?" she asked, staring at me, hands gripped on the metal fence posts.

"I'm just going to the car to put some movie players in for you!" I replied, trying to sound happy and calming.

"Are you coming back for me?"

I found the question strange but focused on my task. "Yes! Of course! I'm not leaving. Just doing something in the car."

"Are you giving me away?"

"No." I was stunned this time and looked directly at her. "I just met you, and I never want to give you away." I could tell that she did not like the fence posts between us. "You can watch me; I'm not leaving without you." I opened the DVD player box in front of her and hastily attached the screens to the back of the headrests on the front seats. Then I uncurled the cords and attached them, never sitting inside the car as I worked. Cheyenne remained fixed, her hands firmly gripping the fence posts, her gaze attached to my every move. Though I was never more than six feet from her, I sensed her desperation to remain fastened to my side.

At least I wanted to think that her desperation was for me. She smiled almost eerily whenever I looked at her. She was beautiful, but her smile appeared painted on, rather than genuine.

There was something there and in her emerald eyes that suggested an insecurity, or desperation; I wasn't sure. But it was there.

"Done!" I announced, closing the doors of the car. After insisting they use the restroom, we were soon back on the road. I only had three DVDs with me, two that I had purchased when I bought the DVD players and one I had swiped from my in-laws' house. I hoped it would be enough.

The girls quickly picked up that I would stop whenever they said they needed the toilet. After one such stop, not even halfway into the trip, they called out that they "didn't need the toilet anymore" as they ran to the play area next to the restrooms.

"I totally fell for that," I said aloud to no one—both girls were busy squealing with delight, bellies down on the seats of swings, legs kicking in utter joy. Though their happy noises delighted my heart, these additional stops worried me. I began to fret about how long the drive was taking us, still determined to get home that day. Luckily, it was a bright day and the roads were almost empty as we drove north along the coast. There were occasional fellow motorists, but not enough to make the drive demanding, which was a blessing as my travel companions distracted me.

Between DVDs, Cheyenne chatted with me, smiling and asking where we were going. "To Queensland," was all I said, trying to keep things simple. The situation was complicated enough for the adults, and I hoped to keep things as uncomplicated as possible for the children. Reesey was quieter. Her speech was less developed compared to other two-year-olds I'd known, but I assigned it as a symptom of shyness and uncertainty and presumed she would speak more when she felt more comfortable.

As we drove, I occasionally asked questions. "Which tree over there is the tallest?" or "what does that cloud look like?" Both girls would look, but Cheyenne usually answered. Together they were cute, and as I drove, I loved hearing them begin to sing along to the songs in the movies they were watching on repeat. Around 4:00, I pulled into a solitary rest stop along the highway. I had never stopped at this place before, but along with fuel amenities, it promised a small choice of restaurants, and I hoped for a children's play area.

I was wrong. It was more like a food court in an airport, with restaurants surrounding a shared dining area. Though different from what I expected, selections of chicken nuggets and french fries were in abundance, and I needed a break from driving. So we ordered and sat down to eat. Realising that this was the first time I'd been able to sit with them in a relative moment of peace, I decided to ask them about themselves. "Cheyenne, what is your favourite food?"

"This is," she responded simply, her mouth full of a combination of everything we had ordered.

"What about you, Reesey?"

"This is," she responded tepidly, casting her eyes downward. Her voice sounded sad, and I wondered if she really liked what she was eating.

"Are you still hungry?" I asked. No response. "Do you want something else to eat?"

"Can we have ice cream?" The response came from Cheyenne, but I saw Reesey's mouth curl into a smile as soon as Cheyenne spoke it.

"Yeah," said Reesey, fully grinning for the first time since I had met her.

"Sure," I said with a smile, "after we finish our food."

I tried again. "Reesey, what is your favourite colour?"

She ignored me. I asked the same of Cheyenne. "I don't know," was her answer. "What's a colour?" I was stumped; I had never known toddler-age children to not know the names of at least a few basic colours. Between bites of fresh strawberries, nuggets drowned in ketchup, swallows of cordial, and my own veggie-laden burger, I began to point out colours. "The strawberries are red, dark red in some places, lighter in others. Where else can you see red?"

"Ketchup?"

"*Yes*! Well done. Where else?"

They pointed at most red things, and sometimes other colours. I would correct and tell them the names of other colours and challenge them to spot those colours in different places. This went on for the remainder of the meal, focused on primary colours and pink. It became clear that they both preferred pink. Bright pink, pale pink, pastel pink, neon pink—they happily pointed out every kind of pink they could find until we were all giggling.

It felt a little like Christmas; there was something magical about seeing and sharing the names of the colours with the girls! I was feeling blessed and a little re-energised. After using the facilities, we exited the restaurant omnibus with ice cream cones in hand, ready to drive the remaining distance.

Cheyenne had quickly picked up on how to start and stop the DVD player with the two screens, but I asked her to wait until they finished eating their ice cream cones. As they licked the ice cream from their cones, and arms, and anywhere else it had dripped, I ventured to ask them something that had been on my mind. "So… um. My name is Sherrie. But I would like to be your forever mummy. So… um… what name would you like to call me?"

Michelle said that they called her Mummy, because they had copied her children and she could not be bothered to correct them. I did not want to confuse them or do something that would offend Michelle. There was only silence from the back, and when I glanced at them, they were licking, but looking at me, so I was sure that they had heard me. "How about 'Mummy Sherrie?'" I suggested.

"Okay, Mummy Sherrie," said Cheyenne between the first bites of her ice cream cone.

"Okay," echoed Reesey.

"Okay," I said, my heart swelling. It felt like a momentous moment. "You can put the DVD player on when you're ready." The DVD player powered on with the $1.99 discs I had grabbed when I made the impulsive entertainment purchase. I'd read Ludwig Bemelmans' *Madeline* books when I was a child, though I could remember little other than she was raised by a nun and she had red hair. While listening to the cartoon movies as I drove, I thought the random choice was fortuitous.

Travelling continued at a snail's pace, but as the sun set, the girls finally fell soundly asleep in the car. My phone rang, and I pulled over to answer it. It was Mandy! Mandy and her two-year-old daughter, Mali, had been staying with us while they waited for their new home to be ready to move in. I was so happy to hear from her and more grateful than ever that she and Mali were staying with us! "How are you doing?" she asked with compassion and brightness. I was so glad to hear her voice— hearing from a friend gave me courage at a moment when I was struggling and tired.

"I'm good!" I said, determined that it somehow be true. "The girls are asleep, so I am hoping to power through the rest of the drive."

"Where are you?"

"Still four or five hours away." I replied, not sure of where I was due to a small detour that took me through a tiny town.

"How are you holding up?" She paused and added, "Really." She could tell from my voice that I was struggling. It had been an emotional week.

"I'm tired," I confessed. "But I bought a Red Bull, and I am sipping it." This was true. The taste was terrible, but I had been slowly swallowing it like medicine in hopes of creating internal energetic powers. "I think I'll be okay," I quickly added. "How are you doing?"

"I'm great!" she said brightly. "Call me in a while and I can talk to you as you drive to help you stay awake. Right now I am going to go to the store. Bruce gave me some money to go and get toys for the girls. Is there anything you want in particular?"

It had been years since I shopped in a toy store and had not even thought about toys. "Um… I don't know… I guess whatever Mali would like?" Mali was only a few months older than Reesey, so Mandy would know better than me what toddler girls liked.

"Maybe a mini kitchen…" I suggested, recalling how much I loved my pretend kitchen when I was little. "With fake food and stuff like that?"

"Okay. I'll do that." Mandy replied. "And do you want me to buy some kid food, too?"

"Yes!" I said in reflex. But the phrase stunned me. *Kid food.* What was that? I was utterly gobsmacked.

"Okay," said Mandy. "I'll be back soon. Call me if you need to talk to me to help you stay awake."

I began driving again. But I was still puzzled. Had the food at my house not been edible for Mandy's daughter? Was I feeding the children something wrong? Mostly I wondered what on earth was "kid food?" What do children eat? I thought back to my own childhood, but could not recall eating anything that was different to what my parents ate, excepting the fiery horseradish sauce my dad liked, and the salted Granny Smith apples my mother ate.

I was alert for the remainder of the drive, praying to stay awake and drive safely in between praying for help and guidance on how to best parent these girls and praying for the miracle that we still needed with all of Australia's anti-adoption laws. But in between prayers, I could not help but keep wondering what "kid food" was. The distraction was probably a blessing in keeping my mind active and my body awake.

It was just after midnight when we finally arrived. Like the night before, the girls awoke as we pulled into the garage. Greeting us in the front room was a delightful play kitchenette, complete with pots, pans, plastic food, and other toys. The girls gazed at everything as though magical fairies had brought perfectly sized playthings just for them. In a near-vacant space by the laundry room that previously only had the skeleton of an unmade bed, there now lay an additional fresh mattress covered in lively cartoon sheets and cuddly blankets that were loaned to us from Loraine, who lived only a few blocks away. Thanks to her and Mandy, the space was perfectly arranged for the girls. Upon seeing the colourful spread, the girls climbed into the beds and went to sleep immediately. They were tired. Maybe even as tired as I was. Looking at my watch, I knew that unloading the car would be a job for the light of tomorrow.

Taking a moment to look in the kitchen, I found boxes of children's cereal, white bread, creamy peanut butter, plum jelly, macaroni and cheese mixes, pizza-flavoured crackers, and a variety of familiar fresh fruits. Kid food. The mystery was solved.

6

MIRACLES

Bruce had taken a long, all-night flight from Chile, arriving home around seven-thirty that morning, just as sleep deprived as I was. The girls were already awake and happily playing with the toys Mandy set up. But the memory of Bruce and his glowing smile as he stood in our doorway with the sunlight shining around his frame is etched in my mind. We were in a new world, and it felt like magic. I was intensely grateful that he was there.

"This is Daddy Bruce," I said, introducing the girls as he stood in the sunlit entry.

He smiled vibrantly and with a soft voice, said "Hi."

"Are you the daddy in the house?" asked Cheyenne.

Bruce beamed. "I guess I am!"

Reesey smiled at Bruce but quickly returned to playing. Mandy's daughter, Mali, and Cheyenne joined in playing while Mandy prepared breakfast. Bruce unpacked his luggage and showered while I unpacked the car, dumping almost everything in the wash. When I came to the oversized teddy bears, I sneakily took them upstairs and stashed them in a closet. I confirmed that the girls needed underwear as well as shoes, so after we all ate breakfast, Bruce and I planned to take the girls shopping. Mandy also needed to do some shopping for their new home, so she and Mali headed out for the day. With Saturday morning inching into afternoon, our tired team of Bruce, the girls, and myself headed out for an adventure!

Strapping the girls in a two-seater shopping trolley, Bruce and I wandered through the children's section of a department store. We had never previously shopped in this section, but eventually we found bubblebath, children's shampoo, non-spill drink cups, and children's tableware. In the bedding section, Cheyenne chose a bright pink bedspread decorated with dancing black and pink butterflies. Reesey chose a black bedspread with huge, bright hummingbirds in every happy colour. Realising that I had no clue about children's clothing sizes, I sent a text to Michelle asking about the girls' sizes. She responded that Reesey was size zero and Cheyenne was size zero or maybe one. Clueless to children's sizes, I was completely unaware of how tiny and underfed the girls were for children who were two and three years old.

Thankfully, the girls went to sleep quickly that night and rose on Sunday morning without a fuss. We were new to the ward, having uneventfully moved in just two months earlier. Uneventful, because it was a large ward, and as we did not have children, we went unnoticed by the majority. The girls were becoming clingy, so after the sacrament meeting, we all went to the ward nursery to join the half dozen children already there. Bruce stepped out for a moment to flag down a member of the bishopric in regard to a calling that had been offered to us and we planned to accept. When he heard the reason for Bruce's sooner-than-anticipated return, this counsellor said he thought we should meet with the bishop.

Thus, in the final hour of church, as the girls had become happily distracted by the other children and the plentiful nursery toys, Bruce and I slipped out for a quick visit with the bishop. Warmly welcoming us, he asked us what was going on. "You need time to adjust to your new life," he said. "Two- and three-year-olds can be a challenge. I think it's best to not complicate your life with a calling at this time." His voice was filled with love and calm. I was a tad disappointed because I had come to find that a calling is one of the best ways to get to know people in a new ward, but I also felt relieved.

Our new bishop also offered us an additional blessing: he was a counsellor at LDS Family Services. The ghosts of my meetings with Michelle and Trent were beginning to haunt my sleep-deprived mind, and some of the things the girls had begun to say made me fear that they had been abused. Our bishop arranged for us to have the first available appointment that coming Tuesday with a counsellor named Zoia, who specialised in working with children. We were relieved, grateful and a little teary as we left his office.

We dashed home and left the girls with Mandy, who had offered to watch them so Bruce and I could go out and shop for proper bedroom furniture for the girls. We knew of a furniture store with an adjoining warehouse, which meant that most items were available and in stock. We borrowed Mandy's truck and loaded it with a bed frame and mattress that matched the single bed we already had, and two matching hutches–one for each girl.

When we arrived back at the house, Mandy fed and entertained the girls while Bruce and I worked to set up the girls' bedroom. Bruce worked on putting the bed frames and then each hutch together, while I dressed the beds with the freshly washed sheets and the new blanket sets that the girls had chosen and I had washed the day before. I folded their new and old clothes, all freshly laundered, and placed them in the hutches and closet. And finally, I placed a giant teddy bear by each of their beds. Tired, but happy, Bruce and I finally invited the girls into their new room.

"Okay. Come on in," I said. The walls and hutches were white, which made the girls' bedding pop in a particularly bright way. Within a breath, their shy smiles turned into gaping grins. They stood, not making a sound, wide-eyed, looking around. They turned to each other, grasped each others' hands, and began jumping, hugging and squealing with delight. They were clearly thrilled. "This is the one you picked out," I said to Cheyenne, pointing to the bed that was flowering in pink butterflies.

Bruce directed Reesey to the multi-coloured hummingbirds. "Mine?" she asked with bright, hopeful eyes. Bruce assured her it was. Soon they were jumping and laughing, pure joy in action where they alternately hugged the giant teddy bears, then raced around, occasionally pausing to gaze at the room. Their room. I smiled in spite of myself, my exhaustion, and my anxiety. Happiness flooded our home, and it felt like heaven.

It truly felt like miracles were surrounding us.

When we first opened our home to Mandy, I naïvely felt that we were helping her with a place to stay. But having her there helping us with the furniture, setting up toys and shopping for "kid food" was astronomically helpful for us. Mandy was a miracle. Our new bishop, who worked with LDS Family Services, knew exactly who to call to set up counselling for the girls, saving us weeks of wait time and administrative processing. Our bishop was a miracle. Loraine, a new friend from the Relief Society and our neighbourhood, the one who delivered the extra mattress and bedding on loan that first night, was a miracle. Bruce's employers, who were generous enough to allow him to immediately fly home, were also a miracle.

Everything at that moment felt like a miracle.

7

ZOIA AND PSYCHOLOGY

"One of you, come with me," said Zoia, in a gruff, almost cold manner quickly adding, "the other, stay here." We'd arrived early and been sent directly into her office. It appeared as though the counsellor was waiting for us and had been informed that this was an urgent, unusual meeting. Her personal office had a desk, comfortable chairs, a bookcase of children's books and bins filled with a variety of children's toys. The girls saw small figures that they could hold in their hands and began to collect them and play. With a nod, we decided that Bruce would stay in the office with the girls, so I followed the clipboard-carrying counsellor to a separate room. This room had a long table, whiteboard and a dozen chairs.

Her name was Zoia, and she was from New Zealand. She had an exotic look about her: rust-brown hair, a strong chin, and chocolate-caramel eyes. "Alright," she started in a business-like tone. "Your name?" I began to give her all of our information but was suddenly reminded that I didn't know the girls' last names. Michelle gave me medical and government benefits cards for the girls, but the surnames on all of the cards differed; one set of cards had Michelle's surname, but the others were different. I shared only the first names for the girls and withheld Michelle and Trent's names entirely. I also shared what little I knew of the natural parents: that they were incarcerated, that I had been told that they were supposedly wicked, and that I had been forbidden from contacting anyone in the birth family.

Suddenly, I just broke down. Through tears, I explained that I was still tired. Not just physically tired, but emotionally tired from years of infertility treatments and the isolation that comes with being childless and Mormon. I sobbed while explaining that I was not prepared for any of this and had not expected to bring two children home with me. But now that I had, I desperately wanted to keep them. I also shared that parenting seemed to come easy to me when I looked after my friend's children, but since this whole situation began materialising, I felt like I was in no way skilled to do any of this. "I don't know how to be a mother," I sobbed. "I want to help them, and I know they need help from everything they've been through, but I don't know what to do."

Her voice became firm, and with perfect compassion, she spoke. "These children have been brought to you," she said. "I meet a lot of people in my work. Parenting isn't always natural, but *you can do it.*" I needed those words. I needed someone to tell me that I could do this. And frankly, I needed to cry. In the counselling office, I felt like I had permission to admit that being a mother maybe didn't come naturally to me and say out loud how scared I was of the improbability of everything that had happened and had yet to happen to have us adopt the girls. "Now," she said after I composed myself, "Let's get back to the girls."

We went back to her office where Bruce was sitting on the floor, patiently playing with the girls. As Bruce and I sat in chairs, Zoia explained that with children, you often watch them as they play. She observed them for a moment, then asked how they played together at home. I hesitated to answer. They did not play well; often, they bit and hit one another. They seemed to scream more than not. "Um. Well… They usually hold their dolls on their hips. They tilt their head to one shoulder and act like they are talking on a phone… complaining about their children."

"Uh-huh," nodded Zoia. "They're modelling what they've seen. What else?"

"They sometimes tell whoever they are speaking to on the phone to 'hold on,' then they violently hit their dolls, and then roughly throw the doll in a corner." The level of violence in the way the girls played had surprised me, but I didn't know if what was going on was normal.

"Okay!" said Zoia, sounding keen to begin real work. "What you need to do is, go and take the doll after one of the girls does this. Rock it, tell the doll you love her. Ask if she is okay. Show them how you are supposed to treat a doll as if the doll were a real baby."

"I can do this," I said with confidence.

"Uh-hum," said Zoia with love. "You can pretend to put down a phone, rock the doll. Offer to feed the doll and so on. Teach them about love using their dolls." Zoia gave us some additional words of encouragement and advice, and before I knew it, our time was spent. We made a standing appointment to see her, and as we left, I felt relieved.

"She knows what she's talking about," Bruce said, as we drove home. "Let's do *everything* she tells us to do." I did. I began to write down whatever questions I had about the girls, then took the list to my appointments with Zoia, where we would discuss each item. Zoia was patient and loving and gave me time to make notes as she answered each question.

Our first sessions almost entirely reflected my learning how to work with children who were dealing with attachment disorder. A very broad description of attachment disorder is when a child fails to form and develop normal "attachments" to primary caregivers in early childhood. This can have severe long-term consequences that can result in social anxiety and relationship problems that last well into adulthood. For the most part, treatment is found in developing a positive, loving, relationship with a permanent carer.

Zoia was as opposed to corporal punishment as I was, but because that was the only form of discipline the girls seemed to know, Bruce and I needed to define boundaries and consequences, plus focus on positive behaviour. Following Zoia's enthusiasm about celebrating kind actions, I taped a large sheet of paper at knee level in the kitchen where Bruce and I added stars and hearts when the children said "please" and "thank you," helped with cleaning up and were kind to each other. "Timeout isn't just leaving a child alone for blocks of time," Zoia taught. "It gives them a space to *think about* what they have done wrong, to correct the behaviour." The timing was also precise, she instructed. "No more than one minute per year of age, otherwise they'll forget what the problem was in the first place."

Bruce and I began calling these spaces "think-about-its" rather than "time outs" because we quickly learned that a "time out" at Michelle's house meant locking the children in their room for hours. We did not want to echo abandonment, so when one of the girls misbehaved, we quietly sat with them on the bottom step of our carpeted staircase for only two or three minutes. We then simply stated what was wrong, such as, "We don't hit our

family. Sisters are best friends, not people we hit."
We would tell them we loved them and ask them to
repeat what we had spoken about.

This was not easy. Sometimes our tempers
flared and sometimes we needed to hold the
children gently but firmly in place for those two
or three minutes. Sometimes they were defiant and
spent the entire two or three minutes screaming
at such decibels that I was sure I would have
permanent damage to my ears. And sometimes they
kicked or even bit us. But for the most part, I found
that the girls just wanted to be hugged and rocked
and told that they were loved, even when they made
mistakes. "Don't we all crave this?" I reminded
myself of those calm and sacred moments.

We found that the most violent episodes of
them biting and hitting each other occurred after
video calls from Michelle. Zoia recommended being
as distant as possible from Michelle, but because
she was the girls' legal guardian, I felt trapped into
accepting Michelle's dwindling but still present
demands to have video calls. In one of these calls,
the girls' actions were spiralling until they were
hitting themselves as well as each other. "We have
to go," I finally said, my patience entirely spent with
Michelle's ongoing reminders of how daft I was at
everything. At that moment, Reesey bit Cheyenne
with so much force that she drew blood. "They are
biting each other, and it's getting bad..."

"Just bite them back," said Michelle with a laugh. "That'll teach them! They don't do it when they get bitten back enough. Just keep biting them till they stop!" I was horrified by this! I stammered a goodbye, ending the call in a tornado: the girls hitting and Michelle's parting advice. I had no desire whatsoever to bite a child and found the concept repulsive. Besides, they already bit each other. How was my biting going to help?

I kept slogging at "think-about-its" while Bruce was at work, and we both kept at it when he came home, but this seemed to have no effect on the girls' biting. One afternoon, I placed Reesey in "think-about-it" after she bit Cheyenne, again. After two minutes of redundant talk, I turned to stand, where Reesey bit me on my backside. In pain, I screamed at her to remain in 'think-about-it,' and marched to the bathroom. I locked the bathroom door, sank to the floor, and began sobbing. I stayed there for almost half an hour, crying, exasperated, and tired. I was also becoming angry. I was angry that even speaking to Michelle for a moment triggered the girls into violence. I was angry that we couldn't just "file adoption papers" and it was all done in a week like in fictional TV movies. I was angry that I felt so alone. I was angry that Zoia's advice in this case was not working. I was angry that I had been bitten.

I was being pushed beyond my patience and began wondering if hitting really was the only way to deal with the situation. I often reasoned that people called it "spanking" and "smacking" to make it sound like something... less than a hit. The thing was, I was angry enough that I wanted to hit something, if only to release my feelings of frustration.

My mother generously used a wooden yardstick as a mode of discipline when I was growing up. She swung first, asking no questions, striking us into submission. What I later learned was a coping mechanism, I sometimes felt like I was observing myself being hit, rather than as one who was experiencing the strikes. I also began to have violent childhood fantasies and dreams about beating my mother to an immobile pulp. The dreams should have been nightmares, but I often woke up feeling totally relieved. I was ashamed of having such thoughts, and desperately hoped they would go away. The dreams clung to me all through my school years, and even when I went away to college.

It was there that I finally decided to speak to a counsellor to help me process whatever was going on."It's a normal response," explained the LDS Family Services counsellor I was randomly assigned to through my young adult ward. She taught me that thoughts like this were typical for people who were spanked as very young children, and one of the many, many reasons that striking a child is deeply wrong. "You're normal," she assured me. "You are trying to process the trauma of being hit by someone you love." In learning that this was a "typical" response and that I was not alone, I was finally able to heal. The violent dreams ceased, never to return.

But now with my hoped-for children, my mind was becoming a jumbled mess. Retaliatory thoughts flooded me every time I was bitten or hit or even saw it in my own home. A reactionary, tired, spent, unintellectual part of me wanted to hit back. I vowed to never, ever hit a child, and I knew that physically striking Reesey would only make the problem worse. But exhaustion and intellect are rare bedfellows.

By that evening, I had a very distinct toddler-sized, mouth-shaped bruise on my right buttock. Bruce thought it was funny. I was too hurt and angry to agree and resented his chuckles. After the girls were asleep that night, we did the only thing that we could think of: we Googled. I was too tired to fully engage, so Bruce patiently sifted through parent advice websites until he came across something that sounded almost too good to be true. The website recommended that we firmly use a distinct phrase while making eye contact. What could we lose?

The next time I saw a set of Cheyenne or Reesey's mouths positioned with the intention of biting another person, I raced over, looking at the child in the face, then firmly, clearly and sometimes slightly loudly said, "Stop. No biting. Biting hurts." It was stating the obvious, but I desperately hoped the redirection would work. Within two days of using this magic phrase, the girls stopped biting us and each other. A week later, I was able to chuckle over my bite-shape bruise. And a week after that, the bruise was completely healed.

Maybe I could do this parenting thing.

8

NEW LIFE, OLD ROUTINE

Mandy only stayed with us for another week. Her new home, about a 30-minute drive from us, was ready, and she wanted to get Mali settled in their own space. I was sad to see her go, and intensely grateful for all the support she offered without hesitation. Bruce had been able to not travel to work sites for another two weeks after Mandy left, but this soon ended, and I was on my own. The primary responsibility of the children rested squarely on my independent shoulders. Though I wanted to be a mother, the idea of being alone so much was scary.

Bruce's job paid well, and because we burned through a chunk of savings getting set up for the girls, we wanted to rebuild our finances. But mostly, we knew we needed money for whatever legal hoops and requirements were coming next; changing jobs was not an option at that moment.

So as before, I was lonely. Very lonely. With so many moves, I had struggled to build friendships. Robin was a state away, and we were in yet another new ward. As usual, sans children, or a shared national identity, I had felt like a pariah at church. The irony was that now that I had two children, I was finding that communicating with distant friends over phone and e-mail was a luxury that I simply did not have time for.

Adding to these huge changes was Michelle. As I had been the first to communicate with her, navigating ongoing, positive communication with her fell on me. Though at first she was mostly cordial, she quickly became angry with me for reasons I could not understand. I asked what she would like from me, or what we could do to help her, but she only told me to "mind my own business." Communicating with her was proving to be increasingly difficult. She would text me in spurts, threatening to call the police and accuse me of kidnapping if I did not respond to her texts within minutes, if not seconds. She constantly found fault with me over everything, calling me an unworthy, second-class person, all the while complaining about her financial difficulties, unfair landlords, mounting bills, and her inability to pay. She rarely asked about the girls, and even then, she only asked how much we were paying for things for the girls.

Bruce thought Michelle was trying to find a way to ask us for money or manipulate me into giving her money by berating me. I could not process this line of thinking, as it made no sense to me. Mostly, I felt very impressed—either by a spiritual prompting or my own internal resolve—to not pay Michelle any money, lest it appear as though we were purchasing the children. After all, I was not in the habit of sending even my closest friends sums of money for no reason. And if nothing else, I was unemployed.

On my more compassionate days, I tried to imagine why Michelle was so angry. Though I knew very little of her and her childhood, I knew that her parents divorced when she was very young, and she implied that she experienced only bitter and cold child-custody drop offs and pickups. I sometimes wondered if her penchant for anger and brow-beating was because that was the only life she knew. In a rare moment of vulnerability, she had shared that she had dropped out of school in ninth grade. I was shocked by this, and though she said that the reason she dropped out of school was because she had antagonised fellow students "a bit," I felt deeply sad for her to not have an alternative to dropping out of school to avoid being physically attacked. I wondered why the people in her life had not helped her to finish school when she was such a young teen.

With this on my mind, I believe that her texting marathons were intended to hurt me. I wondered if she was testing me to see if I could manage friendship with her, or if her texting was a way for her to release long pent-up anger. In her text messages, she repeatedly called me an "idiot," accused me of being untrustworthy, and raved about how unfit I was as a parent. At first, I tried to be patient with her for the integrity of the situation; she was their legal guardian, after all. Or so she said. She said many things that confused me, but I wanted to hope for the best, so I grasped the rare occasion when she asked about the girls, if only because those scarce messages did not feel intended to degrade or exploit my increasingly rickety internal sense of worth.

No matter how I tried to unburden myself from her words, the texting and messaging tirades were beginning to crush me. Bruce insisted that I do my best to soothe and maintain a relationship with her, reasoning that she must have some degree of compassion or else she would not have taken the girls in the first place. He was also absolutely convinced that she would keep her word and "step up" to facilitate our adopting the girls. But I began to doubt this. She never texted Bruce, and within a few weeks, Bruce was totally disinterested in hearing the latest beratements, slurs and threats I had received from Michelle. So though I longed to have someone help shoulder the burden of this intense, personal criticism, I stopped telling him about her texting diatribes. Instead, I let the words sink into me, believing that Bruce might even agree with Michelle's opinion of me.

Bruce's absence, both emotional and physical, left me in a kind of social isolation that I had never experienced before in my life. The intense pressure of parenting neglected, traumatised children, not to mention the unknown adoption path, was pushing my anxiety to new heights, and it felt like on top of the complicated jumble, there was Michelle with her phone. She would use her lightning-speed texting thumbs to beat me down with random, vicious, sharp thumps that left deep bruising.

I feared that some of Michelle's words might be true, that maybe I was a terrible mother. Maybe I was unworthy of these children, and maybe I was as worthless as she claimed. I didn't want to admit that maybe this whole parenting thing was too much for me, but mostly, I did not know how stealthy depression is. I became ashamed of how alone I felt and reasoned that I was "just tired." I decided to "power through," believing that everything would be fine … *if* I held it together. It was all on me.

"You need some time to yourself," advised Mandy one evening when she had popped in for dinner. I was so glad to see her! "It's important. Very important. You need self-care." Her voice chorused the *Exponent II* women who'd communicated the same thing when I asked for advice. But I felt confused about what to do! It was as if I suddenly did not know how to care for myself because everyone else needed so much of me. Instead, I did my best to push all of my hurt, disorientation, exhaustion, and loneliness down, down, down, deep inside. That way, I could protect my marriage, heal the girls, soothe Michelle, and keep smiling. *Maybe if Michelle were my friend, and she liked me, maybe she'd stop sending angry, rampaging, and sneering messages,* I wished. In this hope, I responded humbly

to her spew, often asking for cooking advice I did
not need. I breathed deeply whenever the texts came
through, working to keep my growing resentment
in sharp check.

9

IMAGINATION AND HAIR

By this time, three weeks had passed since I brought the girls home with me, and I was beginning to feel a little less isolated. Zoia was becoming as much of a friend as she was a personal counsellor to me; I even had her home phone number. I enjoyed visiting with her and had quickly grown to trust her. But fearing that I would be labelled unfit to parent if I was depressed, I didn't tell her how much Michelle's texts were disturbing me. My focus was on the girls.

The girls were becoming more comfortable with me, which meant that mostly Cheyenne, but sometimes Reesey, began to share some of the uglier things that had happened before they came to live with us. These retellings sickened and enraged me. I wanted to somehow punish Michelle and Trent for what had befallen the girls at their hands. As rage and frustration began to simmer throughout my days, I knew I had to address this with Zoia.

"I think the girls have been abused," I tested at the start of our session. In truth, I knew they had been abused, but didn't know how to introduce the topic. But as soon as I spoke, the rest of the words spilled out. "Sexually abused… and…" Within seconds, I was out of control, weeping sadly and angrily, while I bitterly relayed all the things that the girls described they had experienced.

Zoia interrupted me, raising her hand. "Your job is to parent the girls, *not* to convict abusers," Zoia said with firmness. Her words slapped me to attention. I had begun to focus on documenting the abuse that the girls shared with me, imagining some big court case where my notes would put Michelle behind bars. I was so busy making these notes that I neglected to consider how I could help the girls to heal and feel loved unconditionally. Zoia was right.

With Zoia's words, I was absolved of the responsibility of "convicting" Michelle. I immediately felt happier. I could remove "child abuse conviction" from to my to-do list.

Zoia's advice did not solve the majority of the problems swirling around me, but it did relieve me of *that one thing*. I still refused to admit or share how depressed I was feeling and how neglectful I was becoming with my diabetes care. But I could re-focus on parenting the girls, working with them to feel safe and loved… by me.

I began to re-engage with parenting, which was joyful. I watched the movie *Cinderella*, and when Cheyenne was so terrified of the step-mother's cat hurting the mice, I held her and promised everything would be all right. And it was. We practised somersaults together, and I bought a small plastic pool that I filled with soft, white sand for them to play in. We bought clothes and toys, and I started to teach them the alphabet song. In between texts from Michelle and never-ending laundry, life was starting to become delightful in a way that was new to me.

I also began to notice the girls never seemed to use imagination. It was odd to me that they were possibly unable to "pretend" or "make-believe" anything when they played. They mimicked behaviour they had seen, including mine, but when I suggested that we pretend to be puppy dogs, they ignored my suggestions. I wondered if this was an intellectual disability, or if maybe it was a reflection on me, that I was doing something wrong. I loved the girls and wanted to adopt them, intellectual disabilities or not. But I also wanted to do the best job as a parent that I could, so if that meant getting them into educational therapy, then I wanted to do that, too.

"Um…" I ventured slowly at our next weekly appointment. Zoia's attentive face was open and loving, as always. Every whit of her countenance reflected her desire to help. "I don't know… um… but… I mean…" I wasn't sure how to describe what I was thinking without sounding… judgemental. I mean, maybe I'd been a weird kid who used my imagination too much? I didn't know. Zoia looked amused at how awkward my words were. "Okay. Okay!" I said as I decided to just spit it out. "When I watch the girls play, I notice that they don't use their imagination! They just don't pretend! I mean– is there something wrong with them? Are they intellectually disabled or something?" And then quietly, "Or are they just fine, and I am the weird one?"

Zoia's demeanour changed, and she gave a knowing nod. "I don't mind if they have intellectual disabilities," I hastily added. "But if they need help or special support, I want to get them help as soon as I can." I was worried that my critique might be seen as unfair, or make me look like I didn't love them. "I just loved using my imagination when I was little," I continued, feeling sappy, nervous, and intensely vulnerable. "Maybe I was different? I don't know."

I was shaking my head now, feeling stupid at my crass wording. I felt so much like an insensitive louse that I wondered if I was stupid, or if I needed a swift kick to check my judgement. But as always, Zoia's words were clear and kind. "When you don't know what reality is going to bring you next, it is hard to use your imagination," she said warmly. "It is not unusual for children with their background to not use their imagination. When they feel safe, they will use it. It will come! It just takes time." She said the last part slowly, but also firmly. Very firmly. It would take time.

I was relieved at this news, but also heartbroken. They didn't feel safe, or at least not safe enough to let go and play with wishful, dreamy freedom. Zoia assured me that this was not a personal failing on my part. She continued, "When they do use their imagination, you will know that they feel safe. And that will be wonderful."

I mulled over this on the drive home and well into the evening, wondering how long it might be before they felt safe enough to use their imagination. My bedtime prayer that night was more mindful; I prayed that we would legally and quickly adopt the girls in addition to my growing list of prayer items. I also dedicated my home as a sacred space wherein God would abide, helping to make it a safe space. I prayed for this with all my heart, to the point of begging. Before closing, I also prayed that the girls would eventually feel safe enough to use their imagination.

As it was, almost every evening at bedtime, Cheyenne would grab the largest bag she could find and fill it with toys to overflowing. Sometimes she even used two bags. "I am taking this with me!" she would angrily shout at me as we prepared for the bedtime routine. "When I am not here in the night and in the morning, this is *mine*," she would command with her developing vocabulary. Sometimes she packed dress-up clothes, but mostly, she packed things from the toy kitchen.

I surmised that the girls must have been shuffled from house to house as they slept, so I just smiled and said, "Okay! We bought them for you; they are your toys. But we're not taking you anywhere tonight. You'll be here in the morning, and I want to be with you forever and be your mummy forever."

She would look at me with a confused scowl. Sometimes she would even stomp her foot and shout, "I don't care! These are *mine*." Moments later, after her teeth were brushed and her face was washed, I would tuck her in bed with the bag(s) against the space where she lay. Because the bags were plastic, I did not allow her to have them in her bed. She accepted this and fell asleep with her hand firmly gripped around the bag handles. The next morning, she would unpack the toys in her play kitchen, and then model my food prep behaviour, all without a hint of imagination.

Besides being shuffled around, it was clear that the girls had been hit regularly, though I could not tell to what extent. Cheyenne had what looked like belt-whip stripes across her back, but I had almost blocked them out, distracted by a swelling mass on her lower back that was larger than a golf ball. When she described a belt buckle cutting her, I held my tears and rocked her, saying "That must have been very scary. I am so sorry. So, so sorry."

Not familiar enough to understand what was growing on her lower back, I googled what the injury might be. It was a boil. It was caused by an unwashed, untreated wound that had festered into a huge infection. When I learned what it was, I gently washed, medicated and bandaged the wound twice daily, trying to lure out the infection like I was trying to lure out their imaginations. The boil eventually drained and healed, with patient attention and love.

Reesey did not have an open wound, but I saw sadness behind her clear, blue, beautiful eyes. Michelle volunteered that the reason Reesey's head had been shorn was because Reesey was pulling her own hair out in clumps, leaving welts on her scalp. Even after a full month with me, I could still see some faint, circular marks on Reesey's scalp, just visible under the four millimetres of hair that was trying to grow. Michelle claimed "the doctor" said to shave the toddler's head to stop the behaviour. But I sensed that this doctor, and the advice, were not real.

I was becoming more familiar with toddler life, so at a friend's recommendation, I purchased a Disney movie I had not yet seen called *Tangled*. As I watched this fairy tale with the girls, I saw them fall in love with Rapunzel and her hair. *Tangled* became their favourite thing. They watched it daily, sometimes even two or three times a day. As they watched, they began to play dress up, re-enacting and modelling Rapunzel with the beautiful hair and would tell me that they both were going to grow their hair long to look like her. In this, I began to see teeny, tiny steps towards imagination, and I was thrilled!

Feeling more confident, I took the girls grocery shopping with me one morning. On securing the girls in the shopping trolley, a jovial older man said, "Hello, good-looking boy!" to Reesey. The comment was from a stranger in passing and intended to be kind. But Reesey lowered her head and looked at the floor, a frown spread across her sweet face. None of us responded to the man, and I pushed the shopping trolley briskly away. Reesey glanced at me, then looking down, she said, "I am too ugly to be a girl. I have to be a boy." My heart sank.

I looked at Reesey. She and Cheyenne were truly the most gorgeous children I'd ever laid eyes on. (This maternal bias thing is real and instant!) But at just two years old, Reesey thought she was ugly. "You're so beautiful," I said. "That man was dumb. He's old. Some old people have trouble seeing–he's one of those. If he could see, he would know you and Cheyenne are the most beautiful girls on the face of the Earth."

Reesey looked at me with hope in her eyes. Then she looked away, as though she suddenly remembered what I was saying was impossible. "My hair," she finally said in a clear, distinct, yet hurt voice. "I don't want a cut." Her words were broken but expressed so much; she did not want to have her head shaved.

"Let's make a rule for our house!" I said brightly. "Only you get to say if you are going to have your hair cut. And if you decide you want a haircut, then we will go to a proper hair salon." She didn't respond. Her hair was already gone, so a new "rule" about hair had little effect at that moment. It would clearly be a long time before her hair was long enough to even consider having a cut or style.

I paused, wondering what to say, then spied a model with a pixie haircut on a magazine cover. "Lots of very pretty girls have short hair!" I said, pointing to the magazine. "Let's go and find some things so we can play with your hair!" I had seen new mothers use tape or even glue to put bows on their bald, infant babies. Surely something could "dress up" Reesey's shorn crown? She looked at me in a happy but confused way. I wasn't even sure how I could "play" with her hair; she did not like her head being touched. She would jerk away sometimes if I brushed against her head when towelling her off in the bath, and she rarely let me touch what little hair she had. Still, we went and selected infant hair clips in various bright colours, along with princess crowns, glitter hairspray, and ribbons. Her hair was so short that there was no need to comb it, but we still could put some of these things *on* her hair when she allowed me.

From that second in the grocery store and on, whenever the topic of hair came up, I promised the girls again and again that in our home, they would choose if they wanted their hair cut, and that I would never cut their hair. I continued to call them, "my beautiful," "gorgeous girl," "beautiful darling," and other names and phrases all intended to reinforce just how attractive I knew they were.

This speech did not come easily to me. As a feminist who was suddenly focused on appraising and celebrating female appearance, the words betrayed a part of my soul. But I also understood that both Cheyenne and Reesey had been called ugly for a long time, and those words had hurt. In succumbing to the adage that "desperate times call for desperate measures," I concluded that when it comes to children, love was more important than anything. Children need to feel loved, and focusing on their appearance in a positive way expresses exactly that. I did love them. Every cell in my body loved them with a protective passion that I did not previously know I could feel. I loved them at first sight, and I loved them now, with all my heart.

Cheyenne was happy to have me put her hair in clips or gentle hair ties, but Reesey was more complicated. Reesey seemed to like the pretty hair clips, choosing to attach them to her clothes rather than in her short hair. She still did not like me touching her head, but she allowed me to occasionally put some glitter spray or flower wreaths on her head. More often than not, she would look in a mirror with great anticipation, become unhappy, look away and roughly pull everything off of her head. But every now and again, she would look in the mirror and gaze, revealing the beginnings of a microscopic spark of joy behind her sparkling eyes.

Cheyenne often asked to comb or brush my hair, which I freely allowed her to do. She was becoming more comfortable with me, and I was glad. One night, Reesey asked if she could brush my hair. I was surprised and happy! I readily agreed and hoped that she and I might begin to connect in a way that was similar to my "hair time" with Cheyenne. I handed her a brush and a comb, placed her on the kitchen benchtop, and sat on a chair with my back to her. She chose to use the brush, and slowly began working my hair in gentle but choppy caresses, exploring how best to work through my shoulder-length hair. She happily chattered in gibberish as she stroked, gaining in confidence as she went about her work.

But as she continued, her gentle, playful strokes slowly grew into aggressive, painful lashes. She yanked the brush through my hair roughly and began hitting my head with the brush as she ripped it through my tresses. At that moment, I knew I had a choice. I could step away, chide her and take away the brush. After all, this was the child who left a bite mark on me for weeks. But it had taken so long for her to even hold a brush in her hand that I felt that this moment was important to her. I let her continue tearing through my hair, only turning briefly so she could see that I had tears streaming down my face. Her hand directed my face away, so I turned back, silently submitting to her two-year-old blows.

She continued to strike my head with the brush with increased force, then whipped the brush through my hair in varying directions as quickly as she could. As she did this, she began to speak.

"I'm doing this because I love you," she repeated several times, then began adding, *You are too ugly to be a girl!*" with a vicious staccato.

The words stung more than the physical pain of the moment. This was not love. This was violence. This was abuse. It was anything but love. I was not sure how much longer I could continue taking this, but believing that somehow she needed to release an internal demon, I forced myself to remain in place as she continued to belt my head, rip at my locks, and shout at me.

I didn't know if I was doing the right thing, and my thoughts raced. The only thing I could think to do was pray, so I offered a silent prayer, begging for help, asking if I was doing the right thing. I implored God to know if letting her do this would heal her and also that it would end soon. Very soon! The moment I closed my silent prayer with "Amen," she abruptly stopped.

I felt numb, but slowly stood, still crying. Her arms were open to me, but she refused to make eye contact. I gently lifted her and placed her safely on the floor. She immediately dropped the brush and dashed away as if nothing had happened. She joined

Cheyenne who was in the play area stacking mini plastic pots, pans, and fruit in the play kitchen sink, pretending to wash them.

Emotion pulsed through me, tears streaming down my face. I breathed in deeply, slowly counting, *one, two, three, four, five,* and then exhaled, slowly counting *one, two, three, four, five.* My tears slowed, but were still falling. I listened to the tick of the kitchen clock and began to watch as the second hand moved ever so slowly, counting its never ending revolution. I felt utterly defeated and alone, ready to give up.

Then I heard something.

Meow

Meow

It was Reesey. She was crawling on the floor, meowing. Cheyenne joined in, and soon they were giggling. They were pretending to be kittens.

They were using imagination.

I wept again. But this time, it was tears of joy. With my eyes raised, I breathed a silent prayer of gratitude.

SHERRIE GAVIN

10

HEALING THROUGH PLAY

Bruce and I briefly met our next-door neighbors when we first moved in. On the left were an Australian–Thai couple with adult children still at home. When the parents were travelling, as they often did, the adult children quietly looked after their house, focused on university studies and building young careers.

The Thom family were the neighbours on the other side. Catholic, with six children, they had moved into the neighbourhood shortly before us. The father was in the military, in active service overseas for varying blocks of time starting from two weeks and up to six months or more. The mother, Carli, was bright and friendly and had a fun blog where she discussed home crafts and house management. Most importantly, the three youngest children were girls. It wasn't long before the three girls next door and my two charges were playing together, sometimes at our house and sometimes at their house.

After chatting with Carli one afternoon in her home, I let the girls know it was time for us to go. After some effort, and promises that they could come back and play in the backyard cubby house another time, I prompted the girls to thank Carli for having them as guests. But instead of saying thank you, Cheyenne said, "I'd like to live with you next." For Cheyenne, it was the ultimate compliment. She had little to no concept of a permanent family or home and felt comfortable enough to imply that when we dumped her, she'd be happy to live with Carli. Carli looked startled, and her eyes widened in a kind of shock. After a slight pause, she responded, "Well, I have my own children, but you can live next door and come to play when you like!"

I felt awkward and embarrassed but tried to laugh off the situation while thanking Carli for having the girls. As we walked the few steps back to our house, I reminded Cheyenne that I hoped she would live with me forever and that I might be her forever mother. But she was disinterested, racing ahead of me, anxious to grab a few more minutes of play while I prepared dinner. A few days later, when Carli was visiting us, Bruce and I were becoming exasperated over another behavioural issue with Reesey. With trepid reserve, Carli asked, "Do you mind if I give you a tiny bit of advice?"

"Yes, please!" Bruce and I chorused. We could not get the words out soon enough! With all that we had been managing, my time with adult friends had been severely reduced, and I quickly realised that I had very few friends to ask for advice about children. Bruce and I were both anxious and welcoming of parental advice.

"You're giving them too many choices," she said. "Just give them one or two options, otherwise they become overwhelmed and can't decide." We applied her advice, and it worked. Carli was a godsend! Over the next few weeks, Carli and I became friends. I explained to her the situation we were dealing with, and she offered friendship, support, prayers and best of all, loving advice.

"Go shopping or do outings in the morning."

"Use fewer words and stay on point with what you want them to do."

"They need to play, just play, to burn off that energy."

"Slice the sandwich in quarters so they can easily grab the tiny wedges with their hands."

"Bath toys can make bath time much easier."

These were just a few of the gems of wisdom she shared with me and for which I was deeply grateful. One evening, when the girls were unwell, we asked for her help. She came immediately, gently kissing each of the girls on their foreheads as her way to check their temperature. After assuring me that they had fevers, she offered her recommendations and dosages for over the counter medications and put me in touch with a service that had doctors who did house calls for children. Carli was a miracle, and I whole-heartedly thanked God for her.

Over the next few weeks, I purchased an excessive amount of craft supplies: paper, paints, glitter glue, and crayons. Carli's girls would join us and regularly spent hours creating works of art, painting, and decorating everything from toilet paper rolls to rocks in the backyard. My girls, partly because they were so young, but also because all of these things were new, often watched Carli's daughters create, draw, and paint, then would ask the older girls to help them to do the same. It was beautiful to watch them interact, as the older girls modelled how to share and help one another, while I cleaned up after them, folded clean washing or washed and chopped fruit for snacking. Hearing the happy chatter of children soothed me, especially when Michelle's texting firestorms randomly launched hatred via venomous pings.

Lilly was Carli's youngest, and her sixth birthday was approaching. Her father was away on active military duty, and she sorely missed him. Because of this, and because they were also new in the area, Carli decided to throw a huge party which included setting up a mini petting zoo in the backyard, complete with a pony that children could take short rides on.

Cheyenne and Reesey had never been to a birthday party and were anxious. No matter what Bruce and I said, promising we would go with them and stay by their sides, they did not want to go. They were dressed in party dresses, ready to go, but the unknown was just too scary. Bruce and

I decided to stop pressing them to attend and sat patiently with them. We could hear the party from our house, and it sounded grand. Cheyenne and Reesey occasionally asked about it. "What are they doing?" and "What goes on at parties?" were some of the questions. We offered answers, but nothing inspired them to even have a peek at what was going on. Suddenly, there was a knock at our door. It was Gracie, the eldest of the Thom girls.

"Why aren't you at the party?" she asked.

"The girls are feeling a bit afraid," I explained.

Gracie put out her hand. "Come on," she said. "Come with me. It'll be fun."

Reesey took Gracie's hand, and in moments, we were all walking to their house. It was a tiny moment, charmed by the kindness of friends and the spirit of love.

Upon seeing the girls, the animal carers immediately invited Cheyenne to feed a bottle to the baby goat. Without hesitation, she stepped up and held the bottle. The bottle wobbled as the hungry baby goat noshed away, making it look like Cheyenne might drop it. But she quickly steadied herself, gripping the bottle in a new way, growing both buoyant and delighted in a matter of seconds. In that twinkling, she changed. The painted smile that she had worn as a mask of survival vanished from her face. She was *happy*. Truly happy. Her entire appearance reflected that genuine smile that beamed as brightly as sunrise on a clear day. As she moved around the party, gently holding the baby animals, her giggles turned into belly laughs. She instantaneously grew in new confidence within the blink of an eye.

Reesey followed, feeding a bottle to another baby goat and smiling with a giddy satisfaction that I had not previously seen in her. They took turns riding the pony, playing party games, and holding the baby animals, again and again and again. In turn, this moment allowed their hearts to become enveloped with the kind of wholesome, joyful feelings that all of God's children should revel in and experience in their early years. It was an enchanted moment, blessed by God.

At the end of the party, we walked the short way home, allowing a new kind of peace to envelop us. The Thom family was a miracle, and we were blessed to have them as neighbours.

Within weeks of Lilly's birthday party, I was awakened in the dark of the night to screams. It took me a moment to identify where the screams were coming from, but once I did, I realised it was Cheyenne. She was sweating, crying and screaming incoherently. It was as though she was asleep, but *I could not wake her.* I was terrified, and my heart raced to help her. She seemed paralyzed and no amount of rocking, hugging, or pleading seemed to break her spell. After a few hours, she finally collapsed onto her bed, heavily breathing, completely immersed in a deep sleep. It was an alarming experience, and I hastily added it to the growing list of items to discuss with Zoia, worried that something psychologically dreadful was at hand.

At our next appointment, Zoia's eyes brightened as I recalled the ghastly experience to her. "This is good news!" she said, much to my surprise. "When children are afraid and unable to express their fears, they push the fears down inside themselves. When they start feeling safe, then those scary feelings come up and are released as night terrors," she said enthusiastically.

I was confused. Night terrors were a good thing? She had to be kidding!

"But it's like she can't wake up..." I said, dubious of Zoia's advice. "I'm scared," I said. "I couldn't wake her or comfort her. Nothing I did worked!"

"I know," said Zoia, calmly. "Be patient. She will settle down and go back to true sleep eventually. And soon, she won't wake anymore. She is letting the bad feelings out. This is a very good thing, it shows that she feels safe enough to release the fears deep inside her heart and mind."

I wasn't thrilled by Zoia's answer but nonetheless moved on to another item on my list. "Okay, this is a weird one," I said. "When I first met Michelle and the girls, I noticed that Michelle did not have any photos in the house of the girls. All of her photos, including the family photos, were only of her, her children, and her husband. So I decided that I would print photos of the girls and have them around the house so they knew that this was their house, too."

"Goooooood," said Zoia, drawing out the vowel sound in the way that meant she was preparing for whatever bomb I planned to drop next.

"So our house and their rooms are filled with photos of them and us doing a variety of things from dress-ups to playing at the park. So I also decided to print what very few photos Michelle shared on social media of the girls. I printed the ones that just had the girls– none of Michelle's family. Only three or four photos at most. Then I made a photo album for the girls, so they had a connection to their past," I explained before adding, "I also wanted to show Reesey how much her hair was growing."

"Yeeeessss?" prompted Zoia as she nodded.

"When they were looking at the photo album last week, Cheyenne began to cry. I went and asked what was wrong, and both of them, but especially Cheyenne, were crying about the toys in the photos. They cried about the toys, asking where the toys were. I answered that I thought Michelle gave them away, since she assured me that she packed all of their things in the bags she placed in my car that night. They cried even more asking 'Why? Why did she give the toys away?' Then I told them that I'd buy them replacement toys. But they still sat there, for a long time, looking at the photos and crying about the toys, asking why 'Old Mummy' didn't love the toys. Then they began asking me if we could find and save the toys because they still needed *those exact toys*!"

Zoia nodded understandingly. She was used to my exasperation and did not let it affect her. "When they see the toys, they see themselves," she said. "They don't realise it, but they aren't asking about the toys; they are asking about themselves. 'Why did Old Mummy give them away?' is what they are really asking. It relates to their self-esteem. They are trying to understand why they would be given away, wondering if they are broken, or worse... *unloved*."

I sat dumbfounded for a moment, slowly absorbing and processing the information. It suddenly seemed so clear, but so complicated. I finally spoke, somewhat brainstorming, partly panicked. "Am I supposed to go and somehow try to find those toys to show the girls that they had value and were loved? Or should I replace all of the toys and declare a fresh start? Or..." I paused briefly, owning how exhausted and sleep deprived I was, "Maybe I can just throw away the photos like they never existed?"

"None of those things will work," said Zoia, patiently. "You are a creative person. You've been telling me about some of the stories and games you create with the girls. You can create a story about the toys that will help the girls heal. Use your imagination."

"Every child needs a story about themselves," continued Zoia. "I created one for my daughter which highlighted the strengths and blessings I saw in her. You can do that, too. But for now, focus on a story about the girls' toys."

I contemplated Zoia's advice for a few days, pondering how I might adapt existing fairy tales, and even hoped that the problem would resolve itself. But as the girls again opened the photo album and cried over the toys in the photos, I knew I needed to take action.

Previously, Zoia had recommended that I change the names of the characters in books to Cheyenne or Reesey as a means of engaging them in the story. As such, classic stories in our house were soon adapted as *The Two Little Pigs* (who both outsmarted the Big Bad Wolf) and *Cheyenne, Reesey, and Rumpelstiltskin*, and more. Doing this had worked a treat in engaging the girls in the stories, and had introduced them to reading. I found that I enjoyed working out alternative endings or adding the girls into the stories in different ways. But this was to be wholly creative with the practical application of healing the children's self-esteem! It was not the same as making the *Two Little Red Hens* that worked together to bake bread that they shared with the other farm animals.

Over the next few days, I continually thought about a story. One evening, when Bruce was away for work as usual, I put the girls in bed and began to tell them the story I created. I called it *The Toy*

Fairy. Their eyes were wide with fascination as I introduced the title and remained fixed on me as I began the tale about a fairy who takes lost but deeply loved toys to a toy heaven where she loves them and replaces any lost or broken parts. Then the fairy looks for the right home and magically takes the toys to a new family with children who love them forever. With every word that passed from my lips, a deeper and deeper calm came to the girls. When I finished the story, the girls were smiling peacefully. They quickly slipped into sleep, and for the first time since they came to us, they slept through the entire night.

They never mentioned their previous toys again.

SHERRIE GAVIN

11

GETTING REAL

It had been almost two months since I had brought the girls home with me, so as agreed, Bruce, the girls, and I flew to Sydney so Trent and Michelle could meet Bruce. I did not like being away from the girls, but felt I had no right to request for them to stay with us in Bruce's parents' home. Zoia did not like the idea of us taking the girls back; she said it could be confusing for them. But this is what Michelle and I discussed when we first spoke about the girls, and I did not know how to get out of it. Zoia encouraged me to keep assuring the girls that I loved them and that we hoped that the visit would be short and they'd be back with us soon. Michelle picked up the girls directly from the airport, leaving Bruce and me to fend for ourselves. It was a quiet weekend for us; we missed the girls. We spent most of our time waiting and praying, too anxious to enjoy anything.

Toward the end of the weekend, Michelle suggested that Bruce and I meet her and Trent for lunch at a local shopping centre not far from her home. We agreed and left well before the meeting time, trying to burn off energy and anxiety by walking through the rows of shops. My text history with Michelle niggled at me, but I had always responded submissively, so was not worried about my responses. Because I hoped with all my heart to adopt the girls, I decided to forgive Michelle and blame it on whatever stress she was feeling in her life. Or something. It did not matter. I refused to focus on that over the girls.

In this continued hopefulness, Bruce suggested we pray. We found a quiet corner by the restrooms and offered a prayer. We asked that everything would go well, and that we would be able to take the girls home with us. In closing the prayer, I felt warm and at peace.

Moments later, we were seated at a cafe with Michelle and Trent, ordering soft drinks and snacks. Though we shared mostly small talk, we seemed to genuinely get along well, even if Bruce and I were quite anxious. Trent said that he was impressed enough with us that we could keep the girls "on a more permanent trial." We discussed a little of what this trial might look like, but it was vague. Michelle supported her husband and made no mention of any of the things she had accused me of or threatened me with in her text messages. She only insisted that we never contact the birth mother, Ginny. "Ginny can do no good," Michelle adamantly stated. "She will only hurt the girls."

Trent said little of his sister and rather focused on the biological father. "Career criminal," he said, shrugging. "I don't know what Ginny ever saw in him."

There was some talk about Michelle putting together a type of custody agreement. I am not sure what I expected, but it seemed that with Cheyenne being old enough for preschool, we should have something in place in order to enrol her in school. Bruce mentioned that perhaps we needed an attorney, but Michelle insisted that she could put one together without any legal help, based on what we had discussed. The timing of this new "trial period/custody agreement" was not defined, nor were there any conditions other than that we were required to keep in touch. Trent made a vague promise to "help us out at some time in the future" in regard to adopting the girls, but again, no timeframe was set, no goal created.

As a goal-oriented person, this was unsettling to me. It also bothered me to not have legal advice, representation, or protection, but Bruce motioned me to remain silent on that part. In trusting him, I pushed all thoughts of negative uncertainty away. These things could all be arranged later, I decided, remaining focused on getting the girls back. As things between us began to wrap up, I pressed for a time in which we could collect the girls. "Tomorrow around eleven will be good," Trent said.

"That works for us," replied Bruce, casually. But we were internally elated—we were going to get the girls back! After we parted ways with Michelle and Trent, Bruce and I walked through the shopping centre, holding hands. I felt relieved, but not at ease. Private adoption was still illegal in Australia, with the echoes of the Stolen Generation still reverberating through Australian culture and legal systems. The additional burden of Australia and the U.S. lacking a shared transnational adoption agreement meant that both public and private U.S. adoptions undertaken by Australian citizens and those with Australian visas were subject to strict Australian regulations, which did not include this situation. In all my years of researching Australian adoption laws, I could not comprehend how an adoption was possible. In the meantime, I could not imagine what this (I presumed) U.S. "legal guardianship agreement" would look like. I did know that Michelle wanted to have the power to coordinate everything, but I was dubious of her and Trent's insistence that they could help us to adopt the girls in the future. Shrugging my worries away, I embraced that it was a sunny day and smiled as I treated myself to rummaging through a few sales racks for clothes.

Collecting the girls the next day was wonderful, but chaotic. It was significantly calmer compared to the intense confusion of the night when I first took the girls, but it still felt off. I kept walking on eggshells, just to be safe. I hoped everything would go smoothly, and it did, but everything still felt staged. Cheyenne especially seemed off. "I can count my toes," Cheyenne announced when she saw me. But upon not being able to complete her dishevelled performance, she hid her face in her hands. Michelle grabbed her and wiggled Cheyenne's toes saying, "This piggy is number *one*, and this piggy is number *two*..." Both Michelle and Cheyenne constantly glanced at me through this recitation, as if this rehearsed show was somehow for my benefit.

Thankfully, our time there was limited, as we needed to get to the airport. I was so relieved to get in the car with the girls! "What did you do when you were in Sydney?" we asked as we drove to the airport.

Their answers were timid and limited at first, but the further we drove away, the more the girls opened up. It seemed as though there had been some car trouble that ended up with them getting to have a "ride" in a taxi, which had scared them. But mostly it sounded like Trent and Michelle tried to ascertain Bruce's and my financial situation.

In the days following our arrival back in Brisbane, I decided to focus on the next steps towards adoption. I felt very strongly about pursuing legal adoption and, inspired by the spiritual voice I was sure I heard on the night that I first met the girls, I felt like this needed to be started sooner rather than later. I tried to report the situation to the Department of Children's Services (DOCS) in Queensland (QLD), but because the girls' guardians were in New South Wales (NSW), QLD DOCS told us to contact the NSW branch. Which I did. They told me that QLD DOCS were supposed to help me. I ping-ponged between them a few more times before I gave up.

Next I called adoption services in NSW. They told me that private adoption was illegal, but our situation sounded "interesting." Maybe there was "a way for Americans to adopt Americans in Australia…" the woman on the end of the line mused, yet she was sure that it was not through her department. She told me to call QLD adoption services. The QLD people wouldn't even take my call. I repeated this phone call routine between DOCS and adoption services in each state over the next three weeks, chasing tiny leads that inevitably led to nothing. No one had answers. Our situation was unheard of, or too unusual for them to know how to be of any service.

Lastly, I called the U.S. Embassy. They gave me a phone number for American children in crisis, which I called. Finding that the girls were in my safe but not legal custody, the girls' names (or what I guessed were their names) were put on a list. "But to be honest," said the woman on the phone, "this list has a two to three year wait time. You could also try the state where the guardianship was appointed to see if that is any faster, but Australia might be better since the children are there."

It was disheartening. No one knew the answers, and no one knew how to help. The complicated situation of the children not being in immediate danger, and the absence of legal immigration provisions for those who are classed as "temporary residents who were minors," combined with Australian anti-adoption history, positioned us precisely in a place where Australian law had yet to venture.

The situation scared me. Not having legal protection or a hope of official provisions for the girls was unsettling. I finally decided to contact an attorney we had used in the United States when Bruce and I had looked into gestational surrogacy a few years previously.

"You need copies of the court-mandated legal guardianship that awarded custody of the girls to Trent and Michelle before anyone can take any legal action," Larry explained in a response e-mail. "Without the terms of this document, there is no place to start or to even know the true legal status of the girls."

It was clear that we needed to know what their legal status was in order to create the "custody agreement" that Michelle bounced around more and more often in her texts, and more importantly, we needed it to understand how to apply for adoption. In truth, we weren't sure what the legal guardianship was because we had never seen it. Was this a temporary order until Ginny was out of jail? Was this a shared custody with Ginny or someone else? We had no idea, so could only keep searching for anything that might look like a path to adoption.

For the most part, life was settling into a routine. The girls were becoming more comfortable with us, which meant that they were "pushing boundaries." I should have been happy about this normal toddler progression, but butting heads with two- and three-year-olds is reputably hard even for the most seasoned parents. Most of the time, things were fine and went well. But at least a few times a day, the girls deliberately misbehaved to test me. They began playing a game that they called "babies," and I called "bad babies." In the game, they acted like "babies" and would purposely knock things over, spill things or even paint or draw on the floors or walls. Then they would look innocently at me and say, "da-da," as if they had no idea what they did was wrong.

Even though I disliked it, I guessed that the game was possibly a way to re-create a cut-short babyhood, since Cheyenne and Reesey had been removed from their birth mother when Cheyenne was barely two years old and Reesey was about ten months old.

In addition to boundary-pushing, the girls were eating and drinking better. This brought on new issues. For the first month she was with us,

Reesey refused to drink more than a small cup of any fluid per day. As she became more comfortable, she drank more. And though Michelle assured me that Reesey had been trained to use the toilet, accidents were becoming more and more common, and I was becoming frustrated with nighttime bedwetting. Thankfully, a friend gifted me with a special bed cover that protected the sheets from night time accidents. I didn't know such a thing existed! But even with that, often sheets, the mattress and sometimes even the pillows were soaked by morning. After a week of her wetting the bed every night, I decided to buy some disposable "pull up" underpants for her. Reesey was generally good at knowing when she needed to use the toilet during the day, and because pull-ups were absorbent, yet could be worn like underwear, they seemed perfect for what I needed. What a glorious invention!

At bedtime on the day I bought the pull-ups, I helped the girls dress in nightgowns. "Look at what I have for you!" I said brightly, showing a pair to Reesey. I was sure that I had solved my problem and was looking forward to a calm night of stories and sleep.

"No! *No!*" Reesey suddenly screamed at the top of her lungs, stomping her feet in a frenzy.

I was startled and confused, "But... but..." I stammered. "What's wrong?" I asked, as she began to scream in panic. Then stupidly, I said "They're your size!"

"No! I don't want nappies! I am not a nappy-baby! *I am not a baby! No! Nooooooo! Not a baby!*"
She was screaming, shaking and upset enough that she was bordering on a full-fledged panic attack. I quickly presumed that she had some very negative reinforcement when she had been toilet-trained in Michelle's home. She saw the pull-ups as something that was dreadfully demeaning and that wearing them possibly had violent consequences. Within this handful of seconds, she was in a rage, screaming in opposition to the pull-ups. I was frightened!

"These aren't nappies!" I finally shouted. It was the only thing that entered my mind, but it was all I had.

She stopped screaming but was still shaking. "No, no, no..." she quietly panted, again and again. Cheyenne was there as well but remained silent. She was concerned for her sister but didn't seem to know what to do.

"It's okay," I said, trying to soothe Reesey, internally panicking. Then I spoke in a silly tone in an attempt to disarm the situation. "These aren't nappies!" I chuckled, speaking slowly and deliberately, trying to buy some time to think. She was quieting but still shuddered as she kept a keen focus on the pull-ups. Both girls were hanging on my every word. I had to think fast!

The pull-ups I had chosen were based on size, but also because they were pink, with cartoon princesses printed on the front.

"These…" I was grasping at straws, willing an answer from thin air. "These are princess pants," I announced. "Look at the princesses on the front! This means that only a princess can wear them." I felt as if I was playing an intensely high-stake poker game and had laid all my cards on the table. There was no going back—I was all-in.

There was a pause, as both girls considered what I had said. "Princess pants?" asked Cheyenne. As she spoke, a kind of curious joy and wonder seemed to curl around her words.

"Yes!" I said. Then in an attitude as if to say "duh," I continued. "These are not nappies! Nappies are for babies." Then I firmly said, "You are *not* a baby! But you *are* a princess. So you can wear… princess pants." I smiled as broadly as a gameshow host and tried to act like the pull-ups were as glorious as a princess's crown.

"Can I wear them?" asked Cheyenne, innocently. I was thrilled with relief—even though Cheyenne did not need them, her positive response made me hopeful.

"Are you a princess?" I teased.

"Yes?" she questioned.

"Yes, you are! Well, of course you can wear them!" Cheyenne pulled them on and modelled them in front of us. She clearly liked them and began identifying which princesses were printed on the ones she was wearing. Reesey was still staring at the pull-ups. She had not made eye contact with me since I first pulled them out, which felt like hours ago. My heart was still racing, and the bitter taste of adrenaline was in my mouth, reminding me how intense the moment was for both of us.

She stepped towards me and without a word began putting a pair on. Her eyes were still down and she stood for a moment. Then she looked at Cheyenne. "Mine have Jasmine!" she said, finally releasing a smile. I was so relieved that I felt like crying! Instead, I crumbled to the floor, breathing a huge sigh of relief. I sat for a moment, recovering and watching them dance and giggle. "I like princess pants!" Reesey finally said.

"Me, too!" said Cheyenne.

The following morning, Reesey's sheets were dry. On previous mornings, she would come in and tell me in low tones and with a hanging head that she had wet the bed. But that morning, she greeted me with a bright smile. "Princess pants at night, not in the day," she said confidently. She knew what they were intended to be, but instead of a bad thing, she decided they were fun. And different. And special. They were "Princess Pants"!

Thank you, I whispered to God, again and again.

Within days, Cheyenne decided that the princess pants were not something she wanted to wear every night, but she would wear them without argument when we asked. Better yet, Reesey began putting hers on as a part of her bedtime routine. I was relieved.

Not long after this, I awoke one bright morning to Cheyenne crying at my bedside. "Mummy Sherrie?" she wept. She wasn't screaming but crying big tears in a steady stream.

"Yes?" I asked, still sleepy. I was concerned that she was crying and wondered if she had another night terror.

"I woke up and my clothes were wet and I am sorry. I am sorry, I am sorry…" She sobbed. I was confused, my head still in a state of slumber. She continued, "I pulled the blanket off of my bed to help… and… and…" Her crying continued, but all I wanted to do was hug her. I began to sit up so I could reach out. "I put it in the washing basket and… can… can… I picked out dry clothes to help. Can you please help me put them on?"

I finally processed that she had wet the bed. I did not care about the bed; I was only worried about how upset she was. "Yes! You're not in trouble…" I wasn't sure what to say or do, but I was concerned for her clearly broken heart. Until then, I had never seen her so upset, brave, and scared at the same time. "How about a warm shower to help you calm down?" I asked. "Then you can feel fresh and clean?" She looked surprised and suddenly stopped crying.

She nodded and softly said, "Yes."

"Then you can put on the clothes you picked out."

"Okay…"

I crawled out of bed and turned the shower in my bathroom on for her. She was shivering as I helped her out of her wet clothes and was glad that the warm water was running. After she stepped into the shower, I went and collected her wet clothes and blankets. As I began using a towel to soak up the wetness that had seeped through to the mattress, I became conscious of the fact that she was afraid to tell me that she had wet the bed.

I originally thought she was crying out of her own frustration, but it dawned on me that she was crying from fear. She had dutifully tried to clean up the problem to the best of her ability before coming to confess the situation to me. That is where the combined feelings of bravery and fear had originated, and my heart was sad for her. As I collected the wet bedding in silence, I began to hear her singing in the shower. A sense of warmth overcame me, and I felt like something grand had happened.

My reaction, though mostly inhibited with morning sleepiness, was what she needed to feel safe. I reminded myself of Zoia's advice: "Your job is to parent the girls, *not* to convict abusers." Because of this, I never brought up the wet bed or laundry. After all, it was a beautiful day.

Mother's Day was looming. Such a complicated church day! Though many church speakers have praised all women as "nurturers" and in recent years, many perfunctorily state that motherhood is not limited to those who give physical birth, I have found that neither the Mormon culture nor reality complies with these statements.

After years of listening to church talks that spread patchwork theology based on mortal fertility, peppered with jokes of men's incapability at parenting, hence women are saddled with the primary burden, and largely being snubbed by other church women on Mother's Day, I stopped attending church on that Sunday. Instead, Bruce and I usually chose to indulge in a late breakfast at my choice of restaurant on Mother's Day, from which I would send texts or e-mails to fellow childless Mormon women that expressed my love, compassion, and shared trepidation.

But this Mother's Day was different. The words I heard on the night that I met the girls rang in my ears: "I have put this in place for you. If you want to be a mother, do this now. It is your choice." When I could remember this moment, I believed that these girls were to be my daughters. And no matter how much I thought that day might be the same as any Mother's Day before, it was different. I broke into tears as the Primary children, including Cheyenne and Reesey, sang a song for mothers during the sacrament meeting. It was as if, for the first time in my life, there were children singing for me. Absolutely for me. I was shocked to tears, confused, and even angry that it felt so different to other Mother's Days. The anger was because what I suspected all along was true: Mother's Day does not encompass all women. Not even a little bit.

Wiping away the anger were friends. Those who had children and those who did not texted or e-mailed to wish me a happy "first" Mother's Day. These dear friends offered words of love, admiration, and support in ways that meant more to me than diamonds.

Bruce always purchased gifts for me on Mother's Day, just as I had purchased Father's Day gifts for him. These gifts were usually practical—such as a blender or new running shoes. But this year, he gave me a necklace. "I thought you deserved something special," he said. "This has been hard on you, and I thought you needed something that you can keep, no matter how this turns out." His words spoke to the fact that we did not know what the future held. But for that day, it was my Mother's Day. First, last, or only—it was different.

It felt like the whole world finally included me in Mother's Day. Except for Michelle. By then, subtle threats began feeding through my phone again. I sent her a Mother's Day gift with a card signed by all of us, which she acknowledged but did not thank me. "I am a real mother," she texted instead. "Not you."

Within days, the angry texts increased. "*Stop* teaching them the alphabet. They'll learn that at school!" and "You're not their mother. They go to bed at *six*," which came from what I thought was a harmless report on what the girls and I did the day before. Feeling brave one morning, and sensing that Michelle was in an almost agreeable mood, I queried about getting a copy of the guardianship decree. "It's permanent," she texted, dismissing me. "I made sure of that. You don't need it. Everything goes through me." I did not believe her. I could not imagine her legally "making sure" of anything. I was caught in a rip tide: riding luscious waves in a sea of near-maternal bliss, yet dangerously too far removed to see land, occasionally threatened by a power-hungry shark.

When the girls first came, I was not familiar enough with children's growth charts to understand they were significantly smaller than average. When this became clear, mostly as a result of church members who were surprised when I told them the age of the girls, I also wondered if the biological mother or father might be physically small. I wondered a lot of things, especially about the biological mother. I wondered why she was in jail. I wondered why Michelle had forbidden me from contacting her. I wondered what her medical background was—such as if she had allergies or a history of heart disease or diabetes that I should watch for.

As I pondered her situation and how it related to me, Bruce, Michelle, Reesey and Cheyenne, time seemed to be passing very slowly. I wanted to know these things. I wanted to adopt the girls and feel free from the worry that they could be taken away. But time was also passing quickly. The girls seemed to grow overnight. I could almost allow myself to believe that the girls were simply malnourished, rather than being small. Within two months, they were both wearing size two, and even the size two was starting to look small on Cheyenne. They craved dairy, so I indulged them with milk, yoghurts, and cheeses. Reesey's hair was a centimetre long now, and whispered of possible curls. This gave her confidence, and she began gazing at herself in the mirror as she decked herself out in bows, crowns, ribbons, and hair clips. Cheyenne's smile no longer seemed forced or pasted on. Though she sometimes said that she would still be okay if we gave her away, I reassured her I never wanted that.

Small steps continued to bring the girls closer to me, but also invited even more boundary-pushing. Both girls quickly careened into a tenacious streak that began to try me. They were both very strong-willed, and I searched for ways to manoeuvre this in a positive way. Though my efforts had a slow, steady, positive effect, the obstinate behaviour and tantrums were still present, and maybe even growing in Cheyenne.

One Saturday, it seemed like Cheyenne was bouncing between Bruce and me, fighting with us over every single thing and throwing tantrums over details that I could not understand. I wondered if it was her developing personality, or maybe she was trying to get out all of her toddler angst before she turned four years old? We had placed her in "think about it" a few times, but it seemed like minutes later she would pick a new fight and we were back at square one.

As night fell, her fighting, tantrums and screaming were increasing. Because Bruce wasn't home often, and because he and Reesey were enjoying reading books together, I was left to battle with Cheyenne. She was assigned to "think about it," for three minutes so she could try to process why screaming was not okay in our family. "I love you," I told her for about the hundredth time that day, "but it is not okay to scream or yell or scratch or throw things. We use words, not yells."

My words were measured and soft, mildly hinting at the fatigue I felt. But besides being physically tired, my patience was wearing thin. I just wanted her to go to bed so I could have a break. It didn't seem like an end was in sight, so I sat on the floor, my eyes on my watch for three minutes, blocking her exit from the "think about it" space I created in a hallway.

She began screaming and pacing, eventually shouting about how much she hated everything and how everyone hated her. I knew something else was going on with her, but I did not know what it was, nor did I know what to do. "No one hates you here!" I protested, penning a report in my head for my next appointment with Zoia. "We love you!"

Suddenly she looked at me with broken, tear-filled eyes. "Then why did my mummy give me away?" At that instant, I knew exactly what was going on. She was dealing with the trauma of abandonment. "What is wrong with me?" she moaned, seeming to give up all hope. "Why didn't she love me enough to keep me?"

I knew this was an important moment, so I thought fast. "She has four children of her own," I said, vaguely reflecting on Michelle's claim that the dynamics between her children and the girls weren't working. "She did want you…" I began, but paused. I was adamant to never express in any way that she, or Reesey, were unwanted. "And she loves you. But she was very busy taking care of her children."

"But… then why…" Cheyenne began crying steady tears. It was as if she were utterly defeated, and my heart broke watching her reel in such an emotional state. She stopped pacing but began throwing her body and her arms down again and again, as if she were releasing dense waves of exhaustive feelings that were too heavy for her to carry any longer. "The other mummy. The one *before* Old Mummy. She gave me away. Why did she give me away?"

I was shocked. Until that moment, I wasn't even sure if she remembered or knew her natural mother. Cheyenne was barely two years old when she came to Australia with Michelle, and Michelle claimed that she never spoke of Ginny to the girls, keeping them away from her.

"I don't know," I said. It was true and honest. I didn't know why Ginny was in jail, or why she had made the parenting choices she had made. I said it simply, but my eyes began to fill with tears. "I am so sorry." I opened my arms. She came to me and I began rocking her, while simultaneously patting her on the back between her shoulders. Zoia had taught me to do this as a physical way to help release endorphins that would soothe the child. As I sat and rocked her, Cheyenne continued to sob quietly in my arms. She burrowed into me, seeming to give me the enormous weight she had been carrying, possibly for as long as she could remember.

"I think they made very dumb choices," I said suddenly and with thunderous firmness, at a decibel louder than I had permitted myself to use in earlier tantrums. "And I will never understand why they would give someone as beautiful, smart, strong, wonderful, and perfect in every way, as you are… away." I paused, still rocking her, and prayed in my heart to know what to say next. She had stopped crying, but was still cradled in my arms. I felt strongly that speaking negatively about Michelle or Ginny could only result in problems. Even calling the choices "dumb" felt too strong, and I regretted it.

I silently prayed to know what to say that would be truthful and might alleviate the pain she was feeling inside of her heart. The Spirit came over me, and I felt a prompting. "I don't know why they gave you away," I said again. "But I am so thankful because I get to be your mummy for now." I only knew failure when it came to my attempts to become a mother. I couldn't promise something that I could not comprehend how to accomplish; I could only bring myself to focus on "now" as my time to mother her. I wanted to say that she would be mine forever. But doubt won and my lips would not make those words.

"We are going to fight like dragons to get to be your forever Mummy and Daddy. Because I never want to give you away. I'll fight anyone who tries to take you!"

She looked up at me and smiled when I said this, completely ending her tears.

"Really?" she asked with a giggling coyness. "Fight them? Punch them?"

"Well… I don't punch. But I will fight like a dragon to make sure you are safe. And, I am very thankful that I get to be your mummy right now."

"Okay," she said. I stopped rocking her and gazed into her eyes. Soon we were both smiling at each other. Within the hour, she was in her bed, wearing her favorite pink pyjamas, listening to an amended fairy tale where she was the hero.

By June, I stopped initiating contact with Michelle. Her communication continued to slither into my life in texted furies that randomly attacked my phone with acidic anger. These diatribes emotionally and intellectually drained me, every time. More often than not, it felt like she saw me as a way to placate her need to feel powerful by being outright mean then trying to coerce me to admit that I was a daft, lesser human than her. Occasionally, the messages were almost friendly, reminding me that they were very poor, or sharing with me how someone from her church ward or stake was victimising her. It was in one of these rare, yet placid, messages that Michelle told me that the girls' birth mother, Ginny, had been released from jail.

She claimed to not know Ginny's location and to not be in communication with her because, Michelle said, Ginny cared more about herself than checking on her children. Michelle firmly repeated that I was to have absolutely no contact with Ginny whatsoever. "The girls are not safe when they are around Ginny. She is selfish, wicked, and doesn't care about them. Stay away from her," Michelle angrily texted. "She will hurt the girls. I am their guardian. *Not* her."

I was coming to the conclusion that truth seemed a malleable substance with Michelle, so I was not sure what to believe. Yet Michelle was my primary source of knowledge in regard to Ginny. She described Ginny as a drug addict who was abusive to the girls, sexually indiscriminate, emotionally manipulative, and just plain void of all morals. Ginny was, after all, in jail, convicted of a crime—or possibly several crimes? I didn't know. I had found Ginny's mugshot online in a search of inmates, so that much was fact. I was not expecting the Facebook friend request to come from Ginny. But it had.

The girls were playing with toy cars in a small plastic pool that I had filled with fine, white sand as I scrolled through Facebook on my laptop. As soon as the request came, I instinctively looked at them as if to protect them. My heartbeat quickened, and I began to feel so much anxiety that I started to become physically ill.

And yet... she was the one who had given birth to these two precious children. I took a deep breath and pondered as I watched the girls play. Cheyenne and Reesey are so perfect, I thought to myself and smiled. I loved their voices, their faces, their noses, their little toes. I knew I was biased, but I gave in to the bias, revelling in parental prejudice.

I turned back to the computer screen, saying a prayer in my heart. I had prayed for Ginny hundreds of times over the past few months. I had added her name to the prayer roll of the Brisbane temple, along with the names of Michelle and Trent, as well as Bruce, myself, and of course, the girls. I prayed that Ginny would find enough peace that she would be open to our adopting her daughters, that she might have compassion and help us. I prayed that she would get whatever help she needed in jail, that she would be safe. I prayed that her heart would be softened and she could be free from any addictions or bad habits. In my most compassionate moments, I also prayed that if need be, and we were not able to adopt the girls, that she would be in a position to be their primary carer again, rather than Michelle.

I had supposed that one day I would be in some kind of communication with her, but I thought that was years away. I took a breath and looked at the friends we had in common. Interestingly, and importantly, she was *not* connected to Michelle. I leaned back from the computer and looked at the girls, listening to them giggle, chatter and play.

"Let's make believe this is water and can stop cars!" squealed one, pouring water in the sand.

"Okay! And the car can fly and drive. And this sound... rrrrrooooooo!"

Hearing them happily play helped to calm me. I was feeling queasy but decided to not respond to the request until I could discuss it with Bruce.

As usual, Bruce was away working the week, but we spoke most evenings, so I went back to scrolling and "liking" photos. But I was distracted, thinking about Ginny. I suddenly realised that my main concern was all about Michelle. Her demeaning interactions, her vague threats, her real threats, her anger towards Ginny and especially her anger towards the girls caused me to dread even the smallest communication with her. When I removed Michelle from my thoughts on the situation, I had no qualms about being in communication with Ginny.

As I mulled this over in my mind, I thought of my friend, Amanda. She was my first college roommate, and we grew to become very close friends, so close that she spoke openly with me about her family background. She was adopted by her stepfather when she was young, and never recalled ever interacting with her biological father. She expressed how much she loved her "real" family, meaning her adoptive father and his parents.

But after she married and had her first child, she admitted to me that she wished she had some kind of communication with her biological father. "It's not because I want them to know me if they don't want to," she explained. "It's because when I fill in medical records for my son, I can't answer if there is a family history of heart disease or cancer or anything! I feel powerless because I just don't know." As a lifelong diabetic, I know how important medical records are. My friend's simple desire to provide medical information on behalf of her son impressed me enough that when she spoke those words, I decided that if I adopted, I would be in communication with the biological family.

I already knew in my heart that I would accept Ginny's friend request. So with a simple click, we were connected on Facebook.

12

WORDS

For the next couple of days, all was quiet. The
sun was shining, the girls were happy, and I heard
nothing from Ginny. Even my phone was silent, free
from Michelle's angry text messages. In this peace,
I found myself trying to imagine what Ginny was
thinking. I wasn't sure what to expect, but I hoped
that contact with her would be positive. I imagined
that she was searching my Facebook posts and
profile, and I didn't mind. My life was rather benign
before the girls, so my profile was a collection
of photos of my dog, a few news articles I found
interesting, and recipes that I was "saving for later"
but never seemed to find the time to actually make.
Since bringing the girls home, I had significantly
more photos and posts, all starring them.

In the midst of my musings about Ginny, the
memory of a friend named Melissa came to mind. I
met Melissa when we were both in a student ward
about a decade earlier. But for the fact that we
were assigned as visiting teaching companions, we

would not have met, as we moved in different circles. But we got along really well, which was important because visiting teaching companionships could be complicated, especially when assignments involved women who were dating or were interested in the same men. Melissa and I never talked about the men we found interesting or wanted to date, for which I was very grateful. Her gospel focus made me look forward to visiting teaching. She was not afraid of the more challenging topics of racism, lack of education, sexism, and even adoption. I was grateful for her candor, which was always warm and enveloped by the Spirit.

One afternoon all those years ago, Melissa and I were sitting at my apartment talking about our visiting teaching assignments and other things. The topic of future families came up. I already knew that I could not carry a pregnancy, but I avoided the topic of infertility because of the associated "nosy fascination." This was the phrase I created when someone, usually a church member, seemed unable to contain themselves when they found out something unusual about another person. For me, that thing was that I couldn't have children. They would attack me with a verbal, fertility-driven interrogation, which always led to awkwardness and the end of the friendship. It was too hard for me to carry my own burdens as well as the awkward, silent sympathies of others. I learned early in my adulthood to say that I was "open to" or "interested in" adopting as a means of gauging friendships, but mostly it was for social and emotional survival.

Some of the Mormon women I shared my infertility with acted like there was something deeply wrong with me, perhaps even sinister, and distanced themselves from me for reasons I still do not understand. Well-meaning Mormon male friends sometimes tried to offer me priesthood blessings to "cure me." Other times, they shared that they could only see themselves parenting a child that they were biologically connected to, or others stated that they were only interested in adopting from the same ethnic and racial background, which didn't sit well with me. Though I appreciated the honesty, I sometimes allowed these responses to cause me to think less of myself. I wavered in the belief that there was something spiritually wrong with me, or that I had sinned in some way that I could never identify. As a result, I tended to not date fellow church members, mostly because a much higher percentage of my non-Mormon friends were not as prone to nosy fascination and were free from the infertility judgement that can be caused by years of Mormon cultural indoctrination of women's primary role.

I did have true friends, those who were both Mormon and not, male and female, gay and straight, who shared my heartache rather than offering cures or judgement. This protective circle of true friends was small, and I rarely let new people in.

Melissa was still not in this group; our friendship was too new. But she and I shared a spiritual connection. "I'm interested in possibly adopting someday," I tested that afternoon. And because the Spirit was abiding in our conversation, I ventured further. "I'm not sure I can have children," I said, still giving myself an out. "So I like thinking about adoption." I was trying to sound passive.

Melissa moved her head but kept her eyes on me. It was as though she physically positioned herself to look away, and possibly even leave, before she spoke. Finally, she firmly but reverently said, "I am adopted." She paused without taking a breath. "Both me and my brother." I immediately knew that she was expressing something about herself that she regarded as holy; it was something she protected and rarely shared.

"I actually know that I can't have children," I said, speaking my secret in a space that was enveloped by a spiritual calm. "If I become a mother, it will be because of adoption." The conversation that followed was like a breath from heaven. She shared that her biological parents had provided a type of dossier about themselves for her to know about them. They'd listed music as their shared love, and she smilingly told me that she believed they were the reason she had a music scholarship and a superb singing voice.

"Were you ever interested in meeting your biological family?" I pressed. I was worried about adopting and giving my heart to a child, only to have the child long to find someone else and call them "mother." I already felt the bitter pain of judgement and rejection associated with infertility. Did I need to prepare for the possible rejection of my adopted child?

"There was a time when it really bothered me," she said. "My brother was different. But I had a hard time when I was a teen."

"What did you do?" I asked.

"I read about my birth parents from the file they provided. And I knew my mom was always supposed to be my mom," she said, meaning her adoptive mother, "so it wasn't about that. I always knew my parents loved me, and I knew that we were sealed together. But I couldn't understand why I was given away."

She paused. In this, I knew instantly that Melissa and I carried similar burdens of judgement. We both wondered at times why we weren't loved enough, either by God, or by birth parents. For me, I wondered why of all the miracles in my life, fertility was still out of reach. For her, she knew that God loved her and brought her to her real, adoptive, permanent family. That part was easy. Knowing how or why her birth parents chose that path haunted her as a teen.

"One night, after I was really unhappy and really struggling, I had a dream," she continued. She looked upward, as if she could see heaven. "In the dream, I was in the premortal life. I was there with a group of friends and we were all so excited to go to earth!" Melissa glanced at me to see how I was reacting. I was in awe, transfixed by her words. She smiled peacefully. "I knew we were all very close friends. So we all stood there, and we could see down to earth. We were so excited! Happy, laughing and smiling, looking at the people who would be our moms and dads. I was so excited when I saw the people who would be my parents! But I learned that my parents couldn't have children. *And I knew they were supposed to be my parents,*" she said with fierceness. "I suddenly felt very alone—how was I going to get to my parents?" She stopped and looked directly at me as she asked the question. "I *knew* that they were my parents." she repeated. "But there was no way for me to get to them, so I stood there, alone, in heaven, wondering how I was ever going to get to my family on Earth."

She paused again and checked me. I wasn't sure I had breathed since she started. It wasn't a sense of curiosity that gripped me; rather, I knew she had experienced a personal revelation. I was in the very sacred, privileged position to have her relate it to me. Her face shone as she continued. "After a moment, one of my good friends came and touched my arm. 'I'll help you,' she said. 'I'll help you get to your family.' *I knew that she was my birth mother.* She was one of my very close friends in the spirit world, and she sacrificed for me to get to the family that I was meant to be in. I woke up the next day and never worried about my birth mother again. I know that she is a friend. An eternal friend."

The Spirit was undeniably strong as she spoke, so much that I was, and still am, absolutely certain that her dream came from God. I believed every word of it was true.

Like many student ward visiting teaching companionships, our partnering was short-lived and ended between semesters, roommates, and temporary housing. But I have always been convinced that we were put together for me to learn from her. Her words filled me with courage that regardless of my reproductive ability, there was more than one way for women to become mothers *by divine design*. Even if that meant that some women would sacrifice their hearts and their bodies to be the vessel through which some children are placed in their earthly families.

So when I thought of Ginny, I believed that she was a friend. However, she had also been convicted of a crime that landed her in prison. I knew I would have to keep my wits about me.

Before I received the Facebook friend request from Ginny, I secretly e-mailed our attorney, Larry. Larry was now working for the church and had processed adoptions for members of the church in the past. I explained our current situation in an e-mail and asked what we needed to do. Larry responded almost immediately, explaining that we needed the children's birth certificates, a copy of the guardianship agreement, and most importantly, another attorney. "Because the children are from another state, and I am only licensed as an attorney for Utah adoptions, I can't help you. But I can recommend an attorney I have previously worked with."

We were more than happy to take his advice, and within days, I was communicating with David. David was a devout Pentecostal Christian, and I was grateful that we could openly speak about praying for adoption. Larry graciously bowed out of this newest affiliation, and David set out to obtain as much knowledge as he could from the information we provided. This is how we had become aware of (now defunct) state-based Department of Corrections inmate searches, where I had found Ginny's mugshot. He also found and sent us information on the birth records for the girls. (I discovered that Michelle had given an incorrect date for Reesey's birth, something I chalked up to being forgetful rather than deceitful.) We also gained access to the girls' full legal names.

David's next goal was in finding and obtaining a copy of the guardianship that named Michelle and Trent as primary carers of the girls. "It would really help if we had some kind of contact with the birth mother," he had written in an e-mail. Within days of this, Ginny's friend request came through on Facebook. I was sure that God's hand was in the timing.

After what seemed like a lifetime, but was only about three days, I sent Ginny a private message. I was not sure what to write, so I kept the message simple. "Hi! I think I have your daughters. Is there anything you'd like to know about me?"

She responded within a few hours with a short message that acknowledged she was the biological mother. I replied, asking if she would like to speak with me. "Yes, when's a good time?" she messaged. We set a time for me to call on the coming weekend. I thanked her, crossed my fingers for good luck, and prayed with all my heart that all would go well.

The Queensland sun was as bright as ever on the following Saturday morning. It seemed like the grass was the most perfect shade of green with the cooling weather, and sunny-yellow lemons and cheerful blood oranges were just starting to spring from the trees in the backyard. The lemon myrtle that lined the left side of our house blessed us with the most delectable fragrance. The fluffy pink pillows and velvety pink blankets strewn in the family room had become fixtures in a short amount of time, adding a rosy blush to the otherwise neutral tones in our decor, and they made me smile. Bruce was home for the weekend and assured me that he would keep the children engaged while I was on the phone.

I went upstairs to our bedroom and closed the doors. Opaque curtains graced the windows at the front of the room, offering both light and privacy. Because of this, I only partially opened the blinds on the left side of the room to help keep the room cool from the sun. I knelt down and prayed with all of my heart to be prepared for this conversation. When I closed my prayer, the room was still, and I was at peace.

I positioned my laptop on the bed where I had knelt to pray and slowly keyed in the phone number, then paused. I took a breath and looked heavenward. "Help me," I begged.

I clicked to dial.

"Hello?"

"Hello. Um. This is Sherrie. Is this Ginny?" My voice was bright, and my heart was racing. I wanted the conversation to be happy. I wanted everything to be happy!

"Yeah," she replied with a delicious southern drawl.

"How are you?" I asked.

"I'm fine, how are y'all?"

"I'm good!" I was nervous, but I loved her voice! She spoke as if she were a romantic heroine in the opening scene of a new Tenessee Williams play, sitting on a porch swing with a cool drink in her hand. I suddenly realised that I didn't know what else to say. I anxiously tried to recall all of the engaging conversation starters I had used when I was single, mentally ticking down the list of "what is your favourite music" and "where did you go to school," all the way through to "what is your favourite restaurant." But all were too stupid to utter.

I rolled my eyes thinking of how dumb all of those things seemed at that moment. A mild panic was setting in. "The weather is beautifully sunny here today," I finally said.

"Oh, it's nice here, too."

"What time is it there?" I asked, silently cursing myself for not making some kind of notes or something to help the conversation.

"It's about seven," Ginny said. "What about for y'all?"

"Just after ten on Saturday morning," I said, but my mind was racing. Dang it! I know where she is from, so I can't ask her that. I can't ask where she does her hair or anything. Oh, this is a mess! Then redundantly, "It's really a pretty day."

"That's nice."

"Oh, and I mean *we're* good," I said, correcting myself for only telling her how I was doing. I was butchering the conversation. "Bruce, my husband, is fine and the girls are good. He's looking after them right now."

"How are the girls?" she asked. The girls! Of course she would ask about them!

"They're great. They're playing outside right now," I said. With that, a calm came over me. I still wasn't sure of what to say, but before I could think, I asked, "Do you want to say hello to them?" It was an impulse, but it felt natural.

Within moments, I was downstairs with the girls, and we were all looking at a blank screen on my laptop. The girls had spoken to Michelle and

Bruce's parents in video calls before, but because I called Ginny's phone, all they could see was a blank computer screen. I prompted the girls to speak. Cheyenne was shy and kept her hand in her mouth but mumbled a few words. Reesey obediently said hi, but they would not stay still for the blank screen and quickly went back to playing outside under Bruce's watchful eye. "They've run outside again," I said apologetically to Ginny as I returned upstairs to my bedroom for some privacy. "Do you have access to a computer and we could video call?"

"Um, no, not right now."

I was feeling more confident, so instead of guessing what to say to initiate conversation, I decided to turn the conversation to her. "Is there anything you'd like to ask me?" I said brightly, and with purpose. I was ready.

"I guess you'd like to adopt them girls?" she said. I was floored by her directness but glad for the honesty.

"Yes!" I said. "Very much so! We love them very much!" Until that moment, I did not know if she was in favour of having them adopted or if she knew that adoption had been discussed with Michelle, Trent, or us. "Are you okay with that?"

"Yeah. I know I messed up. I've made some mistakes, but if they are happy with y'all, that's what's most important." Joy washed over me, partly relief, but also it was an enormous step towards the legal process of adopting. I wasn't sure how, but I could only think this was a positive thing.

"We love them, and we'd love to adopt them," I said. "Is there anything you'd like to know about us?"

"Are you going to change their names?" Ginny's question caught me off guard. I had not considered changing their names; the thought simply had not occurred to me, between all of the needs of the girls, the legal issues and the uncomfortable situation with Michelle.

"Uh…" I floundered, thinking as quickly as I could. "Well, we'd like them to have our last name," I sputtered.

"Okay," she said with a paced brogue that made the word sound long. "But not their first names?"

"Well, they know their names," I said. "I think it would be confusing for them to change their names," I said with firmness. I quickly added, "And I really love their names—they're beautiful!"

Ginny and I continued to talk for about twenty minutes, mostly about what Bruce and I liked, and what Bruce did for work. It was small talk, but important. She asked how we knew Michelle, and how we had come into contact with the girls. I told her about our mutual friend, Robin, but was careful to not speak ill of Michelle or Trent. "I think they tried hard, but six children is a lot," I said, trying to gently explain the situation.

"I don't think she really wanted them," Ginny replied with sudden strength. Before that moment, her responses were in a sing-song Southern style that seemed too good to be true. But this time, her response was firm. With a mountain of willpower, I held my tongue. I wanted to speak ill of Michelle— to share all that unkindness I had experienced from her and more. But a gossipy relationship with anyone was the last thing I needed or wanted, so I steered my mind away. "Well, I want them!" I said with a laugh. "They're perfect!" I wasn't sure if this was the right thing for me to say, but it seemed like anytime Ginny and I spoke of Michelle, the conversation felt clouded with negativity.

Ginny giggled, easing my mind. I wondered what Ginny thought about Michelle, but was too cautious to ask. I had more important questions. "Is your family okay with having us adopt the girls?" I ventured. "Like your mother—is she okay with it all?" I knew that Ginny's extended family might contest the adoption if they wanted to keep the girls, and I did not want to become involved in a lengthy and expensive legal battle that would break everyone's hearts.

"They're fine with it," Ginny responded. "We all want what's best for the girls, and right now, they look really happy with y'all. Cheyenne looks just sweet on you!" She was referring to a photo I had put on Facebook where Cheyenne and I were hugging and smiling at the camera. It was a beautiful photo of Cheyenne, with her real smile.

My heart sang! With this, I began to relax as we talked. "Are you okay if I get an attorney to begin the paperwork?" I ventured. She said that she was, so I asked where she was living, and if she was working. I made the conscious choice to not ask Ginny about prison. I did not want that part of her life to become a part of my relationship with her. She told me that I could use her mother's address and that she was looking into going back to school. I was sincerely happy for her and told her so.

"What about the father?" I finally asked.

"Well…" she said. "I tried to do the right thing. Settle down and have a family. But that didn't work out. He's still in prison. I don't think he even knows who *his* father is." Just as I had for Ginny, I'd googled the birth father's prison information as soon as I learned his name. Kyle's mug shot was of a skinhead with tattoos; he looked older than his recorded age by at least a decade… and he looked scary. Very scary. His rap sheet was even scarier. It included a long list of burglaries, auto thefts, drugs, various assaults, and multiple other charges that made me feel ill.

"Do you think he'll want the girls?" I asked Ginny, pushing aside thoughts of Kyle.

"I don't think the courts would let him have them 'cause he can't give them a home. And his record."

"Okay…" was all I could think to say. I was still processing the information. "Where is he now?" I finally asked.

"Oh, he's still in prison."

"Do you know when he's getting out?"

"No, I am trying to stay away from him."
We had been on the phone for nearly an hour by
that time, and I sensed it was time to go. I was
both energised and spent—I was happy that the
conversation was going better than I had imagined,
and also exhausted. "Now... are y'all going to
disappear on me as soon as the adoption is done?"

"No," I said, surprised at her question. "I'll
keep in touch. If I was adopted, I would want to
know who my birth mother was. It seems silly for
me to not be in contact with you."

"Thank you," she said with a calming, humble
croon.

"Well, I better get going..." I began.

"Me too."

"Just message me on Facebook or e-mail when
you want me to call."

"Hey, um..." she began. Her sudden inflection
suggested she had something she had possibly meant
to say sooner. I was silent. "Some things people have
said about me..." she started, then hesitated. "Don't
believe everything you've heard," she finally said.
"I've made some bad decisions. I own that. But not
everything people say about me is true."

I did not know what to say to her about this.
She knew that my only source of information about
her had been Michelle and Trent. And just as I had
chosen to not ask about prison, I had also chosen to
not speak ill of Michelle or Trent. But her statement

made me wonder if I had been withholding too much. I quickly decided that this was not the time to broach that subject.

"Okay," was all I could think to say, then "judgement is… not my thing. At least, I try not to judge. I am happy to get to know you personally. People talk and gossip. Real life is better."

"Yes," she breathed, and I sensed a hint of relief.

We said our goodbyes, and I went downstairs. The girls were quietly eating macaroni and cheese and watching *Playschool*. Bruce looked at me hopefully. "Well?" he said.

"It went great!" I said, tears brimming in my eyes. "Really good. Really, really good. She said she was okay for us to adopt them!" We stood for a moment, hugging. "We'd better let David know."

"Yes," said Bruce. "But let's not tell Michelle and Trent. And let's go slow, as they still said they'd help us." It annoyed me that Bruce seemed convinced that Michelle and Trent would help us, but he wasn't on the receiving end of Michelle's hateful texts. So I hoped, rather than believed, that he had more clarity and possibly charity regarding them. At that moment, I chose to pause any thoughts of Michelle and Trent from my mind, and allowed myself to revel in the bliss of the conversation with Ginny.

SHERRIE GAVIN

13

TREADING WATERS

Being a New Yorker who started swimming lessons
at the ripe age of seven, I'd never considered toddler
swimming lessons for the girls. But as an Australian,
Bruce was all about making sure the girls were safe
around large bodies of water. Reesey was small
enough that I was able to take her in the "Mummy
and Me" classes, where parents and children sang
songs as we bobbed in circles in the chest-deep pool.
At the end of each song, we mimicked holding our
own breath, then gently blew in our toddler's face
to get them to hold their breath. We dipped the
child's head underwater for a maximum of two
seconds and immediately brought the child up, all
while smiling and laughing to help them get used
to holding their breath underwater. Other basics
like the "safety crawl" (using arms to move along
the edge of the pool) and properly getting in and
out of the pool were repeated for weeks before we

stepped up to practising back floats, face floats, and of course, kicking. Joyful and copious amounts of kicking and splashing!

I loved this part of the lessons, and even loved having the girls play in the pool afterwards. Though swimming days could be hard with my energetic and newly-happy toddlers, I enjoyed taking the girls to a toddler pool space where the water was only about 12 inches deep so they could play and "swim." They did this for hours, stopping only when I required them to eat or when they needed the toilet—always with pressing urgency!

They loved the pool! In turn, my time swimming with them became a powerful way in which we bonded. I also loved that I was able to engage socially with other women who had children of the same age and were in the same classes. This was a new experience for me. I was already convinced that having children was required for entry into most social circles, including church, but I was surprised at how poorly I seemed to engage. When women began speaking with me, I sometimes responded awkwardly, talked too much and/or too little, and generally had a clumsy time. The oddness of my own behaviour frustrated me, and I wondered why it seemed so hard to speak with people outside of work. I realised that my new social circle was entirely because of the girls. But I also grew to understand that the girls were not just ice-breakers; they were a social dissertation in progress. After all, I looked like a mother, which

altered my social appearance; I carried a large bag
(or two) everywhere I went. I was up to speed on the
latest Happy Meal toys, knew the playgrounds with
the best protective gates and knew exactly which
times the educational children's TV shows were on.
I looked like a typical parent.

"We are in the process of adopting," I became
adept at saying, "so they are in our care and we're
working out the details." For the most part, this
statement sufficed. People seemed to understand
that the girls' situation was unique, which made the
girls into mini-celebrities. With this, they ended up
getting additional positive attention from almost
everyone who knew our story. Almost everyone.

Reesey's first swimming teacher was a dream
come true. Ros was familiar with the foster care and
severely lacking adoption systems in Queensland
and was very sensitive and supportive of all of us.
She was also a no-nonsense teacher who kept the
kids in line if they pushed behaviour boundaries in
the pool. She was safe, in every sense of the word.
Reesey progressed to the next level of lessons and
was soon in the pool with Cheyenne, with Ros as
her teacher, and I watched on the dry sidelines.

Midway through the second pool term,
Ros took a week off from work, and a substitute
teacher was arranged for Reesey's lesson. I had not
seen Sammi teach before, but I wasn't worried. As
many as four classes were going on in the pool
at any given time, and the teachers sometimes
traded classes to better suit their skills, the

kids' personalities, and their schedules. Neither Cheyenne nor Reesey had had lessons with Sammi previously, and to help them feel more at ease with her, I stopped at the front desk to introduce ourselves. I was carrying Reesey on my left and holding Cheyenne's hand on my right. "We are in the process of adopting the girls," I explained as I introduced them, as I had dozens of times previously. "So they sometimes have a hard time when they meet new people…" I had a huge smile on my face because I thought adoption was wonderful and I was happy to be sharing their story with others, but also asking for patience when they disobeyed out of fear.

"Oh, you *poor thing!*" Sammi interrupted, clearly taken off guard.

I was offended. I took her comment personally, as if I, or the girls, were unworthy of adoption. The girls were not "poor" from being with me! They were better off! She was transfixed on Reesey's face. "Well, it's actually a really good thing," I continued calmly.   "Adoption is wonderful…"

"Oh, you poor thing! Oh, you poor thing! Oh, you poor thing!" She began to repeat, interrupting me. She was sounding less and less in control of herself, and began shaking her head. People around us started to stare at her. Reesey cuddled closer to me. I don't think she comprehended what was going on, and neither did I, but I could tell that she sensed that she was unsafe. "Reesey's just fine and happy," I said brightly, trying to soothe Reesey.

Cheyenne looked up at me, very confused and a little frightened. "We're okay, Cheyenne," I said with a smile, pulling her a little closer.

"*You* poor thing!" Sammi squealed at Cheyenne, "You poor thing! You poor thing!" I had no idea what was going through this woman's head and did not care to find out. "Let's go get ready for class," I said sharply and marched away to the safety of the change rooms. I was angry with Sammi but pushed my anger down to help the girls get ready for the pool–even if it meant they would miss their lessons and we directly went swimming in the toddler pool. Sammi's reaction was capricious at best and traumatising at worst. What was she thinking?! Her reaction appalled me to the point of anger.

Before the interaction, Cheyenne and Reesey were excited and happy to go swimming, but after Sammi, their faces reflected fright. I was shaken as well. The encounter was awful, and I was not sure what to do. We already had our swimming attire on, so I encouraged the girls to use the toilets, which gave me a moment to think as I helped them. Almost immediately, I had clarity: I did not want Sammi teaching my girls. I did not want her anywhere near me or my hoped-for daughters.

When the girls were finished washing their hands, I headed toward the pool manager's office. In doing so, we passed where the girls' lessons were about to start, yet I did not see Sammi. Anywhere. I scanned at least three times just to make sure.

There was a different teacher in place of Ros, and it was not Sammi. It was Jo, a teacher we had seen and been swimming with before.

Cheyenne and Reesey happily jumped into the pool, appearing to forget about the incident with Sammi, and began paddling as instructed by Jo. I normally sat and watched the lesson and chatted with other mothers, but on that day, I decided to walk to the front desk and complain to Tori, the pool manager, about the offensiveness of Sammi and her bitterly inappropriate words.

Tori's office was a glass-encased space to the side of the front desk, where she had a view of both the front desk and one of the fifty-metre pools on the other side. I could see that her office door was open, and she was facing Sammi. Though I could not hear, I could see that Sammi was speaking. Tori noticed me out of the corner of her eye, reassuringly nodded, and waved at me as if to say, "I got this," then closed her office door.

I was relieved! But I still needed to decompress. The encounter had angered and hurt me. "Adoption is a miracle," I thought, and then out loud, I muttered, "if we can even do it." My thoughts raged in silence inside my head: What is wrong with that woman!

But mostly, I felt sad. Why did she think adoption meant it was appropriate to cry out "poor thing" repeatedly to a child? I really wanted to just go and watch the girls swim. I didn't want to fight, or explain why adoption is good, or even complain. I took a breath, chose a diet cola from the shop refrigerator, and went to pay at the front desk. I could no longer see Sammi in the office, or anywhere. After I paid and as I headed back to watch the girls swim, I saw Tori rubbing Sammi's name off the white board that listed the swimming teachers and classes.

I never saw Sammi again.

I always wanted to thank Tori. But at that moment, I was too close to tears. Anger tears, hurt tears, love tears, protection tears, frustration tears, relief tears, all of the tears! I walked back to where the girls were swimming, forcing my tears to stay inside my eyes while I slowly sipped the bubbles in a bottle of diet Coke.

The experience with Sammi had shaken me, even if she was someone I never saw again. The truth of the matter was that she was a manifestation of my fears. As a youth, my mother introduced competing concepts in regard to adoption, both for and against, with her own religious outlooks determining which side of the fence she stood on at any given moment. My mother once helped an unmarried, pregnant teen to place her child for adoption. The process had been informative to my devout mother; she felt divinely situated to help an infertile friend to become a mother, always ending her retelling of the story with a spiritual climax of her personally handing the newborn into the arms of the adoptive mother.

When I entered adolescence, my mother amended the story as a forewarning against premarital sex. It was an exhaustively repeated lesson, and as a result, breaking the law of chastity was not something I planned to do. But what also happened in my youthful mind in place of the pro-chastity message was the development of the idea that adoption was a price to be paid for the woman who fell pregnant out of wedlock. There was a brief mention of the irresponsible father, but the emphasis was on the loss of female virtue and the wicked label branded on unexpectedly pregnant, unmarried women.

When I discovered that it would be impossible for me to carry a pregnancy, I was devastated. I was still fuzzy on some of the facts about sex when surrogacy and adoption became topics of discussion at my doctor's office. My mother was also distraught—possibly more than I was. "I don't know why Heavenly Father would do this to you," she would bemoan, shaking her head. Her reaction confused me: had she not claimed to be instrumental by divine design in placing a baby for adoption? Weren't Joseph and Emma Smith adoptive parents? Didn't the doctrine of the church, which taught that mortality means we are imperfect in varying ways, suggest that infertility was a mortal thing and not a curse from God? Hadn't my youthful Stake Young Women's President spoken memorably and meaningfully about the son that she and her husband were "finally able to adopt"?

With all this confusion, I eventually needed a break from my mother and from the church. As a young adult, I changed my phone number without telling my mother. But the church remained. Specifically, the women of the Church. Not everyone, but a handful of holy soldiers, especially a visiting teacher named Julia, who embodied one of the closest examples of Christlike love that I can imagine. More than just Julia, other visiting teachers, mentors and friends testified that the Spirit spoke to them that I would be a mother. I trusted these women. I trusted these women because when they spoke these words, they spoke words that were powered by divinity.

I still had to choose for myself what I believed. Would I choose to listen to the people like Sammi who believed adoption was somehow horrific? Or to those who believed I was a lesser being because of infertility? Or would I choose to listen to the Julia group who filled my soul with light and promise? Mostly I listened to the Julia group, but sometimes the poisonous darts of self-loathing pierced me, usually when I least expected it, and the Sammis would win a battle. Even with this, somewhere deep inside me, I was yet determined that I would win my war for motherhood.

SHERRIE GAVIN

14

NURSING

"If they ever ask for a bottle," Zoia advised one session, "be sure to give it to them." Things were progressing with the girls, thanks in many ways to our ongoing visits with Zoia. But this advice seemed random… and weird.

"Okay," I said questioningly. After all, the girls were two and three years old.

Zoia must have sensed my scepticism. "It means they are wanting to connect with you. Don't force it; they are connecting already. But just if they ask." I was quite convinced that they would not ask for bottles but accepted the advice and moved on.

The next day, I found myself at the grocery store with the girls. They played in the shopping trolley while I placed milk, apples, and a variety of other items around them, chatting away about the yummy things we would be eating for the week.

"What is next on our list?" I asked the girls brightly. They could not read, but I would still point to the words on the shopping list. "Princess pants!" I said and slowly made my way to the aisle with baby supplies. I parked the shopping trolley on the opposite side of the "princess pants" and took my eyes off of the girls to reach the top shelf. As I turned around with the package in hand, I saw Cheyenne standing and holding an item she had grabbed. It was a bottle.

I was a little startled but accepted that perhaps Zoia had not only been an astute counsellor, but an inspired one as well! "Isn't that a cute bottle," I said nonchalantly, as I wedged the princess pants in the trolley's undercarriage.

"Bottles are for babies," Cheyenne said blankly. Reesey stood and grabbed a bottle.

"Bottles are okay for everyone who likes them," I gently responded. Wary of forcing a bottle on her, I calmly asked, "Would you like a bottle?" Cheyenne pondered, and Reesey was silent.

"I'm not a baby," Cheyenne said, matter-of-factly.

"That's okay," I said. "You don't have to be a baby." I looked at some of the varieties and colours, noticing a package of three twist-top bottles in green, blue, and pink. "Would you like a bottle, Reesey?"

"On the shopping list?" she hummed, knowing that if it was, we were allowed to get it.

"Well, um… I forgot to write it on the list." In finding my pen, I said, "I'll write it on there now." I glanced at Reesey as I wrote. "Shall we get it? Then you can cross it off the list?"

"Yes!" She smiled. I pointed to where she could cross off the word I had just written, and added, "Big girls have bottles sometimes, Cheyenne."

Cheyenne mirrored my smile and happily replied, "Okay!"

That night, I sat in a rocking chair in their bedroom. I was armed with two bottles. Reesey wanted her bottle straight away, but I invited Cheyenne to sit in my arms while I rocked her. She agreed, and I began to sing a Shirley Temple song that my father used to sing to me. I didn't remember all of the words, so I made up what I couldn't recall. "Animal crackers in my soup…" I sang as Cheyenne sucked her bottle. Within moments, she was sound asleep. I carefully cradled her, stood and placed her in bed, bottle gripped firmly in her hands. I laid next to Reesey in her bed and watched her slipping to sleep between bottle slurps. "Thank you, Mummy Sherrie."

"You're welcome," I cooed.

As I watched her drift into sleep, I thanked God for Zoia's advice. Without Zoia's words, I would have not purchased the bottles, and maybe even would have chided the girls as "big girls" who should not want bottles. But there they were, fast asleep while I silently watched, savoring one of the sweetest moments in my life.

"The day after we saw you, they asked for bottles!" I enthusiastically shared with Zoia at our next meeting. "And I rocked them to sleep, and sang songs…" She was genuinely happy for me, and as usual, she patiently worked with me as I ticked off the list of things I wanted to discuss.

As I paid the receptionist on my way out, Zoia called out of her office, "Mummy!"

I stopped and turned. "Let the children just call you 'Mummy,'" she said, walking me toward the door. "And Daddy. Just Mummy and Daddy. Not Mummy Sherrie or that business. You are their Mummy. It's confusing for Mummy Sherrie and Mummy Michelle. Just Mummy. You are Mummy."

I nodded, in a bit of a haze. The advice had seemed to come out of nowhere. I longed and dreamed of the day that someone would call me "Mother" or "Mummy" or anything of the sort! Even being called "Mummy Sherrie" was a treasure. Still, I was anxious. I was robustly aware that the adoption might not go through, so the idea of having the girls call me "Mummy" and then losing them filled me with dread, for me and for them. My heart was most certainly "all in," but in my mind, I was plagued with doubt. I rebuked myself for this, believing that I was worse than Thomas (John 20).

The last thing I wanted was to ever hurt the girls, so I decided to leave it up to them. As I drove home from our counselling session, I casually said, "You can call me Mum." Then I paused. "Or Mummy. Just Mummy. If you like." My heart was pounding, though I was trying to sound as if they had no pressure on them whatsoever.

"Are you going to be our mummy?"

"I am working on it." It was the truth!

"Mummy, can we get ice cream on the way home?" asked Cheyenne, testing, maybe even teasing me.

"Yes," I giggled.

"Thank you, Mummy!" chorused the girls from the backseat. My new moniker fit perfectly, so perfectly that I became teary, filled with the utmost joy. It seemed unreal—*and yet it was real*. The two cherubs in the backseat instinctively, unquestioningly, had called me their mother. At that moment, I was even more motivated to make sure that I would be their mother, lest this moment become a lie.

Filled with new fierceness and determination in my soul, I dried my eyes on my shirtsleeve just in time to pay for and collect the ice cream cones in the drive through.

SHERRIE GAVIN

15

OBLIGATIONS AND INVITATIONS

Setting up a routine was one of the things that
my Exponent Blog sisters uniformly advised me to
apply into our new toddler life. At first, I created
a poster with words and a few images that was
quite detailed and included reading time, play time,
painting, getting dressed, brushing teeth and so on
down, nearly to the minute. I was naïve and quickly
learned that this was fantasy. It took some time, but
within a few months of trial and error, I was able to
create a more realistic routine that was laid out on
a large poster with images of the activities that we
planned to accomplish on certain days, including
church, swimming, Zoia and toddler library days.
It was a skeletal approach to life, but one that kept
us on track. The routine poster was also helpful for
Bruce to switch to home-mode after being away at
work.

This was a hard-won thing, so when a few
friends from other areas suggested they would
like to visit, we kindly declined. It wasn't that we

did not want to see them or that we didn't need the help, but the girls were still adjusting, and we were learning how to be parents. Moreover, Zoia had identified that the children had experienced sexual grooming, and I was working with the girls to redirect these taught behaviours. In addition, nightmares were ongoing and there were still occasional lapses into violent behaviour between the girls. The only individuals that we could not refuse were Bruce's parents. I pushed back when Bruce told me that they wanted to visit, but he was sure that everything would be fine.

Bruce's parents briefly met the girls in Sydney when we went to meet Michelle and Trent. They understandably wanted to develop more of a relationship with the children and soon arrived after a long drive from Sydney. The girls were not interested in them at all. Within a day, the routine was ignored and the girls were out of balance. Reesey began wetting her pants while Cheyenne was more aggressive, telling Bruce's father to "Get out! Go away!" Though they wanted to spend time and get to know the girls, they were almost strangers to the girls, which triggered the girls to be angry, frightened, protective, aggressive, and territorial. Though I was trying to be a thoughtful host, I was also stretched. Bruce was away for the week, and no matter what I said, his parents did not seem to understand that the girls needed to get to know them on their own terms.

OBLIGATIONS AND INVITATIONS

When Bruce arrived home for the weekend, his parents offered to look after the girls so he and I could have a night out. Though it had been a rough week, we grabbed the offer, anxious for uninterrupted time together. We enjoyed a quick dinner at our favourite Mexican restaurant. Even though Bruce's parents really wanted to put the girls to bed, we were home before 7PM, confident that we would need to be home for them to relax enough to sleep.

When we arrived back, Bruce's father met us at the door, visibly upset. "We told them that we are leaving early tomorrow and that it was our last night here," he said. "And Cheyenne told us, 'I hope you drive off in a car and crash and die tomorrow.'" Because I was somewhat conditioned to some of the more violent things they said sometimes, I wasn't surprised, but I was disappointed. "They don't know you yet," I tried to soothe, but my words were useless. As expected, the girls were still awake, so I excused myself to put them to bed. Between cooing the girls to sleep, I could hear Bruce's voice, but could not make out the words. His tone sounded apologetic and defeated, not his usual, cheery self. By the time the girls were asleep, I joined him to find that his parents had gone to bed, resolute on an early start.

They left before the sun was up the next morning. Bruce and I rose to see them off, but we all said very little. The girls were still solidly asleep, which given the hurt feelings, was possibly a good thing. In the falsely fluorescent dim of our porchlight, I could see Bruce weeping. His heart was broken.

"I hope they didn't take those words personally," said Zoia compassionately at our next appointment. As usual, Bruce wasn't able to attend, so I was relaying the events to her. "They did," I said downheartedly. "Is there anything I can do?" I was asking for advice about my in-laws, something that was new to our sessions. "Bruce was crushed. He wanted the girls to feel loved and safe with his parents, and so did I! But... it just... wasn't. I don't think the girls are ready."

"Attachment is something that can be hard to form in families where the children have been traumatised," explained Zoia. "The girls are still learning to trust you, and they do! I've seen it! But it is still very new. You can never take these things personally."

I knew this, but I had been unable to effectively relay it to Bruce's parents. "But... how would Cheyenne think of saying 'drive off and crash and die'?" I asked. "They don't see TV shows with this kind of thing... or books." I had searched my mind to understand where such a violent idea would have entered their minds.

"Someone would have said it to them," said Zoia, matter-of-factly. "They are repeating what someone has said to them. Not TV or a book. Or you." I wanted to be relieved at this insight, but all

I could feel was sadness. Who would say something like this to a child? But at Michelle's admission, they had been shuffled around a lot.

That night, I called Bruce and relayed Zoia's take on the situation to him. "It wasn't your parents. Someone has said this 'driving and dying' thing to the girls. They're just repeating it. They probably don't know what it means and certainly didn't mean it towards your parents. They only knew that those words had power." Bruce seemed softened by Zoia's insight and was relieved to know that the girls' behaviour towards his parents was amenable. But I could also tell that he was tired; the visit had not been good, and given all the unknowns ahead, we needed his family to support us.

Still, I could not help but feel that a silent earthquake had fractured the earth between Bruce and me. He needed privacy to mourn and recover, and I was struggling to see any light at the end of the tunnel.

Thankfully, communication with Michelle was becoming less and less frequent. However, when I did hear from her, she was always demanding, cruel, and ferociously judgemental. She refused to hide her animosity toward Ginny, or me, and dotted every communication with various attempts at pilfering money from me. Bruce still encouraged me to maintain contact. "You're the main person," he said. "So even if she is—like she is—you are in the best position to maintain communication with her."

I did not agree. "Bruce, there is no way for her to help us. We know private adoption is illegal here. The adoption has to go through the U.S."

"But the immigration side is something they could help us with," he countered. "I think she will help us in the future." He was impatient with me for not shaking off Michelle's demanding texts and verbal insults as well as he thought I should, though he had not read or heard about any messages in months. He responded that this was the only tactic and that my ideas about pushing back on her were unreasonable. He assured me that subjecting myself to Michelle's draconian word spew was "a part of my responsibility." No matter how much I disagreed, he would not hear me, which caused me to feel dismissed and hurt.

One of our wedding gifts was a book called *The Five Love Languages* by Gary Chapman. We finally got around to reading it by our third anniversary, and it made a positive difference in our marriage and my life in general. In reading the book, I learned that my primary "love language," or the way in which I process feeling loved, is through "words of affirmation." It also means that in addition to feeling loved when I receive positive or affirming words in any form, hateful words can be poisonous to me. Bruce identified his love language as "quality time," which was also not an easy thing to accomplish with his current employment situation. Nor was it easy at home. It seemed like all we did was catch-up: listing the foods Reesey tried and vomited, retelling the most recent nightmare of Cheyenne, recounting updates on swimming lessons and playdates. It was not an easy time for either of us, but most alarming was how much it felt like we were disconnecting as a couple.

"Would you like a girls' shower?" Becky, a woman in my previous ward, asked timidly one day. In the past, I had thrown baby showers and attended baby showers armed with generous gifts for women I hardly knew. I also knew that I had purposefully not been invited to some ward baby showers and later was told that it was because the hostess did not want me "to feel sad" about not having children, even though I felt even worse being excluded! I also knew that many adoptive mothers did not have baby showers because of the very real chance that the biological mother would change her mind at the last moment. By my early twenties, I understood that baby showers were yet another method by which women divided themselves. And yet, I still wanted one.

Becky recognised that whatever kind of mother I was at that moment, a baby shower might be appropriate. She was an angel! Her thoughtfulness in asking me what I wanted was balm to my soul, healing at least a decade of cold shoulders and mindless presumptions. "Yes! I'd love a girls' shower!"

"Oh, good!" replied Becky. "Just let me know who'd you like to invite. And where?" Within a few minutes, we settled on a large public park Becky had invited us to previously. At that time, Cheyenne and Reesey were very clingy and did not want to play with other children. I found it hard to speak with the mothers, but I was grateful to be invited. By the time of Becky's offer of a shower, the girls were becoming more confident that I would not leave them, plus they liked Becky. That was the most influential thing: Becky. The girls felt safe with her, so though they might not engage with anyone else, they would at least feel safe with Becky being there.

Becky made cute invitations, and I was surprised when people asked what gifts the girls might like. I had not thought of gifts, and though some were startled when I relayed the girls sizes, Becky did not blink when I told her that the girls were only sizes one and two. They were eating copiously and growing, but they were still much smaller than children of similar ages.

Good weather is one of the blessings of living in Australia, and the day of the planned shower was beautiful. Cheyenne and Reesey played with Becky's boys within view, and they were having fun. My friend Nina brought her mother and sister and gifted books for the girls. Carli brought a gorgeous mini tea set. It was ceramic, and therefore breakable. "It will help them to learn to be careful with plates and cups," she explained. "And because it's so pretty, they will work hard to use it properly." There were other gifts, mostly small things that the girls could grab and play with immediately—blowing bubbles, chalk, and other fun things that kept the toddlers and preschoolers all engaged.

Becky's gift was different: it was a pad of paper and a pen, intended as a bedside notebook. "I keep cards by my bed," she explained. "And when my kids say something silly or funny, I try to write what they said on the cards. It's a good way to keep a record of the bright parts of your days, because you read them again and feel good. The kids also like reading them when they get older," she explained, her eyes shining. "They'll go and read the cards and laugh and ask if they really said those things when they were little. It helps on the hard days, and it's a fun keepsake for everyone." I was touched by this simple, personal, and big-hearted gift. It was a gift for the entire family—the invitation to focus on the positive and to keep a sense of humour in the adventure of parenting. I loved it.

As the party wound down, Becky and I tidied the picnic tables we had been using, and I moved to get the girls into my car. Becky had been loading her son's bikes into her car when she noticed I was about to leave. "Oh, Sherrie!" she said, "Come here for a moment." Inside of her car were giant, black rubbish bags. She began to open them, and then proceeded to pull out brand-new girl's clothes.

I was dumbfounded. "You shouldn't have…" I stammered.

"Oh, these are just the giveaways," she shrugged. "They're from ages ago. Are you interested?"

"Yes! Please! Thank you!" The words stumbled out of my mouth in a rush, and I wondered where she might have kept such an amazing stash of unused toddler girl's clothes. I was gobsmacked by her generosity! I could not think of how to ask how she had come to have them as I loaded bag after bag into the back of my car, thanking Becky again and again and again.

At home, the girls had a bath. After they were dressed, I washed the new tea set and placed it on their tiny, plastic, pink table. I filled the teapot with chocolate milk, and placed some dainty biscuits on the matching plates. The girls happily sat, hair drying in the warmth of the afternoon, pouring and sipping from teacups, pinkies raised. As they happily chatted, I went and unloaded the car. After washing and putting away the picnic things, I began to open the giant black bags from Becky. The clothes were divine! Even better than I had first realised! Pleated dresses with petticoat-lined skirts, matching sets of tops and shorts that were cute, frilly and feminine. Cheyenne and Reesey appeared at the site of the first lacy dress. "Who are those for?" asked Cheyenne.

"For you! And Reesey!" I replied.

She blinked. "Me? And Reesey?" She didn't seem sure.

"Yes," I said brightly. Reesey remained quiet, looking at the items but not touching them. She seemed to enjoy putting bows and ribbons in her hair but rarely wore them outside of the house, and even though we had purchased some floral and pink clothes for her, she still wore many of the hand-me-down boy's clothes that she came with.

"Is this mine?" asked Cheyenne, picking up a pink and black butterfly-printed dress with a matching bright pink cardigan.

"Let's check the size," I said. "Yes! It's a size three. Cheyenne size!"

"Can I put it on?" she asked, excitedly.

"Of course!" I scooped her up onto the kitchen counter and helped her put the dress on. She beamed!

"Ya know…" I said, "Fashion models walk on a thing called a catwalk. And our kitchen counter is a little bit like a catwalk. Models walk on it and turn around so everyone can see how pretty they look. Do you want to—" Before I could finish, Cheyenne was standing on the counter, taking a few steps, then turning around. She was in heaven! I took a quick photo, then helped her hop down.

"Reesey, it's your turn!" I said with enthusiasm.

"My size?" she said quietly, not looking at anything in particular.

"Um… let me see…" I pulled out a dark blue floral top with white lacy sleeves and matching pantaloons. "This is your size. Want to try it?" She remained quiet and I helped her put the outfit on.

"It fits," she said quietly. She usually kept her head down when we looked at clothes and didn't bustle much when getting dressed. Cheyenne was fussier— she liked skirts she could twirl in. "And it's gorgeous on you!" I said enthusiastically. She slowly raised her head, revealing the most jubilant smile I had ever seen on her face.

"Pretty!" she said.

"Very pretty!" I said. The little girl who once said that she was "too ugly to be a girl. I have to be a boy" was beaming! Her entire demeanour reflected the perfect joy that can only be found in being completely satisfied with one's self. She was enchanting and radiated happiness in that outfit. I was only allowed enough time to take one blurry photo before she and Cheyenne were off pirouetting through the living room and dancing on the wings of childhood dreams.

Bruce was working locally that week, which made the night feel extra special. The girls were still twirling, leaping and singing when he arrived home for dinner that evening. When Bruce was home, dinner was always my favourite time. At Bruce's suggestion, we each took turns at dinnertime sharing our "favourite things" from the day. Similar to Becky's nightstand notebook, it was an opportunity to remember the good things. Bruce and I often went first, in part to set an example, but also to remind the girls what we had done that day.

"My favourite thing is that Daddy is home, and this yummy dinner and the girls' shower," I said. Bruce's "favourite things" list was similar, but he included the hugs the girls gave him when he arrived home from work.

"My favourite thing," began Cheyenne, "is right now. And my dress. And the park. And the party. And…" She listed everything from the entire day. It was sweet to hear!

"My favourite thing," stated Reesey, "is me. I'm a girl. Pretty girl. And the party." It was simple and short, yet related the difficult path of self that, at less than three years old, she was already working through. Bruce and I both verbally agreed that she and Cheyenne were very pretty.

"You know there are even more clothes…" I mentioned.

"More?"

"Yep."

"For us?"

"Yes," I giggled. "We'll look when I can't see any more carrots on your plate."

Plates cleaned, we all went to the girls' bedroom where I had placed the bags. We helped the girls into princess pants and pyjamas, then separated the clothes according to size. The girls squealed with delight and jumped with joy! They held the clothes like treasures, and we helped them to fold, hang, and put them away. As we did so,

Cheyenne spied something crawling outside of her bedroom window, and squealed in fright. "Will it get me?" she asked with real concern.

"Noooooo…" said Bruce soothingly before I had even seen what caused the commotion. "Just a little gecko."

"Where?" asked Reesey. Bruce pointed to the tiny lizard, and we all looked.

"It eats the yucky bugs like mossies," he said, using the Australian term for mosquitoes. "It's a helper."

Cheyenne was not convinced, but was confident enough to not scream again. "How is it a helper?" she asked.

"Geckos eat the bugs that like to bite us. And the flies that buzz and land on our food," he explained.

"They don't eat people," I added. "They help people!"

"Did it come from Becky?" asked Reesey. "A helper?"

"From Becky's bags?" asked Cheyenne. "Becky is a helper."

"Yeah," said Reesey. "Becky's Gecko. A helper!"

"A Becky Gecko?" said Cheyenne.

"Yes!" agreed Bruce, "a helper gecko, just like Becky." I smiled and giggled, making a mental note that this naming would be the first entry in my bedside notebook.

That night, my home was utopia.

16

PARTIES AND PLANS

I asked Ginny for a copy of the guardianship agreement, but she did not have it. "It was made when I went to jail so a lot of my papers got lost," she explained. Bruce pressed me to ask Michelle again for the document. I did so, with trepidation.

"You don't need that," Michelle immediately texted back, but I tried again, suggesting we could use it as the foundation for the "custody agreement" she said she wanted. She curtly replied, "That's none of your business. I'm in charge. Not you." I wasn't surprised at her rejection, but I felt like Bruce was disappointed in me for not getting the document. He spoke to me as though I was not doing my best to appease Michelle, and I was at odds with him for not understanding how difficult it was to flatter someone who seemed to think of me as her personal dupe. I began to feel angry at Bruce for pinning me in this position.

Michelle originally stated that she wanted to take turns travelling to each other's residences to spend Easter, Christmas, and the girls' birthdays together. It was not something I wanted to do, but as time progressed, it became clear that she only wanted us to deliver the girls to her, when she wanted, and at our expense. I guessed that this might have been a reflection of Michelle's childhood experience as a part of her parents' divorce, but I had no intention of playing the part of the ex-spouse in a relationship that had never happened. I dreaded it. If I did something that struck her as wrong in any way, such as stating one of the girls liked a particular kind of yoghurt that Michelle deemed unfit for children, she threatened to call the police and accuse me of kidnapping until I appeased her. It was exhausting.

Bruce was hopeful of creating an agreement that somehow supported Michelle and Trent's undetermined "trial period." I disagreed with Bruce on this for many reasons, including that it could take years to somehow get through all of the international red tape if we processed this adoption in the way that Michelle suggested. Based on her langage and messaging, it sounded like she expected to adopt the girls so they could remain in Australia, and then she would have us apply to adopt the girls from her. But there were too many complications, if only because Ginny expressed to us that she did not want Michelle to adopt the girls, so would not give permission. That, and the fact that private adoption is illegal in Australia. If this was Michelle's plan, it could never work. But whenever I was brave enough to voice my concerns and point out how legally unfeasible Michelle's implied plan was, Bruce dismissed me.

Something else was niggling at me. From the first night I shared with the girls, I felt intensely impressed to strictly abide by the legal processes in Australia and the U.S., and to be lawful. "Honesty is the best policy" had proven to be constantly true for me, and I had no desire to bend any rules, especially when it came to my hoped-for daughters! As it was, Bruce and I were not knowingly breaking any laws, but I suspected Michelle might be receiving government financial support on behalf of the girls. If this was the case, the fact that the girls were not living with her would be problematic, and she would possibly lose that government-provided income. Bruce and I might even be held in contempt for not disclosing to the government that we were wholly providing for the girls.

Mostly, based on what I could Google about the girls' visa status, as non-citizens and non-permanent residents, they did not qualify for government concessions. But when Michelle originally handed the girls to me "on trial," she handed me Australian government concession cards *in the girls' names, but with Michelle's surname.* I brought this to the attention of our attorney, David. "We think that the guardians, rather than the birth parents, will offer more resistance because we suspect they are getting welfare in the girls' names," I wrote in an e-mail to him. "Getting a copy of the guardianship agreement could be hard going through them, for this alone. And we think that the guardians really only want money from us, if something like that is possible or legal."

Responding to my e-mail, David promised me that he would begin searching for a copy of the guardianship, with Ginny's help. In regard to my comments on money, he added, "Sometimes we need to think outside the box. We can't be involved in buying a child, but maybe there is a way to structure a package deal that is a win-win. I know my comments are a bunch of clichés and semantic mumbo-jumbo, but keep your mind open to a 'creative' solution. Certainly, a court would look at them [Michelle and Trent] with suspicion since they are not actually caring for the children, and especially so if they are collecting money under false pretense. Keep careful track of the interactions, even if it's just notes that you make about each phone call. It could be very helpful in court." With this message, I felt like at least David was on my side, even if no one else was.

Cheyenne's birthday was coming up, and I dreaded the idea of flying or driving to take the girls to Michelle's home. Flying with them had already proven to be problematic: sans court orders or anything reflecting some kind of guardianship, or their identity, we had no way of proving we had any permission to travel with them. We might be asked at the airport to provide documentation, and lacking that, the girls might end up being removed from all of us. My only hope was that with Cheyenne's birthday happening to fall during school holidays, perhaps Michelle would have other plans that did not involve us.

In Australia, schools run roughly on four ten-week terms, buffered with two to four weeks of school holidays between terms (similar to U.S. year-round schools) and a bit longer break during summer, which falls over Christmas and the New Year. "Do you have any school holiday plans?" I timidly asked Michelle in a text. "We're trying to budget for everything."

She responded that she had some day trips planned with her children and was looking into various activities, *only for her children*. This message filled me with hope and even a smidge of courage. "Bruce is going away for work that week," I texted, "so coming to Sydney would be hard. Would you mind if we rescheduled?" Almost immediately she responded that our not coming would be fine and worked better for her. A few minutes later, as if an afterthought, she texted platitudes about how difficult this would be for her, but she was willing to sacrifice all of her feelings so long as we made sure to let her speak with Cheyenne on her birthday.

I did not believe her when she professed "how emotionally difficult" things were for her. She never asked about the girls. Nor did she ever ask to speak to them when she called or texted me. Observations aside, I was ecstatic! I desperately wanted to have a birthday party for Cheyenne, and now I felt free to plan something wonderful. Or at least as wonderful as my budget would allow.

When I shared this news with Bruce, he was thrilled. "Hey, the girls can come to the resort in Yeppoon!" he said, referring to a training session he was running the week after Cheyenne's birthday. "The cost of the room is covered, and while I run a training session, you can play with the girls in the pool, or even have them in the resort's childcare. I'll be there in the mornings and evenings to help out with breakfast and bed time. It'll be a holiday!" This sounded glorious! Before the girls, I had joined Bruce on a previous trip like this and enjoyed working on my thesis in such a beautiful location. The rooms were spacious suites of two bedrooms and a full bathroom. Located oceanside, it hosted a quiet, lapping beach where you could see a part of the Great Barrier Reef. It was not hard to decide to absolutely go for it.

I wasn't sure if Cheyenne had ever had a birthday party. I knew she had family birthday dinners with Michelle and Trent, but I did not think she had ever attended a party where there were games and guests of her choosing, and I wanted to give this to her. There were two motives for me. In reality, the adoption might not happen, so this might be the only birthday we would ever celebrate with her. I also wanted to satisfy my own whimsy by pretending she was mine and indulging in all of the things I had dreamed about giving her if I was lucky enough to become her mother.

"Who should we have at our party?" I asked.

"Mandy and Mali!" Both girls chorused. They quickly added Carli's daughters and a handful of other names, including Ella from swimming lessons.

"What kinds of games would you like to play?" I asked.

"Games!"

"Okay, but what games? Like 'pin the tail on the donkey'?"

"Okay."

They clearly didn't know what that game was, so I moved on.

"Um… maybe 'pass the parcel'?"

"Okay." They obviously had no clue what that was either.

"Are we going to have party bags?" Cheyenne asked. Reesey chorused the request behind her. I was surprised but chuckled that they knew what "party bags" were. These are small bags filled mostly with candy and handed out as parting gifts at the end of a birthday party. They are very much a rite of passage in Australian childhood. Being diabetic, or perhaps because it didn't seem common where I grew up, I was not raised with a party bag expectation. But I was eager to give Cheyenne and Reesey a fun birthday party, even if the idea of giving toddlers a bag filled with candy did not appeal to me. I agreed to the party bags and began contemplating candy alternatives. After Cheyenne chose the flavour of cake she wanted (chocolate), I knew that party planning with the toddlers had gone as far as it could.

Bruce and I decided to have Cheyenne's birthday party on a Saturday, a few days before her actual birthday. We planned to have the party mid-morning, then load the car and hit the road for Yeppoon. Yeppoon was about an eight-hour drive north, but we thought that having the party in the morning would wear the girls out so that we could have them watch a movie or two on the car DVD players, then sleep for the majority of the drive. By arriving late on Saturday, we could all relax on Sunday together at the resort.

I wanted the party to be everything that Cheyenne could hope for, so I clandestinely began serious party work when the girls were at daycare for the two days a week and after they had gone to bed. Even though it was Cheyenne's birthday, I decided that Reesey should be a part of the celebration as well. I made matching birthday dresses for them with pink Japanese silk fabric that was on sale. I had never sewn such small clothes before and found it challenging to work the slippery fabric to create the tiny dress sleeves. But I was determined and stuck with it. I drew a poster of Rapunzel and made a stack of paper crowns so we could play 'pin the crown on Rapunzel.' I bought an assortment of bouncing balls, plastic pastel-coloured hand mirrors, glittery plastic combs and even some candy for the party bags.

The day before the birthday party, I stocked the car with snacks and children's DVDs and secured packed suitcases for myself and girls, hoping to make the transition from party to car as smooth as possible. The cake I made was cooling as Bruce and I fed the girls, bathed them and tucked them in bed, chiding them that if they did not fall asleep quickly that the party might not happen. They fell asleep remarkably quickly, allowing me to lay a plastic pink tablecloth before I slathered rich pink icing across the layer cake, finishing with a pinch of white icing that spelled out "Cheyenne" and "4."

That Saturday morning was bright. Even though July is in winter in Brisbane, our tropical location blessed us with a sunny day, with only the slightest chill. Bruce and I dressed, each of us wearing pink shirts. We were ready!

Reesey woke and, before leaving her room, dressed herself in brightly striped socks, lavender polka-dot shorts and a striped sweater vest that almost matched her socks. She was dressed to party! What was most striking, though, was her smile. She was clearly excited for her sister's birthday, and her grin illuminated everything around her. Cheyenne dressed as well, in a bright pink tee and light pink shorts, but she was more timid, even shy, or maybe hesitant that the birthday party wasn't really going to happen.

After breakfast, I led the girls to the laundry/ sewing room. "I thought that since you are princesses," I began, "and this is a very important occasion, that you might need some proper dresses." I showed them the matching perfectly pink mini gowns, graced with plastic pink snap necklaces and pale pink slippers.

"Is that for me?" asked Cheyenne, mesmerised.

"For a birthday?" said Reesy with her developing vocabulary and amazement in her voice. They stood and stared with smiles on their faces.

"Yes," I said happily. "I thought you both needed something special for this occasion."

"For me? And for Reesey?" asked Cheyenne.

"Yes. You and Reesey. Is that okay?" Cheyenne nodded, unable to speak as she slowly began to comprehend that they each had a birthday dress with matching jewelry and shoes.

"And me!" said Reesey. "Me?"

"Yes," I giggled. "Even you. Is that okay?" She nodded enthusiastically.

"Shall I help you dress?" I asked.

Within minutes, each girl was dressed in her pink gown. Reesey's was a crumb large on her, but as the sewing pattern was only sized from three and up, I did the best I could. She didn't notice one bit and was all smiles! Cheyenne's dress fit her perfectly. They were over the moon!

Carli's daughters thankfully came by before the party. The eldest, Gracie, offered to do Cheyenne's hair. Cheyenne happily agreed, and within moments, both Cheyenne and Reesey were having their hair styled. Reesey's was still short, but it could hold some tiny pink clips—at least for a moment. It was rare for her to allow anyone to touch her head, and I was grateful for the tiny miracle when she gave Gracie permission to style her hair. As the girls played, I put some finishing touches on sliced finger sandwiches and a fruit platter, finishing just in time for the party to start.

The first game was 'pass the parcel.' This is a traditional English game where a toy is wrapped in newspaper or wrapping paper, then another toy is added and wrapped, and another and so on, for each child playing the game. The children sit in a circle and music plays as they pass the parcel around the circle. When the music stops, the child holding the parcel unwraps one layer, receiving the prize in that layer. It was clear that Cheyenne didn't care if she received any of the gifts in the parcel, happily passing it along, bounding in her chair to the music, all smiles.

As the party progressed, sometimes tears welled in my eyes. The girls were so happy that life felt like perfect charity, the pure love of Christ. At that moment, I could tell that Cheyenne felt absolute joy and love. She knew that she was special. It was a sacred experience.

'Pin the crown on Rapunzel' was confusing for the smaller children who had never experienced it, but they all had smiles. Even though I had a prize for the "winner," no one was interested in the prize. Who knew that being blindfolded and spun around was a satisfying game on its own?

Among many generous gifts, Mandy and Mali give Cheyenne a small pink tent. "This is for sharing," Mandy assured both girls, "It's more fun with sharing." The tent was assembled in seconds and became the prime source of entertainment until we cut the cake. As we sang the birthday song to Cheyenne, she pumped her legs in complete joy, nearly bouncing off her chair!

Her smile was blissfully frozen in place as if she were under a marvellously magical spell. It was an enchanting day, a day that Michelle knew nothing about, and it was blissfully absent of hateful texts.

Mandy generously stayed afterwards to help clean, as Bruce and I packed last minute things for the drive. We loaded everything in the car, only slightly later than we hoped. I felt happy! The party had energised me, and I was excited for a few days away. I dressed the girls in pyjamas, even though it was three hours before their official bedtime. We hoped that they would be tired enough to quietly watch a cartoon movie in the car for the first part of the drive, then after a quick dinner stop, they would sleep.

As I fastened Reesey's seatbelt on her, I saw her slip her pink ballet shoes over the enclosed footings in her onesie, as if she were Cinderella and taking off the shoes would somehow break the spell.

She maintained a constant and a firm grip on her party bag, but her smile had turned into a look of worry.

I dismissed this, thinking she was just tired.

SHERRIE GAVIN

17

WAVES OF EMOTION

Everything was going to plan when we stopped at a fast-food restaurant about two hours into our drive. The girls had no interest in food when there was a new playland to explore, so Bruce and I were able to relax, eat and prepare for the drive, estimating that we would arrive at the resort around 11PM. When it was time, I took the girls to the restroom while Bruce bought a couple of kid's meals for the car. We began driving again, happy to hear the girls munching on their food and happily chattering to each other and sometimes us.

About an hour later, we pulled into a rest stop to refuel the car before the long-haul drive. This rest stop was typical of hundreds of others along the wide-spread Australian roads, but yet, seeing where we were walking, Reesey began to cry. This was not a small, tired, weeping cry, but a panicked bellow. "I don't want to go to the toilet..." she wailed, confusing me. Bruce looked at me as if he expected me to be able to solve the problem. Then Cheyenne also began to weep.

"Um… are you hungry?" I asked Reesey.

"Noooooooooooo!" she moaned. "I don't want a holiday."

I was baffled, so I tried to redirect. "Shall we look through the shops and see if there is a treat you'd like?" I asked.

"Noooooooooo!"

I was thoroughly perplexed but tried again. "Okay… let's see if there are some toys?"

"I don't want the toilet!" she shrieked.

"We're not going to the toilet," I tried to redirect. "We're going to look at the lollies." She settled to whimpers but seemed alarmed. "Is there anything you might like for a treat in the car?"

"No, no, no, no…" she said, shaking her head and nuzzling into my shoulder. Bruce shuffled Cheyenne to me so he could pay for the fuel.

"Would you like a treat?" I asked Cheyenne.

"No," she said quietly and distinctly. "I don't want a holiday."

"Um… but…" I sputtered. "Um… holidays are fun! We'll see the beach!"

"I don't want a holiday," repeated Cheyenne, her eyes now brimming with tears.

"Um… Okay… Um… Are you sure?"

"Yes. No holiday."

I was thrown by their reactions, so I attempted again to redirect "How about… ice cream?" They refused. I was so confused by the whole situation that only then did I notice that I had been shaking my head. I gathered my thoughts and tried to redirect. "How about we try to use the toilet?" I said brightly, trusting that they were more tired than I realised.

"No, no, no…" Reesey began crying again. She was crying enough that I felt eyes on me from the other customers in the shop.

"No!" By this time, Cheyenne began crying again, too, and this time with gusto. "I don't want to go on holidays!"

I decided to get out of the shop as the girls were beginning to make a scene. "But… but… holidays are fun!" I said as I moved, still perplexed as to what was going on. "So… uh… let's go to the toilets and we'll go on a vacation." I slipped in the American term, hoping that would trigger a happy, or at least happier, response. This did not work. Frightened, desperate sobbing soon ensued from both girls. "Vacations are fun!" I said. "It's a vacation. It's fun! Lots of playing and games… what games would you like?" Wails of grief were my only response. Until that moment, there had only been a few other times when I felt completely at a loss as to what to do. I racked my brain trying to recall or discover what Zoia might advise, but other than redirecting and reassuring, which I had tried, I was stuck.

"Should we head home?" I asked Bruce, my own panic brimming.

"I want to go home to Brisbane!" yowled Cheyenne, overhearing me.

"No," he said. He was clearly flustered as well, but his tone was steady. "It'll be too much driving back and forth—I still have to get there for work." Then, collecting Cheyenne in his arms, he asked her, "Don't you want to go on a holiday?"

"*Noooooo!*" She shrieked in terror.

He looked at me. "Have they been to the toilet?"

"No, neither of them." I looked at him, searching for some kind of answer, or calm, but he was looking at me the same way. I despise the idea of a child crying themself to sleep, but we were stuck! It was already dark and getting later by the second. "Let's just strap them in the car and go," I said.

Bruce agreed and, carrying the visibly and audibly distraught children to the car, we secured them in their seats. As we drove on the highway, we were intensely focused on the road as a means of trying to block out the unnerving screams of the children. After a torturesome fifteen or so minutes, they began to cry less. I wondered if they were dehydrated, but I put the thought out of my mind—I just needed the quiet to try to process what was going on. Within another twenty minutes, the cries became occasional whimpers, and then finally, they collapsed from exhaustion.

Bruce and I drove in complete silence for a while, intensely alert, listening to the sound of the road as we drove. "How are you?" Bruce quietly asked, just above a whisper.

"I'm okay," I answered in kind. "How are you?"

"Good," he replied in a steady voice. "What was that about?"

"I don't know," I breathed. I was fretting about what would happen when we reached the hotel. "Bruce?" I finally said.

"Yeah?"

"Are you okay if I pray?" We had prayed just before we pulled out of the driveway at home, but I was troubled enough that I needed to feel like there was something more than just us at that moment.

"Yes, please."

In a soft voice, I offered a prayer, asking God to protect us in a typical travel prayer. Though still whispering, I then began to pray in a firmer, more distressed voice. I prayed that the girls would sleep for the rest of the drive, and that they would not scream or cry when we reached the hotel, and that somehow, everything would be okay. Bruce and I both breathed, "Amen."

The phantom of desperation that haunted us since the rest stop almost lifted, and we drove on in relative peace for the next four hours. We were only thirty minutes short of our destination when Reesey stirred, partly awake and partly asleep. "Mummy, peas hold me," she asked, unable to pronounce the "l." "Mummy cuddles, peas, mummy cuddles…"

"We're almost there," Bruce said to me, meaning that he didn't want to stop.

"I know…" I said.

"Mummy, peas… Daddy, peas…"

"Bruce," I said gently but firmly. Bruce got the picture. He pulled over and I reached inside the car to unbuckle Reesey's seatbelt. In a second, she was on my lap, nuzzled in the fetal position against me. We sat there for a moment with the car running. It seemed sacred; I could tell that she felt safe there, and I did not want to disturb her. But we were so close to the hotel! Bruce and I discussed for a moment about driving with her on my lap, which was against the law.

"I don't feel good about that," said Bruce firmly. "She needs to be secure in her seatbelt."

"Reesey," I whispered, "I am going to hold you again like this soon, but you need to wear your seatbelt in the car." She resisted with a quiet "no," but that was all. No wailing, no tears, no screams. Bruce went around to my car door and gently opened it. He tenderly lifted Reesey from my lap in a smooth and soothing motion. He placed her in her seat, while I turned inside the car to smile broadly and lovingly at her. Though she whimpered slightly on the remaining drive, she seemed to be drifting more in than out of sleep.

We finally arrived, the clock ticking close to midnight. Bruce knew the building well. He pulled into the underground parking garage, close to the service elevators. I stayed in the car while

Bruce retrieved the key to our room and a luggage cart. I held Reesey and he held Cheyenne as we manoeuvred the cart loaded with our belongings into the elevator, and then on to the room. The girls were wide awake, but silent. We were relatively silent, hoping to keep the girls calm, the only sound being the squeak of the wheels as we made our way along the corridor.

"Oh, what a nice suite!" I said, opening the door and showing them the room we planned for them. "Isn't it nice?" The girls were silent, eyes open with wonder. "Look—in here, these two beds are for you." Cheyenne was on her feet now, exploring the space. "This is our room?" she asked. "Yes." I smiled. "I'll show you mine and Daddy's bed," I said, "come!"

"Oh, it has such a good tub!" I said, passing by the bathroom. "Do you think that tub can make bubbles?"

"I think so!" said Cheyenne, with some happiness. I gently placed Reesey on the floor by the queen bed. "What do you think?" I asked her.

"Same room," she said, still seeming to process everything, looking at the children's bedroom that was adjacent to the primary room that opened to a balcony. This room had a queen size bed, couch, TV and table.

"Yep. We are sharing the same room, toilet in the middle! But you're lucky! There's a door in your area, so you won't hear me and Daddy snore! But we can leave it open and you can come here anytime you want." Reesey's eyes remained wide, visually exploring and processing the space. Cheyenne was also absorbing the situation, but a smile had spread across her face.

"What bed do you want, Reesey?" she asked.

Reesey stood still. "You are on holidays?" she asked me.

"Yes, we are on holidays." I said as calmly and lovingly as I could, still full of worry. I began to pull the blankets down on the twin beds, just low enough for the girls to slip inside. "But Daddy will work the day after tomorrow in an office." I placed Cheyenne's butterfly pillow on one bed and Reesey's dragonfly pillow on the other. "I'll be here with you. They have a beach and a pool; we'll go and check them out, okay?" Reesey assessed the situation, looking around with surprise in her eyes. She still had her pink ballet slippers on over her footed pyjamas, party bag in hand. "Okay," she said simply. Within about fifteen minutes, after a goodnight kiss and prayer, she and Cheyenne were sound asleep.

Bruce and I were tired, but we set the room up so we could find what we needed in the morning. We would eat at the breakfast bar in the morning, but I laid out colouring books, pencils, and toys on the coffee table. Exhausted, I climbed into bed. "They must've traded the girls at rest stops," said Bruce with a yawn, meaning Michelle and Trent. "And called it a 'holiday.'"

We knew that Michelle had often offloaded the girls to different people. Now we suspected that they must have met at rest stops for drop off and pick up. But unlike the others, we were playing for keeps. And if the experience at the rest stop was anything to go by, the girls wanted to stay with us as well. "That must've been why they were crying so much," I agreed. "They thought we were giving them away, permanently or temporarily. They didn't know what it really means to go on a holiday as a family. They didn't know that we were staying with them."

"Tragic, isn't it?" said Bruce.

"Yes," I whispered, then fell into a deep sleep.

Normally, Bruce and I attend church even when we are away from home. But Yeppoon did not have a local Latter-day Saint church, so we planned to relax, recover and spend Sunday together. Mid-morning we made our way to the breakfast bar, enjoying a new, "family" kind of experience. It was a happy chaos, filled with discovery of every breakfast food imaginable. Enticing offers of baked beans and pancakes and eggs and cereal and fruit *all at the same time* was entertaining in itself! After we finished the meal, we decided to go for a walk on the beach, so Bruce played with the girls in the lobby while I went back to the room to quickly grab sunscreen.

There were two women in the room when I arrived, a housekeeping trainer and her protégé. I giggled at how different this room looked compared to when Bruce and I had stayed here previously. Strewn across the floor were coloured pencils, toys, and non-spill plastic children's drinking cups, and in the bathroom proudly stood a large bottle of strawberry-scented, no-tears, hypo-allergenic bubble bath. "We have children," I said to the housekeeping staff with a brilliant smile. The women barely hazarded a single nod to me and went about cleaning the room, oblivious to the miracle.

But I knew. It was a miracle that the girls were in our care. It was a miracle that we'd had a birthday party for Cheyenne. It was a miracle that Reesey had settled and learned that "holidays" could be a very good thing. It was a miracle that Bruce's work allowed us to share a hotel room in a lovely resort. We were a living blessing, and that bright Sunday morning, I dismissed my impatient adoption timeline and basked in the moment.

The resort looked out onto a beach that could be accessed through a short and romantic earthy path past a small, non-denominational wedding chapel. With children, the walk was a trail of adventure and discovery. "Look! A church!" said the girls, seeing the building. "Look! I see the ocean!" "Look! It's a bug!" "Look! I see clouds!" "Look! My feet have sand!" Sticks, leaves, pebbles and even variations in the colour of the sand were detected, handled, examined, and discussed. The short walk was taking a satisfactorily long time; it wasn't enough to wind me or make me want to return to the hotel, but rather it made me appreciate the beach in a new way. It had been a very long time since I had noticed the variation in grasses as we neared the water, and how some grains of sand sparkled, where others remained cloudy and earthy. I revelled in it.

We finally climbed down a small sandy hill where we stashed our shoes and saw the lips of the sea bringing soft, wet kisses into the shore. The girls were cautious, Reesey holding my right hand, and Cheyenne holding my left. They would rotate between holding one of my hands and walking independently, depending on how confident they felt or how distracted they became with items they were still gathering or examining along the walk. They would sometimes hold Bruce's hand, but not as often as they held mine. They were still getting to know him.

In some ways, I was getting to know him as well. Though we had been married for more than ten years, we were becoming different people since the girls came into our lives. We discussed politics and the news less often than we discussed what time Playschool was on television. Professional aspirations, musings and plans fell by the wayside altogether. We also shared fresh memories from our childhoods that were previously unknown to each other and had only been triggered by having children in our home. These were all simple, delightful things—like my memory of swinging in the backyard of my childhood, in my underwear, chomping on celery as though it was the most delicious snack in the world. And Bruce's memory of sneaking the carob dog chews from his mother's cupboard thinking they were chocolates. Children opened a new format for learning about each other.

"Would you like to put your toes in the water?" I asked the girls when the sand was wet and close to the gentle surf.

"Is it safe?" asked Cheyenne.

"No," said Reesey. I smiled and tried to stifle a chortle; she often said "no" as an automatic response to new things that she very much wanted to try, but only on her terms.

"It's okay," said Bruce. "We can just walk in the wet sand for a minute." We were accustomed to their being hesitant; besides, it was only a lukewarm, Australian winter day. We were wearing shorts and t-shirts but not swimwear. Only northern hemisphere tourists would think of this as swimmable, I mused to myself. Surely the girls wouldn't—

Splash! Reesey plopped her foot squarely in the water. It was very shallow, probably only a centimetre deep. Then she let out the silliest, happiest laugh I ever heard from her. "Cooooooold!" she said with a snigger and giant grin. Before I knew it, Cheyenne was in the water, too. Within seconds, both girls slid their wet pants off to just undies and shirt tops, splashing and playing. They ventured out little by little, with Bruce and I both keeping a sharp eye on them. I was happy to not get wet so was content to not chase or splash in the centimetres-deep area. Bruce waded in more closely (almost to his ankles) and began to teach them a game. In this game, they would chase the small waves as they recede back to sea but not go too far out. Then when the sprays began to roll back onto the shore, the girls would scream and run towards the dry sand.

They were thrilled, filled with squeaks and howls of delight in the game that nature seemed to create just for them. Bruce was running back and forth with them, fully engaged in the game. They would all run toward the water, then pause, yelp, and run back. The girls did this again and again, gaining confidence but never running out far enough to be submerged past their feet—their own running and splashing was enough to soak them. Bruce continued to run with them back and forth, until he allowed himself to indulge in his developing hobby of photography and began snapping photos of the girls.

I loved watching them all, but stayed dry, relaxing and enjoying the utterly charming scene that was laid before me: the water was calm and clear, and the sun was shining with only a dusting of clouds. But mostly, the three people I loved most in the world were running, laughing and having the time of their lives. As I watched the girls and the sea, I began to imagine this as a cleansing ritual: the waves reaching toward me, carrying the girls in rapid, tiny steps in front of the fizzing lips of the sea. The water would not subdue the girls, but it could grab the bad feelings, thoughts and memories, plus all of the stress weighing me down, and retreat back out to sea, washing all negativity away. The next crest brought new, bright foam and giggling children; it distilled forgiveness, peace, and love, all of which washed away gloominess and doubt. I felt like this was God's blessing for me on that Sunday morning. In place of the sacrament that I normally would take as a matter of course at church, I was reminded of Christ's atonement in the washings of the beach, salted by the laughter of the children I dreamt and prayed would be mine.

I knew that the girls would soon be hungry, so we decided to head back to the resort. The girls paused and sat for a moment in the sand to put their shoes on but decided against it. The sand was soft, and shoes weren't needed for the short walk back. The sun was enough to warm them, and they chatted as they walked. Bruce and I hung back slightly to giggle at the two most darling girls we had ever seen, walking ahead with perfectly cute, rounded, silhouettes of sand on their rear ends. Bruce took my hand, and we paused for a moment. With tears in his eyes, he said, "That was the most fun I've ever had with them." I squeezed his hand and smiled, not knowing what to say but loving him immensely. He silently blinked his eyes, then we walked on still holding hands, revelling in the moment.

Monday came, and we inspected the resort day care that was only open Tuesday and Thursday mornings because it was off-season. Bruce went to work, while I spent the day at the pool with the girls or in our room watching television, colouring and snacking on fruit. Even though Sunday had eased my overall feelings of stress, I was still dreading the call we were required to make to Michelle for Cheyenne's birthday. Past calls included a tongue-lashing from Michelle about everything I was doing wrong, plus pestering me for money, and when I said I had no money to send her, she sometimes threatened to report me for kidnapping before ending with her reminder that she was a real mother and I was a fraud. In setting up a time for the call, she asserted how much the day was very difficult for her because she was heartbroken to not have Cheyenne with her, and I was selfish to not appreciate her great generosity in not holding me to "our" somewhat verbal contract to drop off the girls for their birthdays. I anticipated being called names and threatened and the girls recoiling into night terrors.

To prepare, I booked the girls into the daycare, and I indulged in a long shower. I spent the rest of the morning praying, meditating and reading scriptures. At lunchtime, the girls and I returned to our room to enjoy a spread of sliced fruit and crustless Vegemite sandwiches. As the girls ate, I reminded them that we needed to call "Old Mummy" because she wanted to wish Cheyenne a happy birthday. When we finished, we moved to the room balcony, partly for improved cell phone reception but mostly to be able to see the beach and invoke the peace I had felt there two days before. I felt physically sick, so I didn't dare take a deep breath lest I vomit. The anxiety of interacting with Michelle was real, but I had to table it. My heartbeat increased as I pressed to dial, causing me to feel slight stings of pain.

"Hello," she said immediately.

"Hi," I ventured. "How are you?"

"Is Cheyenne there?" She interrupted. Much to my surprise, Michelle did not sound nearly as angry as she normally did. I sensed that she had her phone on speaker, possibly in a car.

"Yes," I answered.

"Okay, put her on." The odd cheerfulness from Michelle caused me to breathe more normally, and I handed the phone to Cheyenne.

"Hello," she spoke in a tiny, shy voice. After a brief pause came a chorus of voices from Michelle and her four children, "Happy birthday, Cheyenne!"

"Thank you," smiled Cheyenne, sounding relieved.

"How is your birthday?" asked Michelle, sounding somewhat distracted.

"It's good," said Cheyenne.

"What did you get?"

"A dress and shoes… and a necklace," she said, "and a tent… um…"

"Wow…" said Michelle, absently.

"I made the dress," I broke in as some sort of weird attempt to make it sound like I was thrifty and talented, "and Kmart shoes." I was trying to avoid a mini-lecture from Michelle on how my spending money on the girls was selfish when she and her family were in such constant need of money and blah, blah, blah.

"Alright, well, we miss you. Have a great day! We better go."

"Okay," I said, with surprise turning into shock. "Have fun!"

"Bye, Cheyenne!"

"Bye," said Cheyenne. I was astonished when I heard the phone click.

"Thank you, God," I breathed out loud, looking at the sky. And then, realizing I suddenly had toddlers to entertain, "who wants to go to the pool?"

SHERRIE GAVIN

18

HOPE IS A COMPLICATED THING

Things were almost peaceful over the following two months. David obtained copies of the girls' birth certificates, so we finally knew what their legal names were, and Michelle's spews of hatred towards me were less frequent. When she did choose to belittle me, there were enough days between her outbursts that I was better able to process things less personally.

With Ginny's support, we began the process of removing Michelle and Trent as guardians. This was not a typical part of the adoption process; we had been led to believe that they were in Australia on "orphan visas" as a result of Ginny being incarcerated. Since Ginny was no longer in jail, the visas would have been nullified. We did not know if this was a formal nullification because so far as we understood, the U.S. had no reason to tell the Australian Immigration Department that Ginny was on parole.

The immigration laws around this situation were complicated owing to the strict adoption laws. A few handfuls of non-Australian children could enter Australia on very rare adoption visas. These adoption visas had to be from a tiny list of countries that had adoption agreements with Australia. The United States is not on that list, so adoptions through the U.S. could be completed only if the Australian adoption family moved overseas and could prove that they moved to the foreign country "for reasons other than adoption." The only other circumvention was to process the adoption through Australia and The Hague Convention, which while worthy, is a lengthy and expensive process overseen by the United Nations.

Aware of all this, we watched as another family in our ward, an American family here on the husband's work visa, adopted a daughter in China. I questioned the mother before she left to collect the girl, but she and her husband were sure that everything would be fine. But as she, her newly adopted daughter, and her two biological toddlers went to check in for the flight back to Australia, they were denied boarding for not having the proper visa for their Chinese baby to enter Australia. They had adopted through an American adoption agency, which made sense because the entire family was American. But Australia would not recognise the adoption, because the family had not gone to China for reasons other than adopting. In a panic, the young American mother remained in China with their three children under the age of three while her husband returned to Australia to work with his company to obtain a visa for the newly adopted baby. This did not work out. The mother ended up traveling to the U.S. alone with the three children while the father packed up the family house alone and moved home to the U.S. to be with his family. For right or wrong, Australia's adoption laws were severe, and we knew that we needed to do everything with exactness.

I was sure that Michelle and Trent knew that Trent's sister, Ginny, was out of jail, but I could only presume that they had not informed Australian Immigration, for whatever reason. Michelle maintained that "Ginny disappeared," "abandoned her children," and "refuses to communicate." Ginny and Trent both contradicted these claims, making the guardianship situation complicated. There were a handful of statements on the Australian immigration website that led us to believe that it was in our best interests to legally challenge Michelle's claims to guardianship, but the rest was all hope. So we hoped.

SHERRIE GAVIN

19

COMMUNICATION

Ginny and I maintained regular contact through e-mail, Facebook messages, and phone calls, so when it was Ginny's birthday, I mailed a small package of hand-painted cards and sparkly costume jewellery that the girls made and chose. I was becoming familiar with happiness in a new way, so I also decided to arrange a video call with Ginny. She wanted to see the girls and talk with them. She wanted to see if they were happy.

This was more complicated for Ginny than it was for us; she had limited funds, so she needed somewhere that had access to a computer and internet. She was able to arrange this at her grandmother's home. With my computer fully charged, we connected. The girls did not seem to remember their birth mother by sight, but there was an emotional connection. They loved seeing her, seemed fascinated to know that she was their "tummy mummy," and kept telling me during and after the call how pretty they thought she was.

They were right–Ginny is beautiful! They spent the majority of the time showing off for her by performing somersaults, showing her how well they could "drive" the Little Tikes car, showing her how many times they could spin in a circle, how well they could dance and paint and so on.

"They're happy," she said to her grandmother, matter-of-factly, as the call was ending.

"Yes," Ginny's grandmother responded, nodding heartily. I was so grateful that they could see how happy and healthy the girls were! Cheyenne's hair had lightened with the play outside, and the dark circles that cradled her eyes when she first came had finally released their grip. Reesey's hair was growing, and the new, miniscule length revealed a delightful natural wave that framed her face. Both truly looked cherubic. They were gaining healthy weight and happy confidence.

"I'm ready," Ginny said to me at the end of the video call. "God gave you to the girls. Let me know what you need with the adoption."

I was not expecting this. My heart skipped a beat, and I wanted to cry out with joy and burst into tears! "Okay," I said, trying to sound natural while being intensely focused. "There are some issues with immigration, but we have an attorney; we'll have him contact you if that is okay?"

"That's fine," Ginny hummed with her southern brogue. "I love y'all."

"We love you, too," was all I could say, but the words could never be enough to express my feelings at that moment.

Over the next few weeks, I smiled more than I had in months, but I still longed for better sleep. The girls were trying to learn to self-soothe, but they still woke me to take them to the toilet, ask for another bottle or to rock them. Cheyenne still had nightmares more often than Reesey, but I was becoming more familiar with managing them, which was a blessing for all of us.

Bruce was concerned about visa issues so was just as anxious as I was. I created a new e-mail address, removing my name, and began e-mailing and speaking with Australian immigration lawyers asking for advice. But they told me what I already knew: there were no existing laws for our unique situation. Somewhat exasperated, I finally just asked one lawyer for good, old-fashioned advice. "To be honest," she said with impassioned concern, "I would make sure that the girls are safe. Which means I would adopt them. Their guardians are not providing for them, which puts the children in a position to be exploited. I'd adopt them because then you will be in a legal position to protect them and get them the visa."

She echoed what I felt in my bones, which was that the priority was to make sure that the girls were safe. Not only that, I wanted to feel safe, too. I was tired of fearing Michelle and her threats of accusing me of kidnapping. I was worried that I could not legally enrol Cheyenne in school, or even get medical care for her. The insecurity exhausted me. I had never been in a situation like this before, but in stressful times past, I would turn to the scriptures and prayer to find peace. Prior to having the girls, I read scriptures in the mornings, but that time was now filled with cereal, spilt milk, hair brushing, and washing sheets from soaked princess pants. My scriptures were gathering dust. And though I would pray with the girls, I found myself falling asleep during or before my own prayers. When I tried to read scriptures, the words would blur, and I found myself unable to focus, while meditation immediately morphed into a nap. As a lifelong diabetic, testing and injections were typically second nature to me, even more than praying. But sometimes when I tested my blood sugar at bedtime, I would realise it was the first time I had tested or taken insulin for the entire day.

Being tired, increasingly sick, and lacking the peace that prayerful reflection traditionally brought me, I was becoming impatient with Bruce, and I began to press him about the adoption. "David's started the work," he said. "But we still need to contact Kyle," he added, reminding me of the biological father, who was still incarcerated, failing to earn parole. "And then we need to sort out immigration." He listed it all as if he was working down a rotating checklist that never ended. At the end of each recitation, he walked away from me, avoiding discussion.

COMMUNICATION

I tried to be at peace with the state of being patient, but I was tired. So tired. The stress of everything cloaked restful sleep in a space I could not access. I coped by placing Post-Its throughout the house, car and in my purse to remind me to test my blood sugar and take insulin, all the while chanting, "I am blessed, I am blessed," in an attempt to find the silver lining in my holding pattern.

SHERRIE GAVIN

20

LEGAL WOES

"Dear Sherrie," read the unexpected e-mail from Ginny's mother, "I am so sorry to tell you this, but Ginny is back in jail. She broke parole, and so she'll be back there till she finishes her sentence. She was really happy to be in touch with you and the girls." Though I did not know Ginny well, I loved her. I had not seen this coming, and the news hit me hard. I felt like something had been physically taken from within my soul.

Ginny's mother said she was "not sure" when Ginny would be released and did not tell me what the parole violation was. I previously made the decision to not make Ginny's conviction a part of my relationship with her, so beyond my initial shock, I did not press for information. I asked if there was a way for me to be supportive. I naively began to think I could send her a *Book of Mormon*. "That's contraband," Ginny's mother wrote. "She is allowed to have one personal item, and she asked for a photo of y'all." It awed me to think that she wanted a photo of us with the girls as her single personal item. I could not imagine anything more beautiful in such circumstances as that humble request.

Though this was sweet beyond words, almost immediately I began to feel strange about it. Other than tours I had taken at Alcatraz, the Sydney Barracks, and a handful of other historical "jails," I had never been inside a functioning prison. The idea of a photo of me in a prison had never crossed my mind. So after an initial feeling of honour, a sense of unease developed, which I disliked. As I pondered this, I gazed at the photo Bruce had taken of Cheyenne at the beach where she was running so joyously that both of her feet were in the air. That photo always made me smile. It reminded me of the sacred experience we had as a family at the beach and how I felt at that beach that day—like I had not a care in the world, free from the stress of everything else around me.

I was suddenly ashamed. Why did it matter where she was and what photo she had of me? I didn't know why she was in prison, but the one thing she was allowed, and *the one thing she wanted,* was a photo of us. If she were ill, I would have brought her food or medicine, prayed for her and cleaned her home. If she had car problems, I would give her a ride, and if she were cold, I would give her a sweater, a jacket and a blanket. Why was this different?

I decided that it was not different. She was helping me to adopt her daughters; she deserved better from me. I chose a photo of all four of us and posted it to Ginny's mother to give to her, reminding myself to stop being so judgemental.

International phone calls were not allowed at the prison, so we could communicate with Ginny only through the post or an intermediary, which just made everything feel even more complicated. I somehow felt a deeper sense of unknowing in regards to adoption and immigration. Though I was still sure that I had heard God telling me that this was put into place for me, I felt like I had become unworthy of the blessing. I ticked a list of sins off in my head regularly: I neglected praying, scripture study, and temple attendance, had judged Ginny, had very few kind thoughts, if any, about Michelle, and Bruce and I had turned down the calling extended to us in the ward. This list, combined with everyday failings, multiplied in my mind, and I felt unworthy and disobedient. Plus, I was sure that we needed to pursue the adoption as quickly as possible and was frustrated with Bruce not processing the adoption as quickly as I wanted. I was sure that I did not deserve the girls, nor all the happiness that came from mothering them. Rather than fall into too much despair, I focused intensely on the girls and my time with them.

Parenting suited me and my need for creativity. Storytelling became my vehicle for applied arts; I adapted children's fairy tales to incorporate the girls' names. I added linguistic and social hints that I hoped the girls would learn, such as saying *please* and *thank you*. I included the benefits of sharing and honesty, that it is okay to feel hurt and scared, that it is not okay to act in anger and so on. The girls were progressing in these areas, including swimming. I was growing to love swimming days because the girls became so worn out that my own sleep was less interrupted. While they were in classes, I was able to go and sit and quietly chat with friends or just relax watching them for thirty minutes. I found parenting to be most certainly a full time job.

On one October spring morning while the girls were swimming, Michelle texted me, asking me to pay for medical appointments for the girls' visas. Having been through the immigration process, I was aware of the requisite medical evaluations, but I was suspicious when Michelle claimed that the girls needed "specialist doctors" and that only she would be able to set up the appointments, which she also claimed had to be pre-paid. Further, she did not mention where the appointments were or anything about actually taking the girls to the appointments. I wasn't surprised by the request for money. Bruce and I had already discussed and decided that we would never give Michelle any money but would pay for the girls' visas and whatever else was needed directly.

Responding to Michelle, I asked for the name of the medical facility so we could pay directly. She countered that she also needed to pay immigration costs and unless the money came from her, it would "look funny." I shook my head at this request. I was already convinced that any money given to her would be misused, and if something "looked funny," it suggested to me that this was not the right path, and Bruce and I wanted nothing to do with breaking laws.

Researching immigration and adoption laws had made me familiar enough with the fees that I also knew that the amount Michelle was asking for was more than twice what was required. As soon as she started texting visa "rules" that she claimed had to be followed yet were contradictory and seemed false, I texted, "Can't you push back on immigration? Ask them for a link on the immigration website to verify what they are telling you? Nothing they say is making sense." What I meant was that nothing she was saying made sense, but not being an immigration attorney, I did not know. At that moment, I was more focused on gathering information about the girls' visas, guardianship or anything that could help us. She responded with broken and inconsistent statements, making me wonder if she was distracted while she was demanding this latest amount of cash. "I'm sorry, I just don't understand," I finally texted her. "Can you show me which kind of visa you're applying for? That just sounds outrageously expensive. I want to double check the figures."

"I'll forward the e-mail to you," she replied.

"Thanks," I responded, though given our past interactions, I did not expect that she would forward anything. I was playing along, placating as best as I could in an unfeeling, uninvested way. At least this time she was asking for money for the girls rather than requiring that I bail her out of her latest financial woe or confess my ineptitude and stupidity, lest she call the police on me. "I'll check e-mails later," I continued. "We're at swimming lessons now. Have a great day."

Shortly thereafter, and much to my surprise, there was a forwarded message from Michelle in my inbox. It appeared that she had sent it directly to me, wholly unedited, from the Department of Immigration. It contained the latest correspondence from an immigration agent and Michelle's responding communication. More importantly, it had the date of the guardianship issuance and the date and type of visa that the girls were on!

I felt like I won the lottery! As I sat reading in disbelief and gratitude about the children's current ineligibility "to stay permanently in Australia," I tried to process what was really going on. It appeared that Michelle was no more honest with the immigration department than I believed she was with me. The e-mail included information about the children staying in Australia on bridging visas, but that this did not guarantee a permanent visa for the girls. And given that both the biological mother or the biological father were serving decades-long prison sentences in the U.S., the girls were ineligible for the Australian visa that Michelle and Trent had applied for. It was signed by an immigration representative named Thomas.

Suddenly, some of the things that Michelle said made more sense. Bridging visas are sort of "in-between" visas used as a status between visas wherein the immigrant retains the rights and allowances of their previous visa (sometimes with exceptions) until they are able to obtain a new visa, which may offer different rights and allowances. For the most part, however, bridging visas meant that the girls would not be eligible for any permanent resident or citizen-based privileges. This meant that public school would be an out of pocket expense. When our Korean exchange student stayed with us, I learned that children who are not citizens or permanent residents of Australia needed to fund their own school costs which, at that time, ranged around $30,000 per annum, per child (private schools were a similar cost, or more). Cheyenne was already of the age where she could have been attending pre-school, but because we were not her legal guardians, we could not enrol her. Nor could we afford the kinds of fees associated with alien residency.

It now appeared that Michelle planned to adopt the girls herself, and after the girls obtained permanent visas in Australia, she would try to arrange for us to have some sort of shared custody. Besides being a risky workaround, the far-fetched nature of Michelle's plan included us paying her in advance for everything for the girls, including all visa and school fees, medical appointments, everyday care and travel to take them to Michelle whenever she demanded. The whole thing felt very wrong. Sickened by the thought of my possible participation in anything that was illegal, I was determined to remain honest and within the confines of the law.

Even if it meant I would never be a mother.

21

ALL OF THE HYPOTHETICALS

Bruce and I pondered and discussed what we could do with the contact information and case number that Michelle had forwarded. Before this, all of the state government children's services refused to help us. Those groups were happy to brush us off, citing that this was not their problem. But now we had someone to contact at the federal government level. It felt exciting! I was not sure if there was anything that Thomas could do because he was officially forbidden from offering legal or visa advice; his job was to follow up and inform families where their visa applications were lacking or when the visa was rejected or granted. And our situation was complicated as we were still in no way legally connected to the girls, so we could not obtain copies of their passports, visa records or anything that would help us, or the girls, to be safe.

One step forward, two steps back, as the saying goes.

"What do you think we should do?" I asked Bruce when he was home on the weekend and after the girls had gone to bed. "We could forward the e-mail from an anonymous e-mail account and ask what the best way would be for us to adopt the girls."

"Yeah," Bruce replied thoughtfully. "You need to send him the e-mail as evidence that we are telling the truth about which immigration case this is. Then see if you can call him. The e-mail thread could get too long and be too much."

"So… anonymous or do we just tell him who we are?" I was anxious to be honest and shout my name from the rooftop as the future mother of Cheyenne and Reesey! But I knew this was far too much of a gamble to do this with any kind of confidence and probably too ambitious for Bruce's comfort. "Anonymous is probably best," Bruce replied with measured speech. "But if you don't speak in hypotheticals, find out what you can about the girls. We need a copy of the guardianship for the adoption, though I don't know if Thomas will send it to us; maybe he'll send it to David."

Creating an anonymous e-mail address was easy. I knew that cyber-police could find my location based on my computer internet identification, but I wasn't too worried. We were not trying to break a law; we were in a complicated situation and trying to do the right thing. We did not want to risk losing the girls or having them deported. I already had terrifying visions of them being ripped from my bosom by armed men in black jumpsuits who placed them, tiny and alone, on cargo planes delivering them to dank and dark immigrant holding facilities in offshore Australia. I had no basis for this nightmare, but stress, ongoing reduced sleep and my own creative anxiety could get the better of me from time to time, and my primary motivation was to protect the girls, even if that meant paying for airfare and personally delivering them to Ginny.

I called myself "Anon Mother" in the e-mail address I created. Any information that was requested when setting up a new e-mail account I simply left blank or, if required, I just made it up. Writing the e-mail was fairly easy. I knew the girls' legal names and birth dates, thanks to David's work on securing birth certificates, and now I had an immigration case file number. I pasted Michelle's forwarded e-mail in my message and typed:

> *For my own safety, I have not disclosed my name in this e-mail. I have some confidential information on the girls in this situation. I have called Immigration but was unable to get information on what would happen to the children involved. Is there someone I can ring directly in regard to this, other than the federal police?*

Within moments I had a response:

I am the case officer, and the most cost effective way to contact me is to call *6200 4000 and ask to be put through to me in the Canberra Office. I am usually at my desk, but if you can give me an idea of the general time you will be calling, I can let you know if I will be available.

We agreed on a time for me to call the following day, and suddenly, things felt like they were moving very fast. The visa process is often a detached system of checking boxes and supplying information before proceeding to the next step. But it is a soulful experience because it is about people hoping to begin a better life. It was penetratingly personal for me because I wanted to be a mother, so I was taking a step in that direction, even if it was an immigration visa rather than an adoption decree. Both of these were needed, so any action in either direction felt positive.

I was not sure what to say or what would happen. It felt a little like the first time I spoke with Ginny, but not quite as much pressure. Unlike the phone call with Ginny when I was so desperate for her to like me, my call to Thomas was to understand our options, or hopefully, even procure a plan in which we could progress and even take over the immigration processing for the girls. I phoned and was promptly placed on hold. It was a toll-free number to the general immigration department, and I feared that holding for too long would create such intense anxiety in me that I would hang up.

The hold music was terrible, so I began to pace. Then I stood and began to doodle. Then I started alternating between doodling and pacing. I'd walk from one end of the kitchen countertop and draw a flower, then circle around three times, before returning and drawing another flower. It wasn't much, but it kept me from panicking. After I drew at least five flowers, the phone picked up and I asked to speak with Thomas. Seconds later, Thomas was on the line.

"Hello, this is Thomas, Child and Family Migrant Services." His voice was kind and soft, like a pastor. It made me feel calmer, though my heart was fluttering.

"Hi," I said clearly and distinctly as though my greeting was a statement in itself. "I sent you the e-mail about Cheyenne and Reesey."

"Yes!" Thomas said, sounding keenly interested. "That was quite an e-mail. What information do you have for me?"

"Well, I am concerned about reporting too much and having them deported," I said, testing the waters. "They shouldn't be punished because adults made bad immigration choices and let their visas lapse."

"Australia is not in the business of deporting minors," Thomas said with frankness in his voice. "The primary concern is to protect them from being trafficked. Can you tell me your name?"

"Oh! We also want nothing to do with trafficking. But I want to remain anonymous for now."

"Fair enough."

"Can I speak anonymously and hypothetically?"

"You can speak any way you like," replied Thomas, in a friendly manner. "What can you tell me about the girls?"

"Well, they are not living with Michelle or Trent." I hesitated. "Hypothetically."

"Who are they living with?"

"Me." I paused, then added, "Hypothetically."

"Ah," responded Thomas. "Of course. Are you related?"

"No… but we want to adopt them." I went on to explain that we had made contact with the birth mother in the U.S., and though she had been freed from prison for a time, she had recently been re-incarcerated. I shared that the birth mother did not want Michelle and Trent to adopt the girls, but that neither the birth mother nor we had copies of the guardianship decree, all of which contradicted what Michelle had claimed in her correspondence with Thomas.

"Well, you have given me a lot of information," said Thomas, sounding as if he needed the conversation to wrap up. "Is there documentation you could forward to me of the mother's incarceration? I'll have to look into it, but that could be beneficial."

"Yes…" but then I hesitated. "But let me speak with my husband first." The conversation ended, and I was excited. Even the smallest thing seemed monumental, and having someone official to speak with about the girls felt liberating!

I immediately called Bruce and relayed what had happened. "Let's send him the link to Ginny's inmate record," he said, referring to the link that Ginny's mother had forwarded to me when Ginny first broke parole. It showed Ginny's most recent mugshot and her inmate information as a current resident inmate. Without any other words typed in the message, I sent Thomas the link. Within minutes, I had a response.

> *Can we talk to discuss how the children's mother being in prison may change my e-mail dated 28/09/2012 and the other issues I have to decide for the children's visa applications? Please e-mail me with an indication as to when you might call.*

Setting a time, I called Thomas again on the following day. This time, we had a more lengthy conversation about the entire situation.

We discussed how we hired our attorney, David. How we didn't have copies of the guardianship or the girls' passports. How Ginny was verbally supportive of our adopting the girls. How the laws in Australia did not allow for private adoption. How we were not related to the girls.

How we were looking into leaving the country in order to process the girls' adoption, but could not travel out of the country with the girls as we did not have their passports or legal permission to do so. How we were trying to do the right thing, and how cluttered and confusing that path was.

"You finally have the family you want," said Thomas with a tinge of compassion that could be rare when dealing with government employees. "And you are trying your best to make it all legal."

I breathed a sigh of relief. "Yes," I said. "We're trying everything."

"Okay. I'll get back to you," came his short reply. Within a few hours, there was another message from him, detailing the possibility of a foster placement for the girls with us wherein the twelve month overseas mandatory adoption processing might be avoided. The message should have inspired me, but it didn't. At that time, foster children might have to be as old as sixteen years before the state allowed them to be adopted, with ongoing state required visitation with the biological family. This meant up to a fourteen year adoption process, exposing us to Michelle, the government, and everyone else who wanted a piece of us. Plus, because we did not live in the same state as Michelle, we faced the possibility of having to move. It was a mountain that I did not have the stamina to climb, especially while raising the actual toddlers. I wanted more security and privacy than having to process paperwork in two countries and possibly three states. I also wanted the ability to travel with the girls overseas if our budget allowed. Mostly, I wanted to go to a temple and be "sealed" as a family, which was a blessing ordinance only available to those who had legally adopted children. All I could think of after reading that message was suffering through more than a decade of ongoing government paperwork, checks, and monitoring, as well as needing to maintain a state-required relationship with Michelle. I felt overwhelmed. So overwhelmed that I did not recognise that the black dog of anxiety and depression had not disappeared. Rather, this experience, and the strain on my marriage, had woken it from its nap.

SHERRIE GAVIN

22

BLOOMS IN EMPTY POTS

When he was home on weekends, I worked hard to have Bruce develop a relationship with the girls, which often meant accepting that he ignored my parenting advice in favour of what he had Googled, what fellow travelling fathers recommended and, sometimes, even asking me what Zoia recommended. It felt like he thought everyone was smarter than I was about everything from the best kid-friendly sunscreen to his idea of bedtime routines.

If I pushed for him to read stories for the bedtime routine, rather than putting them in the car and driving aimlessly until they fell asleep, he reminded me of the other meaning for the acronym, FIFO. Instead of "Fly In Fly Out" in relation to mostly men who had families living in areas away from work sites, the slang meaning was "Fit In Or F*ck Off," which is how some men felt when they returned home to a well-oiled family routine that had been lashed into place by the primary caregiver.

In dire situations, if the FIFO parent seemed to undo the family routine, they were threatened with divorce.

Bruce was telling me that he wanted an active voice in parenting, which is exactly what I wanted as well. So even when he dismissed my advice and ignored or tried to rewrite the routine that I found made life calmer, I stepped back and internally beat down my hurt and resentment. Bruce's words were nowhere near as hateful as Michelle's, so I accepted his criticism and slights, remaining focused on the girls.

Our marriage was suffering, but I could not tell if Bruce was aware or cared. The last time I mentioned one of the more painful diatribes to him, months earlier, he responded to me with, "So what? I don't care. *Neither should you.*" But I did care. And it pained me that no one, especially Bruce, ever told me I was doing even the smallest fraction of a good job with anything. By this time, even the tiniest negative comment pierced me like a sharp dart. I remained an unmoving target, while these darts struck and stuck painfully in my heart and mind.

With my mental health rapidly deteriorating, my mind was filled with self-harming thoughts that fed the black dog, where it sat growling in a corner, gaining venomous nourishment. "The black dog" is a phrase coined by Winston Churchill, who used it in a letter in 1911, describing his depression and suicidal ideation.[1] I willed myself into functioning by believing that, without me, the girls would end up back with Michelle, or worse.

One Sunday when Bruce had already left for that week's work, our bishop asked me to come to his office. He wanted to see how I was coping. I confessed that I wasn't as well as I would have liked, but I camouflaged my words with jokes and a smile. I was becoming very astute at redirecting negativity and putting on a brave face. "Why don't you want to just report Michelle to the police?" he asked gently. The truth was, I wanted to. But I felt trapped by my husband's belief that Michelle would eventually "help" us, even if I saw this reasoning as delusional.

After too long a pause, I answered the bishop. "They are a family. Michelle is the mother—they have been sealed in the temple… I just don't want to harm her children. Her children would be hurt if she is arrested. She might even go to jail—I don't know! Aren't we supposed to protect families?" There it was. My religious upbringing had fed an underlying dogma: I believed in protecting families at all costs. My bishop looked downward, and I was anxious to leave, lest I share that I was having occasional suicidal thoughts.

After a pause, he spoke. "Okay," he sighed. His voice was soothing. He then spoke of a family in a difficult visa situation, where the father was afraid to go to the immigration department, lest he be deported, and how expensive the visa process is.

I guessed he was searching to find a way to help us, as he added, "The church could help with some of the finances for these things… probably up to $800." The offer was generous. Very generous! But we were looking at fees that were significantly larger than that, and we still had some savings.

"Thank you," I said. "I think we're okay with the money."

"Does Michelle's bishop know what is going on?" the bishop suddenly asked.

"I don't know," I confessed. "I think so. The children did go to church with them—or at least, I think they did. There is a photo of them in front of an LDS church, and they seemed to know what church was like when we first came here."

"I'd be surprised if he did know. Or he at least might have a different…" he paused thoughtfully "… story. Would you mind if I contacted Michelle and Trent's bishop?"

This idea had not occurred to me! I did not know what their bishop could do, but the thought of someone else helping in any way was soothing. "No. Not at all." The words rushed out, "Please contact him!" I retrieved Michelle and Trent's address, and my bishop quickly found the contact information for their bishop. "It's Bishop To'a," he said as he clicked the number on his phone, pressing it to dial. There was no answer, and I was instantly disappointed.

BLOOMS IN EMPTY POTS

"Why don't you go back to Sunday School, and I'll keep trying to get in touch with him," offered the bishop. I agreed and left. It was almost time for Relief Society, so I sat in the hallway outside of the class area with a few other people. They welcomed me in light conversation for the handful of minutes remaining until we all moved at the change of classes. I spent the Relief Society hour tuning out everything around me. Phone tucked deep inside my purse, I sat in the back of the room, disengaged but smiling. I was meditating in blissful nothingness. Only the occasional chuckle from the class or sound of a baby distracted me momentarily, but otherwise, the calm of the room and the gentleness of the teacher's voice enveloped me in a state of rest. The closing song was in its last verse when the primary-age children began filtering in, looking for their mothers.

Cheyenne and Reesey were not among them, which didn't surprise me. They liked to play in the atrium, an open air space surrounded by the walls of a courtyard in the center of the chapel. When we first came to this ward, we were told that the building design won an award when it was newly constructed, and I could see beauty in the design. Nothing grew in the caked, dry soil anymore, but the bones of the grand planters were still strong, and low enough to be reincarnated as play equipment for youngsters. I loved the space as much as the children did and was a little flustered as to why no one had taken it upon themselves to add plant life to the space. I think I felt like those planters. Like I was supposed to be able to spring life from my body. But even sturdy bones and a willing heart were not enough for me to nest and birth. So the children of friends came to me and climbed in and around me, a repurposed vessel. But now… now I had these girls, and I wanted to give them life! I wanted to heal their scars and see them grow! I wanted to give myself to them so life could be Eden, full of peace, fruitful growth, and love.

As I made my way toward the atrium, the bishop caught me. "Just in here for a moment," he motioned towards his office, and I stepped in. "Bishop To'a noticed the girls when they first came, but he had no idea they were staying with Michelle and Trent permanently," he said without sitting. "He said they didn't always bring them with them to church…" *Probably because they had been farmed out as often as possible*, I snarkily thought to myself. "He did not know they were looking to place them somewhere else, anything about them giving them away or anything! He is going to speak with Michelle and Trent to see what he can do to help the girls. I'll keep you posted."

I had tears in my eyes. "Thank you," I whispered. Within minutes, I was happily running around the stone planter boxes, playing, chasing and eventually calling to the girls to come home with me.

CHAPTER NOTES

1. Attenborough, Wilfred. "Churchill's Black Dog at the Home Office, 1910–1911: The Evidential Reliability of Psychiatric Inference." History 98, no. 3 (331) (2013): 390–405. http://www.jstor.org/stable/24429519

SHERRIE GAVIN

23

GIFTS

Reesey's birthday came with even more anticipation than Cheyenne's. I was grateful that the girls' birthdays wondrously fell within two different school holiday periods that year, as it relieved us from the burden of making travel arrangements to see Michelle. Also, Michelle forgot which date Reesey's birthday was, so the perfunctory phone call was arranged and happened just as quickly as the previous birthday call. When I asked Reesey what kind of birthday cake she wanted, she responded, "chocolate." But she never ate chocolate, so I pressed. "There are other flavours for cake, like vanilla, and pink for strawberry."

"Pink," she said. "I want pink cake."

"Okay–maybe vanilla and pink icing?" I queried.

"Pink. And pink icing." Concerned about strawberries, I made a vanilla cake and icing with copious amounts of pink food colouring, which was happily received. The party was fun and simple, repeating 'pin the crown on Rapunzel' and 'pass the parcel,' but she also liked directing me to the fabric of her choice for the dresses I sewed for her and Cheyenne (pink and pink lace). She impatiently wanted to open presents at the beginning of the party, but I didn't mind. What was most important was that she knew that the party was for her, and she expected good things. Positive expectations, after all, can be a very wonderful thing.

I knew what the package was as soon as it arrived. The women of the *Exponent II* had a tradition that when one of the bloggers gives birth, or is going through a very difficult time such as miscarriage, a family death, or unemployment, the women pool together and have a very soft, faux furry blanket with a giraffe print sent to the fellow blogger. Giraffe print is chosen because giraffes are a matriarchal group wherein the females care for one another and travel together, sharing each others' burdens. The blanket symbolises bonding and a sense of mutual sentiment towards any and all life-changing events. I received a giraffe blanket a year earlier when I was going through my fourth IVF procedure. When that blanket arrived, I felt an intense warmth of relief and love; it healed me and lifted my soul. It is one of the most powerful and symbolic gifts I have ever had the honour to receive.

A month earlier, a loving, compassionate, and careful e-mail had arrived from Emily, asking if it would be hurtful to have blankets sent to the girls. Emily and our *Exponent* sisters knew that our situation was complicated and unsure. They supported me in my quest to be a mother in fasting and prayer on my behalf. In this gift, they wanted to reach out and offer support, but they knew that sending the blankets, previously reserved for births, might be premature. I felt almost selfish at the time but responded in gratitude that I understood the place of love and hope that the blankets were coming from and would be happy to receive them should they decide to send them. Knowing that the blankets were reserved for new babies symbolised a deep hope for me.

I was thrilled when the package arrived full of its tangible goodness. The girls and I opened the box together. Each blanket included a letter written individually to Cheyenne and Reesey that spoke of love and prayer and how much I had hoped for daughters just like them. The letters also contained words of promise—that even if the girls did not remain with me, the blankets would bring them peace and comfort. The letters were written on starry paper, and though I tried to read them aloud, I could not. I was crying far too much, humbled by the perfect sense of compassion, acceptance and love. The letter to Reesey read:

Dear Reese,

We have been so happy to hear of the love you've brought to your new home! Your mummy has waited and prayed and worked to have you by her side for so long. And, we know that you're blessed to be in a home full of love with exceptional parents.

We picked this blanket for you for several reasons. First, we wanted you and your mum to feel the support of feminists—it's no accident that your blankets match! Every time that you are wrapped or wrap yourself in this blanket, know that we are there.

Also we chose the giraffe print for some specific reasons. Female giraffes stay with each other and tend each other's children. They are also the sentinels for the rest of the community (not just the giraffes) and warn others of impending danger. Giraffes are a largely matriarchal group and are affectionate and social. They make lasting social ties and are spectacularly graceful—even other worldly. These are all attributes that we strive to embody in our lives through our faiths. We see them in your mummy and wish the same attributes for you, little one.

Love,

Your Exponent Sisters.

Each girl took one and, after feeling it, wrapped herself in exploration of the buttery soft texture and the shapes of the giraffe pattern. It was midday, so they each took their favorite doll and wrapped it in the blanket, singing and telling their babies that they were loved and safe. The girls never hit their dolls now, and in wrapping the dolls in the blankets, it showed me that they knew that the blankets had a protective strength. That night, each girl snuggled under her giraffe blanket and slept through the entire night. So did I. That day and night were a much-needed miracle.

SHERRIE GAVIN

24

FRIENDS AND LIES

Christmas was coming, which meant that summer was well on its way. I knew of no one in Australia who had an annual live Christmas tree, even though that was common for me in my North American upbringing. Non-indigenous Christmas tree farms were few and far between, making them unreasonably expensive, and mostly the heat of summer made a "live" tree far too similar to kindling. I was in a Christmassy mood, so mid-November, the girls helped me set up a Christmas tree in the living room and helped me sew Christmas stockings for them.

The girls thought the tree looked a bit dull with its false green limbs and my collection of seashell and memento ornaments, so when I spied a drastically marked-down, *bright pink,* artificial Christmas tree at a local craft store, I bought it immediately. It was perfect for little pink girls. It was barely four feet tall and decorated with a simple string of white Christmas lights. The girls made ornaments that complemented the Disney ornaments that they loved best.

With Christmas also came the threat of seeing Michelle and Trent. Though I was glad that they did not see through their promise of coming to see us, they required that we bring the girls to Sydney. I anticipated that such a visit would be similar to last Easter, where the girls were taken from us, leaving Bruce and me on our own. Even if this was just a drop off thing, I was not interested in seeing Michelle. Still stuck on the receiving end of a textual flogging, I feared more interaction with her. I also wanted to spend Christmas with the girls; I didn't want them to ever be away from me, and thinking about not having them at Christmas made me sad. I usually dealt with this by declaring that such thoughts were selfish and reminding myself that I needed to be honest and fair with Michelle and Trent, with Ginny, with the Department of Immigration, and even with their bishop.

I was also under pressure from Thomas at the immigration department to not allow the girls to go to Sydney. He warned that if Michelle took family photos with the girls, and then used them to claim that the girls were still living with her, that her level of fraudulent claims would make things significantly worse for her. As it was, Thomas recommended that we request letters from friends that stated that they interacted with us and the girls and witnessed the girls living with us. Bruce continued to refuse to give permission to process the adoption, sure that somehow Michelle and Trent would "help us" in ways I still could not comprehend.

Burying my anxiety in Christmas-ness, I began to make dresses for the girls. Using some cute cotton fabric and a sewing pattern that I was now very familiar with, the girls helped me cut and sew, anticipating the new clothes that were being made especially for them. After they were asleep in bed at night, I used the leftover fabric scraps to make dresses in the same style for their dolls. This was pure fancy on my part, hoping to dress their dolls in the same frocks as the girls for a surprise on Christmas morning, even though their being with us for Christmas was highly unlikely.

Just after Thanksgiving, Ginny's mother sent me a message telling me that Ginny's grandmother, Ruby, had purchased a ticket to visit Michelle and Trent. She hoped to see Cheyenne and Reesey and to meet us when she was visiting. She arrived in early December and would return to the U.S. before Christmas. I loved the idea of meeting Ruby, whom Ginny clearly loved and respected. Ruby would return home *before* Christmas, which meant that we would be obligated to visit Sydney prior to Christmas, which would allow us to argue against making a second trip back at the end of December. Communication from Michelle regarding this was cordial; she didn't demand we travel to Sydney twice and almost seemed happy to have the girls for a short visit within the period of Ruby being in town.

The only problem was that Michelle did not want to see Bruce or me, nor did she seem to think that we would want, or should have, any time with Ruby. Michelle believed that we should fly in, drop off the girls to her, and after a couple of days, pick the girls up and leave, as though we were a delivery service. "I'm not a fan of this," said Bruce as we were discussing travel plans. "I want my parents to get to spend some less stressful time with the girls and have them swim in their pool and go to church with us on Sunday." I agreed, but I did not know how to make it happen. My experience with Michelle was that she set the rules, and that was that. She asked us to jump, Bruce asked "how high," and I found myself jumping alone until Michelle became bored and left me alone. My people-pleasing skills were spent, and I could think of no creative solution to meet everyone's demands.

"So… what do you want to do?" I finally asked.

"Let's not tell her when our flights arrive in Sydney. Mum and Dad can pick us up from the airport, and we'll spend a day with them before we drop the girls off at Michelle and Trent's," he said.

"Okay, but I'd like the girls to go to church with us on Sunday. How are we going to work that?"

"We can tell them that we are flying out on Sunday, but we won't say when. We'll pick the girls up early Sunday, go to church and fly back Monday morning. We'll fly together to Brisbane, and from there, I'll catch a flight for work. You can just go home with the girls from there."

"She's going to want to know when we arrive," I said, shaking my head, too familiar with her demands.

"Tell her that we're doing her a favour so she doesn't have to drive all the way to the airport. Tell her that we're borrowing a car from my parents, and we're happy to drop the girls off. It's a service."

"But the girls will tell her that we've been in town for a few days," I contended.

"We will tell them that we stopped by my parents' house first. The girls will say the same. Time is irrelevant."

"Okay," I responded apathetically with a shrug. I knew his mind was set, and nothing I could say would make any difference. I was still frustrated with Bruce for his refusal to follow the recommendations of Zoia, Ginny, and even Thomas in submitting the paperwork to begin the process of adopting the girls. I was becoming increasingly detached from him and rarely told him of anything going on in my heart or mind. Pushing back when I disagreed or even mentioning when I needed something fell by the wayside, as I opted for whatever was easiest, which was usually to just go along with whatever he said.

Bruce booked the tickets, and, as usual, assigned me to communicate with Michelle about the trip. I procrastinated contacting Michelle and focused on searching for thoughtful gifts for Ruby and Michelle and Trent's children. I contacted Ginny's mother and asked her about Ruby's interests and hobbies, settling on a bell that was shaped like a koala. I asked friends with children who were of similar age to Michelle's what the interests of their children were, and I decided to purchase a family activity book as a gift for Michelle and Trent. Feeling more confident, I texted Michelle.

"We have tickets! We will be there on December 14th." I had written "we will be there" in the text, which was true, but I neglected to tell her the exact time. Within seconds, my phone rang. It was Michelle. "What time does your flight arrive?"

"Um…" I stammered, totally unprepared, believing Bruce's plan would suffice.

"What is the flight number? We'll meet you at the airport."

"You don't have to meet us at the airport," I said, heart pounding. "Bruce's Dad will pick us up and loan us his car. He also has car seats for the girls, so we won't be bringing car seats with us. You can save the cost of parking at the airport."

"I have car seats," she said, ignoring me. "What's the flight number? And what airline?" This was not going as I had hoped. I knew Michelle would drill me until she got what she wanted, and

I was terrified of speaking with her. I rummaged through my e-mails looking for the message from Bruce with the flight reservations.

"Um... it's Qantas... and I'm looking up the info Bruce e-mailed to me..." I was getting anxious. I am not good at lying. And mostly, I didn't want to lie. But I was feeling trapped. "I know it's..." and allowed my voice to drift off. I was stuck and trying to figure out what to say. I quickly went to the Qantas website and looked at flight numbers, finding that the flight numbers were the same from day to day, depending on the time of the flight. "Our arrival flight number is QF555..." I pretended, "It gets in at about 10:00 Friday night."

"And the return flight?"

"QF528," I lied again. "Leaves at 2PM. We thought we'd take the girls to church with us in the morning, then go directly to the airport." But I did not know how to do what Bruce told me to do, so I forfeited honesty. The irony of lying for the purpose of going to church was staring right at me, and yet I waded deeply into the spew of hypocrisy.

"Hum..." said Michelle. "That isn't much time." Then after a moment, she said, "Our ward is having a Christmas picnic on that Saturday. You can meet us at the picnic and meet Ruby and everyone."

"That sounds great," I said, surprised at the generous invitation. And then, as was my knee-jerk reaction to every church activity of this kind, "Do I need to bring something for the picnic? We can grab something at the shop on our way there."

"It's all covered," she responded bluntly.

"Oh, um… yeah," I stammered, not quite knowing what to say. "Okay."

"Great. See you soon!" Michelle sang into the phone, ending the call. There was a pinprick of relief for a second, but I soon began to drown in increased self-loathing, which had been heightened by my lying. I already felt like everything was my fault. Bruce could not hear me because I wasn't worth listening to. The adoption had not started because I had failed to convince Bruce that it was the right thing to do. And the visa situation was complicated because I wasn't willing to be a foster mother under Michelle's thumb for a decade or more. And I thought that maybe, just maybe, God really didn't want me to be a mother, and it was my fault that everyone was in this mess. Everything was all my fault.

All of the Christmas things I had been trying to do to distract myself suddenly seemed like a flimsy, dilapidated fence standing in a decaying field, securing nothing. I felt utterly worthless.

25

DECEMBER, PART I

I attired the girls in the ankle-length Christmas dresses I had sewn for them and took them to see Santa Claus in a pop-up booth at the mall. Because it was daytime, the majority of shoppers were older, making for a quieter and less crowded time to visit. Their dresses swayed as the girls walked, inspiring them to twirl and dance as they moved. In turn, many of the elderly shoppers smiled, waved and asked them if they were on "Santa's Good List" as they promenaded along. Taking the girls to see Santa lifted some of my depression, and I became almost hopeful that Michelle might be kinder to me with Ruby around. Maybe she would even get me a gift? Or a token of a gift? I dismissed the thought as best as I could. But it was Christmas, so hope swayed my mind.

Our attorney, David, uncovered some interesting information about a report of child abuse that was called in to the local court in the U.S. that accused Michelle of abuse and neglect.

But as the girls were physically in Australia, the report collected dust like a dutiful archive with no administrative path to follow. David also collected statements from Ginny, who disclosed that when she (Ginny) was not in prison, Michelle refused all contact and withheld the girls from communicating with Ginny. This further supported us in submitting an adoption petition. In fact, ongoing communication with Thomas, David, and Zoia was positive and encouraged us to press forward with the adoption.

Bruce was the only one who would not move forward in processing the adoption, fearing that it would have a negative effect on the immigration process for the girls. He still thought that if Michelle and Trent grew to somehow like us, they would help us, therefore making the adoption and immigration process easier. I did not agree, but having grown weary of trying to persuade him otherwise, took his ongoing refusal silently on the chin.

"If they take photos of the girls with them at Christmas and submit a visa application or extension claiming that the girls are living with them, then there is an issue of immigration fraud," warned Thomas, though officially forbidden from offering legal immigration advice. Zoia was also opposed to having the girls stay with Michelle and Trent. This had nothing to do with protecting Michelle from committing a crime but was all about protecting the girls. "They have 'attached' to you and Bruce," she told me. "Having them stay with the other family could traumatise them. It really isn't a good idea." Bruce was not swayed. "We have to keep our agreement with them," he said, referring to a document he created and we signed about shared custody, but neither Michelle or Trent had signed. His focus was integrity, and not being the primary contact with David, Zoia, or Thomas made it easier for him to focus on a tangible, partially signed document than on what I told him.

I dreaded the trip to Sydney but could see no way out. I intellectually scrambled to find something that might make it even a little bit *not terrible.* Having planned to meet Michelle and her family at her ward Christmas picnic on Saturday, I felt a little better. A church picnic always offered a kitchen to do service in or an elderly parishioner to speak with one on one. This thought buoyed me, and I dared hope for the best. In preparation, I booked an appointment with my doctor, primarily to get diabetes medication refills, fully anticipating a lecture on keeping my blood sugar in better check. She noted that my blood sugars "need to be better controlled," but with a seriousness I had not seen in a doctor before, she said, "Heart disease kills more women than men." I remained tight-lipped, afraid I would break down in tears if I told her even a fraction of what was going on. "We need to get your blood pressure down or *you will* have a heart attack." Her words were firm. But she softened, "We need to follow up on this in the new year. After the stress of Christmas, maybe your blood pressure will be better."

I promised her things would improve, because lying was all I had the energy to do.

The Thursday before we left, Michelle began a tirade of texts, once again demanding to know about our flight time. "Aren't we going to meet on Saturday at your ward picnic?" I reminded her, almost feeling faint.

"I'll pick up the girls from the airport. Then you can get them on your way back to the airport on Sunday," she replied.

"But we planned on going to the ward picnic," I tapped.

"I'll get them at the airport. What time is your flight and flight number?"

"We won't have car seats; my in-laws have them." My heart was pounding, I was clammy and anxious, so I paced to try to release my anxiety, pushing down the thought that maybe the doctor's heart attack observations were right. It wasn't working. I was beginning to feel physically sick, so I made my way to the bathroom, pressed my face against the cool tile of the wall and hoped to not vomit. After a pause, she replied. "Ok. Drop them off on Saturday morning." I breathed with relief. *I can do this,* I told myself, no longer knowing the truth from a lie.

Prepped with toys, books, coloured pencils, kids' snacks and sippy cups, we boarded the plane as though we were seasoned parents. As we set up the kids' things in their seat back pockets, Bruce and I switched our phones to flight mode. "We can't let 'Drongo' know what our flights and plans are," Bruce said firmly as I tapped my phone to switch the settings. Drongo was the code name we used when discussing Michelle and Trent in front of the girls. "Make sure that you don't accidentally pocket-dial them."

"Of course," I agreed, barely stifling an eye roll at the suggestion. Besides, I kept my contact list password protected.

The flight was uneventful. Bruce's father met us like clockwork outside of the airport, and we were soon settled in my in-laws' home. Over the past few months, we had spoken well of Bruce's parents, and had been video-calling them so that the girls became comfortable and familiar with them. These investments worked beautifully—so much so that as soon as they saw Granddad, and then Grandma, their reactions were a commotion of hugs, giggles, and happy squeals—the kinds that children make when they feel safe and happy. After some snacks and friendly chit-chat in the kitchen, I excused myself to the bedroom to try and finish an afghan I was crocheting as a gift for my in-laws for Christmas. I had intended to give them the blanket for their fiftieth wedding anniversary, which was the previous October, but hadn't completed it by then, so was extra determined to have it completed by Christmas.

The girls were happily swimming under the close supervision of Bruce and his parents in the backyard. Bruce called for me to bring some towels down for the girls. I dutifully grabbed the pool towels that were stored in a linen cupboard by the bedroom we were sharing and brought them downstairs and outside to the pool. I placed the towels on the picnic table and watched as Bruce perched himself on a plastic pool chair. He placed his keys and phone on the table and began to talk with his parents, sharing with them some of the adoption updates. All felt well, so I went back to crocheting out of sight.

After only fifteen minutes, Bruce stepped into the room. He took a breath. "I pocket dialled Trent," he said. I was confused and stared at him blankly, not sure if he was joking. I uttered a nonsense word in confusion. "I just hung up," Bruce continued. "I don't know if that was the right thing to do. I was talking about Michelle with Mum, and I think he heard. So I called him back, and he said he didn't hear anything. They know we're here." A feeling of nausea began to curl from the pit of my stomach. I instinctively gritted my throat to stop myself from retching but quickly became lightheaded.

"Wha… " I finally breathed, releasing some pressure, but still feeling all of the shock.

"You shouldn't have lied," Bruce said flatly, refusing to meet my eyes. "This is your fault." His words made me angry–angrier than I've ever been in my life. He had asked the impossible, and I delivered as best I could. I was livid with Bruce and terrified of the situation. Had we just lost the girls? Michelle constantly threatened to call the police on us and take the girls back. Would this make her act on her threats? I was near panic.

"What was I supposed to do?" I finally snapped, ready to fight, emotional fists in the air. I was done pressing down, ignoring myself and obeying his commands.

"I told you not to tell them." His voice was angry and sharp. "I didn't tell you to *lie*."

"She kept asking me for the flight number and time."

"You shouldn't have told her. You should have redirected the conversation," came his arrogant reply. "It's not that hard," he added with an attitude that made me want to slap him.

"Then *you* should have called to tell her about the travel plans instead of dumping it *all on me*!" Adrenaline began to kick in. I was in fight mode, livid with Bruce for the pocket dial and then blaming me for the situation. My phone began buzzing with texts, redirecting my adrenaline from fight to flight: I knew Michelle would attack.

"I know you're in town."

"Is this how you think you are going to build trust with me so you can have the girls?"

"I can't trust you. I don't trust liars."

"God hates liars like you."

"You need to repent. You will go to hell for this."

"God hates you as much as I do."

"Liars go to hell, and I will testify that you lied and judgement will put you in hell."

I groaned and stood as my phone buzzed again and again. Trent began texting as well.

"You have not been honest with us."

"You aren't worthy."

"We put a lot of trust in you and you have betrayed us."

"You are a wicked person not worthy of my friendship or trust."

"Is this how you treat all of your friends?"

"God hated you and made you not have children. I can see why. You aren't worthy."

"We can't trust you."

Bruce's phone rang. "It's Trent," he said and turned to walk away so I could not hear his conversation. "I'm sorry, mate," I heard him say as his voice moved out of earshot, "I didn't know that she had told you that." I hated Bruce at that moment. I hated him with an intensity that I had never felt before in my life. But I hated myself more. None of the messages shocked me; I had been receiving texts like these and worse for months. But this time, I was sure we had just lost the girls. I sat down, my phone finally silent. I was sure that Michelle was listening to every word between Trent and Bruce. And then, something in me died. I felt totally powerless, surrounded by shadows of rancour and shame. I couldn't cry. I couldn't move. I felt nothing.

A few minutes later, Bruce returned. "We need to take the girls to them," he said, but the words sounded more like an echo; there was no strength in his voice. "Now." My head began spinning. "You can't come. Michelle doesn't want you anywhere near her property."

I gripped the edge of the bed where I was sitting, trying to steady my thoughts. "So… I am not going to meet Ginny's grandmother?" I said. It was the only thing I could process.

"Not today," came Bruce's reply. "Maybe tomorrow or Sunday." His voice sounded distant and strange, as if we were speaking underwater.

"Can we get them back tomorrow?"

"I don't know when we can get them back." The words all sounded like the shadows of echos. After a moment, Bruce added, "It is what it is. We need to get their things and drop them off now."

Texts from Michelle surged on with a vengeance, complete with direct threats that she would "go crazy on me" if she saw me at her house. Her repugnant texts were meant to cause me emotional pain and hurt, and they usually did. But somehow in that moment, I felt nothing. My head was as numb as my heart. I felt dead inside. I absorbed the hateful words as though that was my job; I was a carcass being stuffed with voracious verbal maggots. Perhaps this is my purpose in life, I thought. My purpose is to absorb all of the hate. Besides, everything was my fault. All of it. I could never be good enough to be a friend, a wife, a mother. I felt dead.

After a few minutes, the messages slowed and my phone finally fell silent. This seemed to give me permission to move, so I slowly walked in a daze down to the kitchen, where I sat at a small, round table and stared at the tiles on the floor. At some stage, someone put a cold drink in front of me. I sipped it, allowing the tingling carbonation and saccharine sweetness of diet cola to soften my clenched throat and start to settle my stomach. "Can I have some?" asked Cheyenne. She was looking at me with her real smile. "Please?" I felt love. Love for her. Love *from* her.

Love for Reesey. Love that brought a miniscule flicker of light through the blackened reality of the previous half hour.

"Yes," I croaked, surprised at how odd my voice sounded. She gleefully climbed on my lap. "I love you," I said, and a tiny smile crept across my lips as I looked at her longingly. She didn't respond, too busy gulping down big mouthfuls of a drink she normally wasn't allowed. The maternal instinct that had slipped into a momentary coma began to prick at me until thoughts about the situation began to form. These might be my very last moments with the girls, and I didn't want to be distracted by anything but them. I chose to not fight with Bruce, which released some of the hostility within me; instead, I would swallow my feelings of betrayal and push through. For the girls.

I surmised that it might be beneficial if I focused on how fun it could be for them to visit Michelle and Trent. "I don't want to go," said Reesey when I told her how lucky she was to be able to go and see Trent and Michelle sooner. "Oh, and I am going to miss you!" I said as brightly as I could, fiercely holding in my tears and the terror in my heart. "But it's Christmas! I think they'll have presents for you!"

Cheyenne just rolled with the punches. "I like Old Mummy," she said with only a hint of the false smile creeping back over her face. "And I like Liam," she said, referring to the middle son. "He protects me."

"It will be fun to see Liam," I said. "And Reesey, I'll be praying for you, and Heavenly Father will be with you the whole time." Within moments, Bruce and the girls were bustling about, getting ready to leave. I thought I would go mad if I stayed at my in-laws' house while Bruce drove the forty-five minutes each way to drop the girls off, so I tried to think of something, anything, to have whatever remaining time with the girls that I could.

Directing the girls to use the toilet before we left, I pulled Bruce aside. "I have an idea," I said quietly so the girls could not hear us. "I'll go with you for the drive, but when we get a block or two away from Drongo's house, I'll say that I am busting and need the toilet really bad. You can drop me at a park or someplace a block or two away from Drongo's house, so she won't see me. Then you drop them off without me. We'll tell the girls we don't want to make them late. And I'll at least get those last few moments in the car with them."

Bruce breathed deeply. "Okay," he said, with his eyes cast down. "That'll probably be good, so we can calm them and be positive about their stay on the drive there," he said, reminding me that whenever they spoke to Michelle on video or phone calls, they fought violently and had night terrors in the days following.

As we drove to Michelle's house, the girls were happily entertained with the colouring books from the plane. They were also excited about sharing the gifts that I had purchased and wrapped for Michelle's family. Gazing out of the window, I cried quietly and intermittently, trying to ignore my feelings. Bruce and I chattered sometimes with the girls, but I was mostly silent. The occasional hateful text came through from Michelle, which I read in numb defeat.

"I am their mother *not* you."

"I can't believe I ever trusted you."

I finally responded. "I'm really sorry," I texted, utterly detached. "Will you need to borrow the car seats?"

"Of course *not*," came her text reply. "I am a *mother. A real mother.* I have car seats."

"This is why God didn't trust you to be a mother. You are a sinner and a liar."

I put my phone in my purse and stared out the window blankly. It was a forty-five minute drive, but it felt both slower and faster, like aeons of time crawled as I sat silently next to Bruce, and yet, it was the most fleeting of moments, as it was the last seconds I likely would have with the girls. "Please Heavenly Father," I prayed silently, "Please, please protect Cheyenne and Reesey. Please bless us that they will come back to us. Please forgive me. Please soften Michelle's heart. Please help. Please just help." Tears came, but I did not want the girls to know that I was crying, so I stopped my silent prayer, took a deep breath and turned towards the back of the car. "I love you!" I said, as if saying "peek-a-boo." The girls didn't look up from their colouring, but responded, "Love you, too." This was repeated several times, so much that the girls stopped responding to me at all. The game was dull, and they were not interested.

"We're getting close," Bruce said faintly.

"I am sooooo busting!" I began. "Can anyone find me a toilet? Let's look for toilet signs!" The girls joined in, and the mood, though awkward, seemed slightly lighter with this "find a toilet" game. "I am so busting that I think I might just go in the park here and Daddy can get me later because I don't want you to be late." Bruce pulled over to the side of the road, a few blocks from Trent and Michelle's house. "Oh! Those bushes look good!" I said brightly.

The girls were silent. They seemed confused but didn't make a sound. They knew something was off. Cheyenne looked at me in a way I had never seen before. I wondered if this was the face she made each time she was given away. Reesey had a grin on her face, possibly amused that I might wet my pants. I hopped out, leaving my purse in the car, but kept hold of my phone. I stepped towards some bushes, then turned and waved. I decided to do a silly dance, jumping and jogging in place, trying to act like a clown that was about to have an accident.

The girls grinned and seemed to giggle, and then Bruce drove away. Staring silently at the car as it turned left onto the road of Michelle and Trent's house, I was alone. Completely alone.

26

DECEMBER, PART II

Praying out loud, I asked God to help me, to protect the girls, to keep me sane. I took a moment to look around to see if anyone could hear me. There was no one in the clearing; it was a lushly green, grassy and flowered space beneath a steep traffic embankment. Above me was a fenced freeway, too vertical and overgrown to climb. Even if there were a space to sit, I was too anxious. I just felt alone and completely helpless, so I returned to prayer, asking that Trent and Michelle would feel love and kindness, that the girls would be safe and come back to us, and that all would be well. I finished praying and felt a little better.

Could Michelle ever be pacified? Would I ever see the girls again? I did not know what would come next, but at least—for a few moments—I was free. Free from receiving hateful messages from Michelle, free from being assigned impossible tasks by Bruce, and free from managing traumatised toddlers. I took a deep breath and closed my eyes. In that blade of time, a single speck of stardust pricked my heart. Hope. I felt a mite of hope and breathed it in, meditating, trying to slow my heart rate.

After about twenty minutes, I began to wonder how long it would be before Bruce returned. I presumed that he would just drop them off and leave, before he was forced out. But maybe Bruce wasn't coming back? I tried to dismiss the thought but wondered if he hoped that I would just disappear anyway. Did I even want him to come back? Our marriage was in shambles, and I wondered if Bruce hated me as much as Michelle did, or more. Maybe they were bonding over their mutual hate of me? I did not know, so I began to wonder what I would do if I were abandoned right there on the side of the road, deeply regretting that I had left my purse in the car.

The girls' well-being was my priority, so I convinced myself that I could stay there at least until dark. At dark, if I was still alone, I planned to walk towards the freeway, and then make up another plan from there. Without realising, I had begun to pace. It was a decent sized space, so I made the decision to walk, and then jog, between two trees that were about fifteen feet apart. After another ten minutes, I added a jump mid way between the trees, as if to climb the embankment. It was a strange routine, but it helped to release some of the cortisol and adrenaline that were still pulsing through my body. After another fifteen minutes, I slowed my more vigorous movements to walking between the trees, but this time circling around each. This way, I was able to catch my breath and keep an eye on the road that led to Michelle's house.

Finally, Bruce's car appeared, and I drew a deep breath of relief. At least I was not abandoned on the side of the road. "How did it go?" I asked as I climbed in the car. "It was good," he said plainly, heading towards the freeway. Entering the flow of traffic until he was driving comfortably, he seemed to relax a little. "You scored," he said.

I was completely confused. "What do you mean?"

"The presents. They all opened the presents there in front of me."

"Oh?" I had forgotten about the gifts. "Good? I think? Really?" I needed more information.

"Yep. Liam asked me how I knew he liked dinosaurs," continued Bruce. "I said that you chose his gift. And the other kids all said thank you and seemed genuinely happy and surprised."

"Oh, I am so glad," allowing myself to feel a drop of relief that in turn watered the microscopic seed of hope that remained in my heart.

"And Ruby loved the bell."

"She did?" Now I was almost excited. I really wanted to leave a good impression on Ginny's grandmother.

"She said she collected bells, and that she didn't have one with a koala on it." I was elated by this information and heard myself chuckle. "Michelle looked angry," Bruce continued. "I think she was jealous that you did so well with gifts, especially because of the gift for Ruby." A tiny smugness came over me; I liked feeling that I had out-shined Michelle. But it did not last. There were two infinitely more important things at hand: the girls.

In a quiet voice, I finally asked, "Are we going to get the girls back?"

"I think so. A time isn't set, but they said, 'see you Sunday' as I was leaving." I sighed a breath of relief before worry engulfed me. I silently prayed that the girls would not be hurt, given their experience at being on the receiving end of belts and wooden spoons. *Please God, please protect them.*

With no plans, nowhere to be, and no children to look after, Bruce decided to pull into a shopping mall he spied on our drive back to his parents' house. The idea of anonymously wandering and window shopping in crowds of seasonal Christmas shoppers was appealing, but we hardly set foot inside when Bruce's phone rang. Many of Bruce's work phone calls were confidential—dealing with injuries and legal responsibilities. I could tell by how he focused his eyes if it was a friend or work calling. Seeing the business look in his eyes, I instantly stepped a few feet away to give him privacy. After a few minutes, his call finished and he walked back towards me. "Michelle wants the car seats," he said, with distinctness and brevity.

This exasperated me. "I asked her if she needed them, and she said no!" I snivelled. "I am so annoyed." I looked at Bruce, shaking my head. "Okay, I guess we'll get back in the car and take them to them now."

"No," Bruce said obscurely. "They don't want you there and they want the seats now, so Trent is going to meet us here in the car park in about ten minutes." The next few minutes were a blur, and I suddenly found myself standing in the heat of the Australian sun, looking for Trent's vehicle. He spied us and pulled into a parking spot that was close, getting out of his car. "Michelle said that she had car seats," I said, wanting to point out that I wasn't the only liar in town, as Bruce swiftly removed the car seats from our vehicle, placing them on the footpath.

Trent ignored me. "Ya know, we put a lot of trust in y'all," he said.

"I really am trying my best," I said.

"Not telling us the truth is the best you can do?" he said. At that second, Bruce moved from beside me to position himself by Trent, physically abandoning me to take Trent's position.

Adrenaline rushed through me again, and it took all my strength to not verbally start recounting all of the lies Michelle had told me. I was also terrified that if I was truthful about Bruce being the one who wanted to conceal our travel plans, then Trent might turn on Bruce and there would be a heated physical confrontation. I was equally panicked that whatever I said could cause us to lose the girls. I had been taking verbal punches since day one, so this escalation should not have been a surprise. I stood, ready to take the punch. Maybe Bruce would join in and beat me as well? I didn't care anymore. Pressing it all down, my palms began to sweat. My mouth was dry and I felt queasy. I stood motionless, not defending myself, feeling set up and abandoned by my husband. I felt like the proverbial deer caught in the headlights, but still trying to protect and please everyone.

"I'm sorry," was all I could think to say, not bracing for the punch. I wanted to be beaten physically into the ground. "I just wanted to spend some time with them and Bruce's parents."

"Well, you're going to have to earn trust back," he said, seeming to back down a little. He picked up one of the car seats and carried it to his car. Bruce picked up the other and followed. I stepped back and was left on the sidewalk alone. Maybe I should have felt relieved that I was not punched, but mostly, I felt stupid. Totally stupid. I waved and smiled at Trent as he drove away, feeling completely detached from Bruce, the situation, and everything.

"Let's go to a movie," said Bruce. "Take our mind off of things." No apology. No checking to see if I was okay. Nothing but the suggestion of a movie. Whatever.

"A comedy," I said, knowing I could not handle anything emotional, romantic, or violent. Bruce consented, and finding that we had an hour before a musical comedy started, we bought tickets and stepped into a restaurant to grab a quick bite. I took a moment to check my blood sugar and take some insulin before eating. As we ate, Bruce and I said very little, except to discuss the best way to bring our remaining drinks into the movie theatre. As time drew near, we went to the air conditioned theatre, sat on cushioned seats and switched off our phones. I took some additional deep breaths, trying to forget *everything*, allowing myself to be absorbed in the movie.

Though I sensed an internal nagging to turn my phone on, I pushed the thought away. I needed a break, and I could think of no one who had any reason to contact me. The world could wait. Within minutes, I allowed myself to be immersed in a silly plot line with a happy ending, where I found myself almost laughing out loud and even tapping along to some of the music. It was a well-deserved break, and Bruce and I walked out of the theatre almost smiling.

Stepping out into the bright sunlight after the movie, I turned my phone on. It instantly began buzzing with an onslaught of more than twenty text messages. All were from Michelle. All were very angry. At first, they were demanding that I apologise, humble myself to her superiority, and prove to her that I could be trustworthy to look after the girls. When I had not responded, her messages became more aggressive. She demanded that I beg her forgiveness, berated me as being deeply inferior to her, and called God's judgement upon me, as though she were God herself. When I failed to respond, she began calling me names and asking if I was hiding from her. Then she began threatening both Bruce and me. "If you don't reply," one of the later messages read, "I am going to report you both to the police for kidnapping. You will go to jail and I will testify against you for stealing the girls!"

"We don't even have the girls with us," stated Bruce in a bewildered voice. At that moment, I realised that I had stopped in the middle of the theatre exit in a shocked daze, nearly blocking the door, totally immobilised. At some stage, Bruce began reading the messages over my shoulder. The movie was over, and reality was blinding me. "We can't be accused of kidnapping when we don't even have the girls with us," he said. He then checked his phone. "I have some messages from Trent, asking why you aren't responding to Michelle."

"I just texted her that we were in a movie and had turned our phones off," I said hastily.

"No one normal turns off their phone at a movie," she replied. Her words dripped through my phone with acidic scorn.

"*Mothers—real mothers*—don't do that. I am reporting you for *kidnapping. I am calling the police.*"

"Mate, we were in a movie," I could hear Bruce say into his phone. I knew he was talking to Trent. Bruce stayed close to me, but most of the words were a blurry echo again. I felt disoriented—

the rush of the day, the anxiety, the abandonment, the fear of being physically assaulted, the bliss of a musical comedy and then the ambush of threats had my head spinning. "We don't even have the kids with us," I could hear Bruce saying. "We can't kidnap kids that we don't have." I began to feel lightheaded, so I found a place to sit and checked my blood sugar while Bruce kept speaking. It was the only thing I could think to do to prevent the possibility of my collapsing. My blood sugar was a little high. This meant that the jittery disorientation was an anxiety attack, maybe even a heart attack. Bruce finished the call and walked towards me. "Are you okay?" he asked, nodding towards my blood monitor.

"Yeah, blood sugar's good," came my half truth.

"Michelle doesn't want us to have the girls anymore," he said with a sort of forced breeziness. I had heard him use this tone before in situations where he was doing his best to remain optimistic and look for positive treasures. "But," he quickly added, "she agreed to talk to me about it before she made a final decision. She's going to call me around six, so we have time to get back to Mum and Dad's."

When we arrived, Bruce's parents were watching television in the living room. Bruce briefly explained what was going on, sounding only slightly less upbeat than average. I stood behind him, refusing to make eye contact with anyone, head down, a mere spectre of my former self. As

Bruce finished speaking, I ghosted through the kitchen on tiptoes, trying not to disturb anything, anywhere, hoping to disappear and cease existence. My mother-in-law, Madeline, always quick on her feet, circled through the living room in the opposite direction, rounding back toward the kitchen, cutting me off in the hallway that connected the spaces. She stopped in front of me, feet solidly placed to block me. "Come," she said, with tears in her eyes. She enfolded me in her arms, and I began to sob.

Bruce's parents are "stiff upper lip" people and don't normally hug or address any kind of emotion. This hug was the first she had ever offered me, and I melted into her arms. It felt like I had not been held by anyone in decades, and that hug meant more to me than anything else in the world at that second. After a moment, I stopped sobbing. She gently stepped back, neither of us uttering a word. With my head still down, I climbed the stairs and went to the bathroom, grateful to be alone. I looked at myself in the mirror, self-loathing filling my soul. My hair was dry and frizzy, my skin was blotchy and uneven, and my eyes were red and puffy from crying. I felt as broken as I looked. I hated myself for being infertile. I hated myself for lying. I hated myself for not managing everything. I hated everything about myself. I splashed cold water on my face, then looked at myself again. "You're not good enough," I said inside my head. "You couldn't do everything that everyone wanted you to do. You're a loser." I slapped my face as hard as I could, allowing the hatred to manifest in physical self destruction. The sting from the slap brought tears again, and made my head throb. It felt like my entire head was burning, and I longed to end it all.

I splashed cold water on my face again, then leaned my face against the cool of the tile wall. I pressed the cheek I had slapped first, then the other cheek. In doing this, I began taking deep breaths, slowly counting, "one, two, three, four, five." Then I deliberately exhaled, counting again "one, two, three, four, five." After doing this for a few minutes, I realised that I was shaking and couldn't stop. Everything was out of control in my life, including my body. I was completely powerless. However, I could not live in the bathroom forever, and I did not want to appear to be unwell. I wanted to disappear, not draw attention to myself.

Confused, all I could think to do was to try and stop shaking. I kept breathing deeply with the intent to try and somehow calm down. Whispering, "inhale... one, two, three, four, five, aaannddd exhale... one, two, three, four, five..." Eventually my physical tremoring slowed, then stopped. I suddenly realised how much my head was throbbing. I opened the cupboard behind the mirror and took a handful of over-the-counter pain relievers. I needed the headache to stop quickly, so more was better, right? And if I overdosed, well... at least I wouldn't die with a headache. Pills in hand, I left in search of a cup, refusing to look at myself in the mirror. As I opened the door, I sensed Bruce, though he was out of sight. He was waiting for me, not impatiently, but waiting. I turned and saw him standing in the doorway of the guestroom with an unopened can of icy Diet Coke. He handed it to me. "She'll be calling me soon," he said, referring to Michelle. "I am going to take the call in here, away from Mum and Dad."

"Sounds good," I said, keeping my eyes down. I chucked the pills into my mouth, swallowing them down with the Diet Coke. I was never good at taking pills without water and added this to my growing list of failures and imperfections.

"Hey," said Bruce gently. "Let's have a prayer," he said. I nodded, and if I were not dehydrated, tears may have even welled again. Dare I hope God would forgive me for lying and answer our prayer? I was too dazed to hope. Bruce voiced the prayer, asking for calm and guidance and that he would know what to say. He prayed for Michelle's heart to be softened and for the girls to be safe and know how much we loved them, no matter what came of the phone call. As he ended the prayer, I pushed out a quiet "Amen," my eyes still facing the floor. I felt a small connection with Bruce at that moment, and he gestured for me to stay there to support him for the call. I surrendered again to his need, and we positioned ourselves on the bed, our backs supported by pillows and with legs stretched out. It was as comfortable as it could be.

A few moments later, Bruce was listening to Michelle. In the silence of the room, I could hear the call clearly without it being on speaker. She was telling Bruce how much she did not trust me. She was telling him how I had lied to her by not giving her access to all of my messages between myself and Trent's mother, and how I manipulated everything she ever said. She detailed every way she could think of in which I was utterly obtuse compared to her: how I was spiritually inferior, a religious fake, how poor I was at parenting, how I was a false friend, how unworthy I was to be a parent, how unfair, prideful, and judgemental I was, and how I was dishonest in absolutely every way, searching and assigning every comprehensible insult to me.

I intellectually knew that this was Bruce's way of placating her; he would agree with whatever Michelle said and hope that she might concede to returning the girls to us. I knew this was his plan and that it had to be done. But knowing this still made me feel ill. Though the conversation was going as expected with the onslaught of hatred unleashed at me, I felt the sting of every word. Michelle verbally demeaned my appearance, lack of fertility, laziness, life of failure, and complete absence of any kind of worthiness.

I willed for my heart to stop. Just stop. I willed myself to be swallowed into the bed, then sucked down through the house, deep, deep into the earth—completely disappearing into nothingness, until I became one with existential oblivion and nothingness. And yet, I was there. In person. In reality. My heart thumped, pounding in my ears with slow, laborious strikes.

Bruce's voice continued to agree with Michelle. "I know," he said quietly.

The phone call ended. Michelle, in all her righteousness, would allow Bruce to collect the girls the next morning. Bruce explained that we would leave for church a few hours earlier than planned. He would drive to Michelle's house but drop me off at a fast food place along the way. Then he would collect the girls, return to get me, and we would all go to church as though nothing had happened.

"Like nothing happened," I whispered.

I needed Bruce to tell me that he didn't actually agree with Michelle. I needed him to take responsibility for pocket-dialling Trent and thank me for being patient with him as he dragged his feet with the adoption. I needed to hear that I wasn't as absent of any value as was just detailed by Michelle. But he said nothing. He seemed to fall asleep quickly, his breath reflecting a regular, though not necessarily deep, sleep. As I sleeplessly lay in the blackness of night, it seemed to me that the only way I could regain some kind of control was to leave. I had a little bit of money in a U.S. bank account, enough for a plane ticket to the U.S. and maybe a little extra. I had friends I could stay with for at least a little while in the U.S., and I could try to block out everything. This tiny fantasy brought enough relief that I was allowed to collapse into fitful sleep.

The next morning, Bruce and I rose very early, in silence. We each showered, dressed and drove without saying a word. Silence was our weapon, but it was also our respite. Bruce chose where he wanted to drop me off, and I knew there was no point in me weighing in on his decision. He had shown that he was not listening to me. This fastfood place was mid-way between Michelle's address and the chapel of the ward we planned on attending. Bruce estimated that I might be there for an hour, maybe more. I silently supposed that it made a little more sense to drop me at a restaurant; then Bruce could tell the girls that I was really hungry, too hungry to pick them up. After all, everyone but me seemed to have permission to lie.

I refused to watch him drive away, walked directly in, and bought a soft drink. Sitting down, I found that the restaurant Wi-Fi wasn't working, and my cell reception was spotty, so I began to play solitaire to pass the time. The numbness of sleepiness began to bubble away with every carbonated sip, and as it did, the black dog began to bark, as if reminding me of my worthlessness. I was still unsure if Michelle was going to return the girls to us. And maybe even Bruce really won't pick me up, I thought. He probably regrets picking me up yesterday. Maybe he will pick up the girls and go to church, then to the airport, and everyone would forget about me. He can do whatever he wants with the rest of his life, with or without the girls. He was a catch, so why not? He could do better than me. Anyone would be better than me.

Even if Bruce did return with the girls, I had no energy to beg, plead, or whatever was needed to appease Michelle. I was broken and wondered if I had the means to kill myself right then and there. At that moment, I glanced out the window just in time to see Bruce pull into the car park. The girls were in the back! I was thrilled! With a burst, I rushed out to the car, desperate to hug the girls. I opened the back door, but Bruce had no time for that. "We're going to be late for church, " he commanded. "So we can get drive-thru breakfast for the girls and go." I obeyed his behest and immediately asked the girls what they wanted to eat. As we ate and drove, Bruce spoke in a quiet voice. "It was as if nothing happened yesterday at all," he said. "She even hugged me goodbye!" he incredulously said of Michelle.

"Old Mummy is really nice," added Cheyenne. "She wanted me to tell you that she is really nice. She even gave us Christmas presents!" Cheyenne and Reesey both held up teddy bears.

"Oh!" I said, possibly overenthusiastically. "Those seem so fun! That was so nice of Old Mummy." But I couldn't help myself. "Did you miss me? I missed you heaps!"

"No," answered Cheyenne plainly. Reesey gurgled something inaudible between bites.

"They missed you," said Bruce, finally saying something for my benefit. "I think they missed out on all of the Drongo drama messing with us stuff, which is good. It's good they had a good time." I was still too numb to process that information.

We arrived at church just as the service was starting. Within seconds of sitting on the pew, Reesey climbed onto my lap. Cheyenne climbed over both of us, put her arms around me and wiggled until she was also sitting on my lap. Each of the girls clung to me, tight fists gripping my dress, legs straddled around my waist. Very soon they each nuzzled their foreheads against my skin in the crook of either shoulder and my neck, where they pressed against me and could feel my heartbeat. That moment carved my heart open, allowing a gush of twinkling love to wash over me.

SHERRIE GAVIN

27

NAVIGATION

I was relieved when our bags were checked in and we made our way to the Frequent Flyer Lounge, where Bruce had membership. Complimentary drinks, sandwiches and snacks were available for all in this restricted area, so we made our way to the gold-class children's space, hands filled with Vegemite toast and apple juice. On the way, we passed a glorious, grand piano being played vibrantly by a skilled pianist, who pulsed the keys along to Figaro's Aria from *The Barber of Seville*. A tenor in a full tuxedo rang out his voice with delight: "Fortunatissimo per verita! Bravo! La la la la la la la la!"

I love opera, and this seemed to be a gift from God! Something this beautiful randomly along our path? The weight of the world was grabbed from my shoulders as I picked up Cheyenne and took Reesey's hand to lead them closer to the music. The pianist was a woman with long dark hair, who perfectly played the song from memory. She was magnificent! The tenor was a tall, thin man with curly blond hair and a smile that reached every corner of the huge space. I stood with the girls, fixed in the moment, a sense of elation filling my soul. The beauty of the music, the sacredness of artistic talent and the enthusiasm of the performers all felt medicinally celestial. I couldn't stop smiling, thrilled at what good fortune randomly appeared at the end of what felt like a completely disastrous trip. I clung to the girls, instinctively moving to the beat, nearly dancing. The girls seemed to sense that this was something magical (it was!), so they listened and watched transfixed by the brilliant performance.

"Let's go," Bruce said gruffly.

"This is beautiful, Bruce," I said in protest, keeping my eyes fixed, my soul healing with every note of the music.

"No, we need to go now," Bruce said urgently. "They are filming this," he said, motioning to a single, professional cameraman aiming his recording device at the performers. "If this somehow gets on the news, then Michelle will know we took a later flight, and," he emphasised, "she will see us in the Qantas Lounge and hit us up for money. She will know we lied about the flight time. We can't risk being seen, and we can't risk them seeing us do anything fun. She'll be jealous, and then she'll attack us."

"But they're not even filming the audience." Yet as I spoke, the operator began panning the crowd's smiling faces. "Okay," I said, immediately lowering my head and turning my back to hide me and Cheyenne. We walked in the opposite direction of the camera to find reprieve, my heart aching. As I sat in the children's play area, I removed the peel from an apple for the girls to nibble on between chasing each other around soft building blocks that were as large as they were. They rumbled, played and giggled within eyesight of both Bruce and me, but just far enough to try and entice us to chase them. I could no longer hear the music, but every few minutes, I could hear applause. At that moment, it was as if everything of beauty was out of my reach. I looked out the window at the runway and began to silently weep.

As soon as we arrived in Brisbane, Bruce helped me get the girls to the car in long term parking. Then he returned directly to the airport to fly out again. But this time, thanks to Zoia and the bed-wetting mattress protectors, I was better prepared for the nights to come. I knew that the nightmares would come again, at least for a few days, until Cheyenne and Reesey processed the Sydney visit. I was not looking forward to facing the nightmares alone, but having no choice, I focused on my love for the girls with every cell in my body. The first night back, the three of us endured the girls' nightmares of vicious dogs attacking them.

Anxious to get them back into routine, I dropped them at daycare on Tuesday, as was usual. The girls enjoyed the daycare centre; they had made friends, and I really liked the women who were involved with them. For that Tuesday, my only goals were to unpack, wash the travel clothes, and go grocery shopping. But instead of shopping, I went home. Something had snapped in me and I needed help. But I was ashamed that I wasn't strong enough to keep taking all of the punches that seemed necessary to get through this, and I found myself formulating a suicide plan. I already hated myself for being unable to carry a pregnancy, and this additional weight of feeling like everyone hated me and blamed me for everything... was I just being narcissistic? I didn't know how to figure it out, and although Zoia was wonderful, I was afraid to talk to her. I was afraid that she might think that maybe I really shouldn't be a mother, especially if I was suicidal.

I held the phone for a moment, then dialed a suicide hotline. The call was immediately picked up, automatically putting me on hold. Calming "hold" music played, but my mind began to race. What if they can trace my call? What if they send the police here and take the girls away? I grabbed a piece of paper and a pen and began listing the things to talk about. Okay... Bruce. No. The girls? No... my suicidal thoughts? No, they'll want to know what started it. Infertility? No, talking about that is stupid and won't solve anything. Michelle? Ugh. And then they'll tell me to ignore her, but then I'll say that my husband wants me to keep in contact with her… maybe go from the start? I was becoming more and more agitated, not knowing how I could even start talking.

"Hello," said the sweetest, calmest voice I had ever heard in my life. The man didn't tell me anything about himself, but his voice was so soothing and radiant, that even his voice seemed to save my soul for a moment!

"Hi," I said, my voice suddenly constricted by tears.

"Can I help you with something?"

"Um…" I choked. "It's just… so complicated…" I was overwhelmed, not knowing where to start.

"That's okay," he said gently. "Just take your time." He sounded worried. But a river of complex thoughts silenced my words and I began sobbing.

"I just…" I sputtered, "It's just… So… it doesn't make… sense…"

"It's okay, it's okay…" came the kind voice. He meant it, but I was imprisoned by fear. Fear of Bruce. Fear of Michelle. Fear of disappointing David, Thomas, and even Zoia by taking the girls to Sydney. Fear of losing the girls.

"I'm sorry, I can't," I blubbered and hung up the phone. I felt completely and utterly stupid, standing in the kitchen alone, sobbing. After a time, I calmed down. I was still anxious to do something, *anything* that could free me from the situation. I remembered the divorce lawyer's office that I had Googled and was not far from me. *Who cares about the backstory*, I thought. *I can just say I no longer want to be married and not give a reason*. I was jittering as though I had too much caffeine but was desperate to do something. Anything. I hopped in the car and put the air conditioning on full blast: December's Australian summer was in full swing. As I drove, I breathed in the cool air conditioning and started to actually feel better.

Seriously? I thought to myself, as I pulled in and saw that the offices were closed for the summer. "I am failing at escaping!" I cried out loud to no one. "What am I supposed to do?" Frustrated, and not sure what to do, I spied a small organic fruit and vegetable shop in the same complex. It was too expensive for me to shop there regularly, but I decided to get out and wander through the small selection of fruits and vegetables for a moment as a means of indulging in something different, even if it was utterly lame.

But it wasn't lame. This tiny change in scenery fed my soul and triggered a much needed change in my train of thought. I took my time, caressing smooth, red Anjou pears, comparing them to the rougher skinned Boscs. I looked at the deep reds and blackish purples of the fresh berries and the bright greens and golden yellows of the varieties of kiwi fruits. Rich orange papaya and deep red watermelon beckoned to me with their juicy ripeness, but I only bought a single bottle of cold water before I decided to drive home. It was in this space that I made a decision. A major decision.

Without permission. Without support. Without bouncing the idea around, without making any kind of plan. I made a decision that finally felt *right*.

I drove home and calmly sat at my computer. I opened my e-mail and began a message. "We are ready to file," I typed to David, implying Bruce and myself. *I guess lying is now my thing.* I shrugged internally. But I was done patiently supporting Bruce's conviction of Michelle's claims for eventual adoption help. The process would not be quick. We needed to challenge the guardianship before we could start what might be a very complicated process. "Let's get this done as quickly as we can," I typed. "Please let me know what fees I need to pay. I have a U.S. bank account and can post you a check from here, but it will take about two weeks to get there. I can also send it overnight express or by credit card. Let's go." I signed off, and clicked send without proofreading.

I breathed a sigh of relief. I might have to fight with Bruce, but I was finished taking punches from Michelle. At this stage, starting the adoption process was self-care. So was a shower, a shampoo, and a crispy green apple from the more-affordable chain grocery store. Feeling better, I wanted to process my feelings through writing, so I began typing an e-mail to Kimberly, my American penpal who lived in another state in Australia. It was in my letter to her that I found myself typing the things that I could not say aloud:

I love the girls. I want to be a mother. But this is not worth it. I have been waiting for Bruce to agree to start the adoption. He keeps thinking that if we are friends with Michelle and Trent, then everything will go smoothly. But Michelle doesn't want us as friends—she wants me as her punching bag—she thrives off of the emotional violence. And I can't shake it because I feel like Bruce does not have my back. So I have e-mailed the lawyer asking to start the adoption.

I am home now, and I am trying to shake this all off, but I am struggling. And Bruce is out of town—again—for work. I feel all alone in trying to protect these girls. It is so much that I don't think I can do it anymore. Mostly, I am not okay today. I needed to admit it to someone.

I took a moment, trying to decide if I should press send or not. It felt like if I sent it, I would be releasing some of my pain from my mind, my heart and my body. But I was shaken—dare I trust anyone? Would Kimberly turn on me the same way Bruce did? I moved my mouse over to the "send" icon and pressed it in place, pondering. I breathed, released, and the screen blinked "Message sent."

28

TALKS

To his credit, when Bruce returned home on Friday night, he sensed something was not okay. Whether he knew that I had vacillated between divorce and suicide, or that I had filed for adoption, I could not tell, nor did I care. But he asked Zoia to call me. The conversation with Zoia was helpful, but I was too guarded to share what was really going on in my mind. Her concerned and patient voice made me feel like someone was there for me, and it gave me inspiration to make another challenging phone call.

Ginny was out of jail. I longed to speak with her, but I wasn't sure how to let her know that I had not been able to meet Ruby. I felt like I failed her but arranged for a time that suited both of us to speak.

"Hi," she said, answering my call, rolling the word from her mouth as if in two syllables. I loved her drawl, and it was a relief to hear her friendly voice. Sticking with my decision to not ask about her incarceration, we chatted about Christmas plans, how hard it was to shop for the men in our lives and what I was planning for the girls. She finally asked about my trip to Sydney. "Um… well…" I stammered, then rushed. "Bruce enjoyed meeting your grandma, and I am really glad that the girls were able to meet her as well."

"Did you take any pictures?" she asked.

I paused, then responded. "I wasn't allowed in the house," I said.

"What?"

"Michelle was angry at me for lying about our flight times," I began, and then rushed into the explanation. "Michelle didn't want us to spend any time with her or the girls in Sydney. She treats us like we are only there to drop them off and pick them up from her. And we wanted to spend a little time with Bruce's parents and take the girls to church. So when she found out that we arrived sooner, she demanded that Bruce bring the girls to her immediately—and she threatened to attack me if I went to the house."

"You didn't get to meet my grandmother?" Ginny said, incredulously.

"No," I said, my heart dropping. "I'm really sorry. I just didn't know how to make everyone happy, and I really, really wanted to meet her." I was worried that Ginny would be angry with me and maybe not let the adoption go through.

Instead, she said, "I can't believe Michelle. Christmas is supposed to be about family!"

"I'm really sorry," I said again.

"But Bruce met her?"

"Yes!" I said with enthusiasm. "He gave her a bell I bought for her with koalas on it."

"At least Bruce got to meet her."

"Maybe I can fly back and meet her someplace, I mean, even this weekend?" The offer was genuine, even if it was a little bit crazy.

"You can't. She's already left."

I was crushed. "I'm so sorry," I said, feeling drained.

"It's Michelle," said Ginny, matter-of-factly. "Trent used to go and Skype me so I could talk to the girls, but only when Michelle was away. She blocked me on Facebook, wouldn't e-mail or call. Trent had to secretly call the girls sometimes and have them promise not to tell her."

"Why?" I asked, confused. Ginny was their mother—why would Michelle not want to communicate with her?

"I don't know," Ginny replied with defeat. "It's her. It's just her. What is taking so long with the adoption?"

The question surprised and thrilled me. "Oh, I think it's just paperwork and the holidays," I said, neglecting to tell her that Bruce still wanted to believe Michelle could somehow help us. "I'll send an e-mail to our attorney and ask. Would you like to talk to the girls now?" Within a minute, the girls were taking turns with the phone.

"Hi Mummy Ginny," Cheyenne said dutifully. "Where are you?" (pause) "Where is that?" (pause) "Where is that?" (emphasis changed, and then a pause)"Why are you there?" (pause) "Are you coming for dinner?" (pause) "Why?" (pause) and then, "Okay, bye!" Thanks to my quick hands, the phone wasn't dropped as she ran back to where she was playing.

"Hi," I said again, chuckling.

"She sounds good," said Ginny.

"They're playing and pretty happy," I said. "Let me see if I can get Reesey."

I called for Reesey to take the phone, which, after some cajoling, she eventually did. She began breathing very deeply on the phone. "Say hi," I prompted.

"Hi to who?"

"Mummy Ginny"

"Who that?"

"Tummy mummy."

"Tummy mummy?"

I could faintly hear Ginny speak, and then saw Reesey react. "Who ahh you?" (pause) "Ohhhh…" then I saw her nodding her head.

"Can you say 'yes' to Mummy Ginny? She can't see you nod," Reesey nodded bigger. "Those are very big nods," I said loudly enough for Ginny to hear.

"Love you! Bye!" Reesey said suddenly, thrusting the phone at me, racing out to play.

I giggled and spoke into the phone again. "They're playing very happily," I explained.

"That's alright," said Ginny. "I better let you go to keep up with them."

"Um… one more thing? Bruce promised Michelle that we would leave all of our communication open only for her over the holiday. So we could not call or video call anyone until Michelle had spoken with the girls. No time was set, so the three days of the holiday—Christmas Eve, Christmas Day, and Boxing Day—were set aside for her. So, I would call you, but…"

"I understand," Ginny quickly replied. She shared that she wasn't sure where she would be for Christmas, so it might be better if we spoke again in January. "I'll let you know on e-mail," she promised as we ended the call.

SHERRIE GAVIN

29

CHRISTMAS

As Christmas approached, Bruce was on the road less. That meant I had a little more freedom to shop and more support in doing things like dishes, laundry and Christmas shopping. The shopping centres were crowded with holiday revellers, yet I enjoyed being a faceless member of the public listening to the tinny sound of commercial Christmas songs echoing through commercial loudspeakers.

Though I am a practising Latter-day Saint, the revelry around the glorious fertility of the virgin birth eluded and even annoyed me, as though fertility were a mark of righteousness that I could never be worthy enough to have. Instead, I loved all the songs about reindeer, and Santa, and even though it was Australian summer, a few snow-related songs somehow seemed okay, too. After all, who doesn't love a cookie exchange with sugared, chocolate-dipped, and green-frosted sweets in various shapes and sizes?

The girls and I talked of Santa and good behaviour and all of the things that sparked imagination. We watched classic Christmas animations and new cartoons, played "Santa Claus is Coming to Town" way too often and I loved it. I was able to table my anxiety and focus on the moment, with the understanding that adoption still felt like a long shot and that this might be the only Christmas we would have with the girls.

We even introduced traditions from our childhood. For Bruce's side of the family, I learned to make proper, steamed English pudding, and we discussed adding a sixpence that was traditional for a child to find within the sweet layers of marinated, dried fruit. Since I was a diabetic from such a young age, many of my childhood Christmas mornings resulted in my having a crisis due to dangerously low blood sugar because I was too excited about playing with new toys to stop and eat something! This gave birth to the tradition of each family member being required to eat an entire banana. After the empty peels were collected, we listened for my father to start playing Fred Waring and his Pennsylvanians' Christmas albums, which gave us permission to discover what Santa had brought us.

By Christmas Eve, the pudding was ready, the bananas were poised, and Fred Waring's well-dated music was set and ready to play. I was worried that the girls might be like me when I was a child and have trouble falling asleep on Christmas Eve, but they fell asleep quickly, allowing Bruce and me plenty of time to retrieve the gifts I had hidden. I wrapped enough gifts for there to be a bit of mystery, but not too much paper waste, while friends and family from near and far had generously sent gifts to the girls. Hand made quilts from Georgia, beautiful books from Linda, LEGO Junior sets from Scott and Lori, and pink ladybug t-shirts from Fiona added to the array of treasures.

Thankfully, it was not very late when Bruce and I finished and made our way to bed. Because of the most recent spattering of raw night terrors, I had moved two single mattresses into our bedroom, shoving our bed to one side to create a sleeping space for the girls. It was not roomy, but with this in place, it was easier for me to respond to them at night when they cried out, and also easier for me to get back to sleep afterwards. As I shimmied through the path to my side of the bed, I was so excited to finally share Christmas with children! Thus, I was the one who had trouble falling asleep!

"It's Christmas!" Cheyenne said, jumping up and down. Reesey was more tentative in speaking, but as soon as she saw my smile, she was jumping up and down, too.

"Yes, it is!" I said. Bruce was awake, too.

"Do we get dressed?" asked Cheyenne.

"Nah… maybe Santa brought you some clothes," I said, stretching out of bed.

The girls knew that they were to sit at the top of the stairs, just like I did when I was little, and wait for Christmas music. I fed the girls each a banana while Bruce went downstairs to turn on some Christmas music. "Oh, you're lucky!" called Bruce. "Santa brought you heaps of pressies! Did they eat their bananas?"

"Yes!" they chorused, their entire bodies bouncing with excitement and smiles. Within seconds, the chimes of Christmas music rang out, and poof! The girls were off, rushing down the stairs. I followed, at first trying to photograph everything with my phone but realising within seconds that all I was going to get was a collection of blurs; I decided to forget photos and enjoy the moment instead. Arriving in the living room, I saw the girls standing and smiling, seeming to process everything, but without touching a single gift.

"Cheyenne, look," I said, directing her to a stack of clothes and boxes leaned against part of the couch, "your presents are here, and Reesey," I said, taking her hand, "your presents are here." They both silently looked at the mound of gifts, yet remained immobile and silent. I was a little troubled but pushed on. "Look at this dress," I said, picking up a periwinkle pinafore, complete with sculpted roses in matching fabric. Each girl had received one, and I thought these might be the first things they were drawn to, being in Rapunzel-like colours.

"Whose is it?" asked Reesey.

"Yours!" I said. After a moment, Reesey asked me to help her put the dress on. I did, and Cheyenne asked for help with her new dress as well. After helping Cheyenne, Bruce and I decided to make Vegemite toast, one of their favourite things to eat, to see if that inspired them to look at anything else. Yet there they stood, munching on half slices of toast, just looking at the wrapped boxes. "Don't you want to unwrap some presents?" I asked. After they thought for a moment, they each grabbed a box, and Bruce and I helped unwrap a toy, then another. They seemed pleased, but not overly interested. In fact, neither girl properly opened or removed the packaging. Instead, they sought for old toys to play with.

Bruce and I decided to set an example. We each unwrapped and removed the packaging of a gift we had each received from Santa, but the girls did not seem to notice. I decided to take a moment to myself, to test blood, get dressed and open a can of American-imported diet Dr. Pepper—my personal Christmas treat. I was sad that Bruce banned us from using the phone or the computer in anticipation of Michelle's call. Had that poisoned the day? *Please let this day be okay*, I silently prayed. I didn't know what "okay" entailed, but at that moment, something was off and I could not figure out what it was. I returned to the living room, where everyone was quiet, the girls still looking but not playing with anything.

"Look," I said pitifully, showing them the dolls that had been dressed in dresses I had sewn for them. "Santa didn't want your babies to miss out, so he brought them Christmas dresses, too."

The girls stared at their dolls. "Who do we give these back to?" asked Cheyenne.

I was thoroughly confused. "Well… no… no one. Your babies get to keep their dresses," I explained, then taking a small wrapped present that I had laid by the doll the night before, I asked, "Do you want to help her unwrap these pressies?"

"They can open them?" asked Cheyenne.

"Yes," I said. "They probably need your help, though."

Cheyenne and Reesey began to unwrap the small boxes. They took the doll clothes out and slowly began dressing the dolls. "You can keep all the presents for you…" said Cheyenne sweetly to her doll. Reesey repeated the same words to her doll. Over the next few minutes, I followed Zoia's example of listening to the girls as they played with their dolls. As I listened, I surmised that prior to their coming to live with us, the girls had not received, or been able to keep, Christmas presents. Any gifts from extended family or friends remained in store packaging, then quickly disappeared. "Can they keep it?" Cheyenne asked again and again.

"Well… yes! Your babies can keep the presents Santa gave to them," I said, still processing everything. It finally dawned on me that the girls were overwhelmed that they had more than one present, as well as the fact that they were allowed to open and keep the presents.

For the next hour, Bruce and I gently helped our cherubs unwrap the gifts, one at a time, removing the packaging and tags. Reesey timidly asked if she could put on another dress. I said yes, helped her, and soon she was running at full speed back and forth from the bathroom to keep looking at herself in the mirror. Each time, she would ask us if we noticed different things. "Do you see? It has a little green here!" and "It's *pink!* Pink! Pink! Pink! Pink!" and "Do you see? When I turn, it flies!" she cried, demonstrating that the skirt was long enough to blossom as she spun in a circle. I loved seeing her feel so happy about herself and the way she looked.

Cheyenne kept looking rather than playing with the toys. "Hey Cheyenne," said Bruce. "Can I please play with the furniture for the doll house?" he asked, indicating a box that had been unwrapped but not opened.

"Yes," Cheyenne answered dutifully, yet as though she still didn't understand that it belonged to her.

"Where should I put the bed?" Bruce asked. Cheyenne answered, and slowly, she began to place the doll house furniture in the places she thought it went best. Soon Reesey began to open and gingerly talk to her toys, asking the dolls if they liked the clothes they received for Christmas. As the day went on, we switched the Christmas music off, happily listening to the lyrical chatter of happy children. The day was filled with laughter, discovery, tasty treats, and blowing bubbles, but soon it was time for sleep. The girls dutifully went to bed, smiling and clutching new toys.

"I think I am going to call my mother," I said to Bruce, passively testing the waters on Boxing Day for us, Christmas Day for North America.

"No."

"I can use my computer, and then your computer will be up for the Skype call, and my phone won't be engaged…"

"No!" he said more sternly. "They are the legal guardians. We have to do what they say."

"But they didn't say to not call our own family…"

"But they did say they would call over Chrtistmas." His voice was rising. So was mine. Bruce had called his parents on his work phone on Christmas day, arguing that it was his work phone and not the primary contact for Michelle. His double standard was angering me.

"They didn't call yesterday!" I shouted.

"They might call today."

"Today is not Christmas. Yesterday was."

"In Australia, Boxing Day is considered a part of Christmas," he said in a mocking tone, even though I had lived in Australia long enough to understand that Boxing Day was a part of the Christmas public holiday trinity.

"My phone will still be free… you can answer it."

"*No*. We can't risk it."

CHRISTMAS

I was too angry for words, and the girls had noticed this discussion in all of its sharpness. So I gave up. I didn't call my mother. Or friends. Or anyone. And like the two days before, I stayed within earshot of my phone and computer, waiting for Michelle to make the all-important contact that she demanded, while Bruce called who he liked. In the silence, I wondered if how I was feeling towards him was turning into hate.

Michelle's call never came, neither did a text. There was radio silence between us. I was both angry and relieved at this. Angry that I had not been allowed to call my mother on Christmas, angry that Bruce continued to place me aside with anything regarding Michelle. Yet there was relief. I did not have to pretend I liked her in a false show of friendliness for the girls' benefit, nor did I have to endure her mockings. The best thing was that I was not awoken at night by screams of night terrors, and I did not have to remind the girls that in our house, we don't hit or bite each other. There were more reasons to be relieved than there were to be angry, but the anger was still there.

SHERRIE GAVIN

30

BEYOND THE JANUARY BLUES

The new year came. I did not welcome it, but putting on a smiling face, I soldiered on. The complications of December meant that I had not been able to do some of the things I liked doing for Christmas, which specifically meant that I had not made a gingerbread house. The recipe is one that had taken me years to develop–not too sweet, not too spicy, and not too dry or hard. I wanted to share this tradition with the girls, and who cares about making gingerbread only at Christmas? So in early January, I made two half-sized gingerbread houses and egg white icing. Then armed with leftover candy canes and gumdrops, we had a blast putting everything together, and then quickly bashing it apart. As I liked to say, "food is a biodegradable art form, so it's okay to totally smash it up and throw it away."

Following the gingerbread house party, the girls were back in daycare two days a week, Bruce was travelling for work again, and I was back to visiting Zoia. By this time, I was so used to pretending that I was okay with everything that I didn't know how to start telling Zoia what was going on in my mind—that I did not want to die, but I didn't know how to survive. That each night I fell asleep dreaming of dying of a heart attack the day after the adoption was finalised. So I did not tell her that I felt like everyone was so ready to "throw me under the bus," that I was numb. Nor did I tell her how desperate I was for that damned metaphorical bus to stop running over me and just kill me already.

But I did tell her about my updated version of Hansel and Gretel inspired by gingerbread making. I told her that in my story, both Hansel and Gretel were girls, that they tricked the witch together, and that when they went across the pond on the goose to escape, they found forever parents. Oh, and the witch had a ton of jewels they kept in their pockets to pay for college.

A week following my visit with Zoia, there was a knock at the door. Opening it, I found that Bruce had sent an exquisite bouquet of a dozen dark red, long-stemmed roses, delivered in a perfectly wrapped box, complete with ribbon. I had never beheld such a luxurious bouquet in person, even at my wedding. I placed them on the dining table.

I wanted to like them. I wanted to love them. I wanted to feel like I was loved and alive and happy... but I didn't. In my mind, I suspected that Zoia instructed Bruce to send them to me, sensing that my marriage was in trouble. I have no idea if she did, or if he sent them of his own volition, but I could not bring myself to feel gratitude, or joy or anything. Depression's grip was too firm for me to feel anything at the sight of the blooms, so I stared at the box and the roses inside. *What is wrong with me?* I wondered. I opened the card. "I love you. Love, Bruce." Short and to the point. Usually more than enough, very Bruce.

But not this time. In my mind, accepting these roses meant that everything was okay. That everything was forgiven, and that I was okay with all of the negativity that seemed piled on me. But it wasn't okay. *I wasn't okay.* I was still deeply hurt over everything that happened over Christmas.

I stood silently looking at the roses, wanting to enjoy them and trying not to blame them for symbolising a heartbreak that I wasn't ready to forgive. "What is that?" asked Cheyenne, interrupting my thoughts. "Ooooh!" cried Reesey as she climbed on a chair to better see the roses. Instinctively, I moved to where she was climbing and helped Cheyenne safely into a chair so she could better see them.

"Roses from Daddy," I said, still processing, still hurting. It was a beautiful gesture, but I could not force myself to believe it was truly for me, or even from him.

"Ohhhhh…" said Cheyenne. Both she and Reesey were mesmerised, smelling, touching the velvet petals, gazing at the glorious buds that were larger than their fists. Their smiles disarmed me, and I softened. "Daddy sent them for you," I said, freeing myself from the burden of a forgiveness that I was not ready to extend. After all, everything I was going through was for them, so the roses should belong to them. They were worth it. They were worth all of it.

I thanked Bruce in a text and on the phone with as much emotion as I could muster. "The girls love the roses," I truthfully told him, though my heart was absent. "They are exquisite, thank you so much."

I wondered if Bruce believed me.

31

CASAMIENTO

For most of January, Michelle texted me very little. I suspected that she was busy with her children being home from school for the summer break because as soon as school started in February, the messaging picked up. Every time my phone beeped, my heart began to beat rapidly, and sometimes my mouth became dry. I started to become nauseous just at the sight of my phone. I did not mention the tirades to Bruce anymore. He had stated often enough that I was taking this "for the team," and honestly, I wanted to be able to take all that she was dishing out. But those words kept that cloak of depression buttoned tightly around me. Occasionally, I was able to redirect her by mentioning something from the church website or asking her about a recipe that she quickly agreed she was superior at making. These interactions were shallow, but sometimes they seemed to soften her.

Bruce knew I had asked David to start lining up things to eventually file for the adoption but had not mentioned a word to me about it. Maybe he was so beaten down by Michelle that he was no longer interested in adopting? I could not tell, and I longed to just talk with him. Our anniversary signalled internal permission for me to get a babysitter. The girls didn't do well with babysitters, meaning Bruce and I could have a quick dinner but never a movie or an activity. Nighttime dates were also out; the girls misbehaved, spent the time frightened, and waited up for us, so most of our babysitters were not interested in coming back. In desperation, I asked their Primary teacher from church if she could watch them because at least she had ongoing interaction with them. She agreed.

Our favourite Mexican restaurant opened at 11AM, and we were the first to be seated. As the food and drinks came, we sat and talked about the girls. "Is this worth it?" I tested.

Bruce knew what I was talking about. "I don't know," he responded, much to my surprise. "It seems like it is a lot more work than it is worth."

"Yeah," I replied, not knowing what else to say but also feeling guilty.

"Maybe it isn't worth it." Bruce's voice was soft. He sounded defeated.

"So what if at the end of this, the adoption doesn't happen?" I asked. "I don't want to be in a contract with Michelle and Trent ever again. And I don't…" I stopped, shaking free from the pangs of guilt for a moment. David had warned us that this could be a very long, complicated process. We might need to face Kyle, should he be released from prison, or there was the possibility of his extended family also wanting to adopt the girls, as well as fending off the ongoing threats from Michelle. "It's not that I don't want the girls, I just don't want to…" I paused. "…keep being everyone's punching bag."

"Same," said Bruce, distinctly.

"So what do we do if we file and the adoption doesn't go through?" We had asked Michelle for the girls' passports numerous times, but she never gave them to us and ended up saying she lost them. When Thomas stated that she also told him that she no longer had their passports or their birth certificates, I presumed she had destroyed them, which was a very real and new problem.

"We'll pack them up and drop them off," replied Bruce. "I'd pay for their flights to go back to the U.S., but because they don't have passports, I don't see that happening unless they are deported."

I couldn't believe what he was saying, and I hated that I liked it, but fantasizing an end to this situation felt liberating. "I'd help them to go back to Ginny," I said. "But if the guardianship is intact even with Ginny out of jail, and they are stuck with Michelle, I don't want to give anything to Michelle." I felt cheap saying that. "No toys, clothes, nothing. She'll just sell them or give them all to her kids anyway."

"I agree," said Bruce. "Give them what they gave us—the girls." I felt terrible, but in such a state of poor mental health, my capacity to endure Michelle was spent. In that moment, one on one, I could finally see how much Bruce was hurting, too. That his mental health was waning from the combination of near-constant work travel and Michelle. "And then, we need to go on a vacation. A big vacation."

"A cruise?" I dreamed aloud. "Or Paris? Or Egypt?"

"All of it," said Bruce. "Any of it." There was hope of life after this experience. It might not be the life I wanted with children, but there was life. I still wanted to adopt Cheyenne and Reesey. I loved them, body and soul. But if the adoption did not go through, I needed to know that I had the choice to be free. Communicating with Bruce that morning was a lifesaver. As we got up to leave the restaurant, I removed that invisible suicidal noose I had been wearing and left it at the table.

32

DISCONNECTING AND PHONE CALLS

Since Ginny was out of prison, she was able to connect with David to sign the documents in support of removing Michelle and Trent's guardianship. Removing the guardianship was the first step in preparing to adopt the girls, and she agreed to go to court to testify in favour of us. Even with this miracle, we had another obstacle: the birth father. Kyle was in prison on a three-year sentence, and presuming that Kyle added David to his approved list of visitors, he would go to the prison to inform Kyle of our intent to adopt. David warned us that Kyle might oppose the adoption, but he noted that Kyle's criminal record would make that unlikely.

Fortunately, David was approved to visit, and he went to see Kyle in jail. David reported that Kyle used some foul language, declaring he did not approve of the adoption. When informed that a free attorney could be assigned to him, Kyle did not demand or even request legal representation. Instead, he used curse words to bemoan that, without being given custody of the girls upon his release from prison, he would have no way to support *himself.* In other words, Kyle saw the children as a possible source of public-benefits income for his own needs when he was released from prison.

David later explained that Kyle's refusal to formally support our adoption of the girls was not an impossible hurdle. "The natural parents and the guardians are in the same situation," David explained. "If Kyle, Michelle, or Trent really cared about having the kids, they would have acted much differently," he explained. He further elaborated that the extended family reported that Michelle and Trent only agreed to take the children if their travel to and from the U.S. for their entire family was paid for by someone else. "Continuity of care strongly favors you, which means there probably won't be any opposition to your adoption," added David. "The hard part is dealing with the technical issues— jurisdiction, visas, and notification of the guardians."

Notification of the guardians. Michelle and Trent had been sent documents from David by e-mail and via international post, but they refused to acknowledge they had received anything from him. We did not need evidence that both of them had possession of the documents; we only needed Trent or Michelle to acknowledge that the documents were delivered to them, but David and I were getting nowhere with Michelle. A signature of delivery was not enough; we needed a "yes" reply. In a text. In an e-mail. In a phone call to our attorney. Just one response. Just those three letters: Y E S.

Bruce decided to contact Trent, even though Michelle forbade us from ever speaking to him without communicating with her first. When Bruce phoned Trent, he stated that he had not received any of the court documents but that he would check with Michelle. In the meantime, the girls' biological father, Kyle, suddenly appeared. He must have been released on parole because he came as a "friend suggestion" on Facebook on a weekend when Bruce was at home. Clicking on his Facebook page, I saw a photo of Bruce, Cheyenne, and Reesey. "I am calling out this guy right here," he wrote in the photo description. "If any ya'll see this guy Bruce Gavin, he kidnapped my kids, so you better beat him down. I'm comin for him." He included a foul list of threats of physical violence aimed at Bruce. I had no idea how Kyle gained access to the photo, but the verbal violence frightened me, and I showed it to Bruce immediately.

"Okay," Bruce said, calmly. "We just need to block him and step up our security on Facebook."

"But…" I stammered, "should we call the police?"

"No. I'm not worried about him. He's a felon, and Australia will never let him in the country." I knew this. I also knew that because Kyle was a felon and he was on parole, he could not even leave the state. But I was still shaken. "But what if we go to the U.S.?" I asked, thinking we might have to travel there for adoption court.

"I'm not worried," Bruce said again. "Let's update all social media security now. And let's follow up with Michelle, see if calling Trent made a difference on if she received the documents or not."

I knew this would be my job, so on the following Monday, after I settled the girls in for an afternoon rest in front of the TV, I stepped into another room where I could pace and relieve some tension while speaking to Michelle. "What are you telling Trent?" she immediately demanded, forgoing a greeting.

"We were asking him if he had received the documents," I said simply. "You did not respond to the attorney, so we needed to check."

"*You* are so manipulative," she said, anger in her voice. "We did not give you permission to do any papers."

"Well, we were happy for you to draw up a custody agreement, but it's been almost a year." I responded, reassuring myself that we had the birth mother's support. "So we thought this might help move things along." What I said was true: for months she claimed she was writing up a custody agreement, but it never came to fruition, and when Bruce composed one with all her demands, she ignored it.

"You are lying. That is all *you* know how to do. *Lie*. You're messing up everything."

"What am I messing up?" I asked.

"This is *not* what we agreed to. *You* are destroying everything!" she screamed. "No wonder God never gave you children!" She huffed, then continued. "Ginny abandoned the girls. *That* is how I am their guardian, *not you*. As far as I am concerned, I can call the police at any time and tell them you kidnapped the girls. Do you want that?"

"Of course not," I responded. "But I don't understand..."

"*Obviously* you don't understand. You are not a mother! They are *my* family. If Ginny gets involved, everyone will be hurt. She is *no good* for the girls. She abandoned them. She will mess everything up, and *you* will go to jail for kidnapping. Is that what you want? Because that is what is happening."

"I don't want to go to jail." My mental health, though better, still was not great, and my patience with Michelle had worn thin. With the added threats from Kyle, I was struggling. I breathed in, trying to calm myself for whatever was coming next, a mild swirl of nausea taking over me.

"You are not being honest with me," Michelle fired. "You never have. You try to manipulate me all the time, but I know what is going on. Do you *want* me to turn you into the police?"

"No," I said, feeling myself careening between anger and apathy, trying to focus on the girls. "I only want what is best for the girls," I said, not sure what else to say. As far as depression went, it had been one of my better days until I called Michelle.

Now I was nose diving in a spiral of desolate shadows. I wasn't afraid of the police; I had not done anything illegal that I knew of. However, if Michelle was getting any concessions from the government while the girls were not living with her, she was risking far more than we were. But even with this knowledge, Michelle was still the girls' legal guardian. Not me. I was a nobody.

"IIIII…," she said, stretching the vowel, "am what is best for the girls. *Not you. Tell me* what is going on."

"We are going through the steps to help the visa process for the girls so they can stay in the country legally." This was the truth. They had overstayed their visas, and adopting them would allow us to legally take over their immigration issues, even if I avoided using the term "adoption."

"You're lying! I know you are. You couldn't tell the truth if it hit you in the face."

"We need to know if you have those forms so we can help them," I said. "And we wanted to help move this thing along."

"How am I supposed to believe you?" Michelle demanded. She huffed deeply and muttered "stupid %$!@#" at me under her breath. "I am their guardian. *You* are not. *They are mine. We* have an agreement."

"We don't have an agreement. Did you send us a custody agreement?" I was poking the bear, just a little.

"You need to pay for our attorney to write the agreement," she declared.

I thought that suggestion was ridiculous, especially after all that Michelle had claimed. Did she also think I was going to pay for her to get a lawyer to sue me? By this point, my patience disintegrated into a vaporous haze of hurt and anger. "We barely have enough money to pay for ourselves and what the girls are costing us with immigration as it is," she prattled on as I said nothing. Having been an immigrant myself, therefore familiar with the process, and being in ongoing communication with the Department of Immigration, and mostly because we had not sent any money to Michelle for immigration costs, I was confident that Michelle had no immediate immigration costs. I paced across the floor as Michelle continued to call me names and berate me.

"You don't even care about them," she continued, jeering into the phone, still muttering. Then aloud, "IF you cared about them, *you* would be a better person. You would *try* to be a mother. You think you are soooooo righteous. You're not! Righteous women have children. You can't do that! You can never care about them the way a real mother…"

"*Biiiiiiiiiiiiiitch!*" I screamed, being pushed beyond what I could take. I was speaking as if in slow motion, like that was the longest, loudest, heaviest term ever expelled from a mouth in the history of the world. The word seemed to take a lifetime to travel from the bottom of my soul to the tip of my tongue before splattering itself out as if excrement.

In shock that I had done this, I hung up. The bitter taste of adrenaline raced through my mouth in an instant, making me regret what I had just done. I was tired of being a punching bag and fighting with Michelle was never what I wanted. I wanted to be a mother. I wanted to feel worthy of being a mother. I wanted someone to tell me that I was worthy, and that God loved me, and that infertility is not a curse. I didn't want to have to keep reminding myself of that in the face of Michelle, church culture and everything else patriarchal that deemed birth as womankind's only virtue.

I did not cry or pray. I took another deep breath, and pressed to re-dial Michelle's number. She answered but said nothing. "I am sorry," I said in a slow, clear, deliberate voice. "It is unlike me to say words like that. I do not usually speak that way to anyone. I apologise."

"You don't deserve those girls," came the curt reply, muttering, "@#$%&! loser," under her breath. "How can I trust you to look after them when you treat me like that?"

"I am trying my best," I said wearily, but as Michelle began another diatribe, something in me died. I could not do this anymore. I could not keep "taking it for the team," keep being called unworthy, keep doing whatever it was I was doing right then—

all while dying on the inside. I wasn't even listening to Michelle anymore, nor was I pacing. I was totally numb.

"You aren't good enough," I heard Michelle snap, slapping me to attention. "You are manipulating me and this whole situation! I should take them back."

"Fine," I said. "Come and get them." I meant it. I was done. I wanted out.

"Fine, but then you have to pay for their airfare back," she said matter-of-factly.

"No. We've paid for everything up till now. Come get them. *Now!* I am done."

Michelle, for once, was silent. Then she hung up.

I took a minute to go and check on the girls. They were comfortably resting on fluffy, pink, kid-sized reclinable chairs. Seeing they were well, I sat in the room with them and tapped an e-mail to Bruce that he could read between work demands. I told him about the call, about how I tried to find out if the papers had been delivered. And I shared that I told Michelle to come and get the girls. Within a minute, he called to tell me that he loved me. His words offered a rush of love and gratitude in my heart, waking the numbness that Michelle had beaten into me. I felt safe for the first time since this saga began.

I also felt like a failure. A failure because I could not deal with Michelle any more, a failure because I finally had a chance to be a mother but

I wasn't strong enough to see the whole thing through. I needed stiff advice, so I e-mailed Kimberly, telling her briefly what had transpired, ending with: "Will you think less of me if I give up? Because I am tired of Michelle telling me that God hates me because I can't have children, therefore she is my new God and I must please her in order to keep the girls. I can't do this anymore."

Kimberly's response came quickly and was to-the-point. "If you are worried about what other people will think, I suggest replying with this: 'We were well into the process of adopting them when we discovered that the legalities were such that we simply could not finalise it.' If those same people ask for more information, just reply: 'Giving up the girls was incredibly difficult and sad for me, and I'd really rather not talk about it.' And if those people keep on pushing, they're idiots. Walk away. Hang up. And don't feel bad about it."

Kimberly's words made me smile and gave me the courage I needed to call Mandy. As a police officer, Mandy could tell me if there was possibly anything to Michelle's kidnapping claims, or if we had an obligation to pay for the girls to return to Sydney. I dared not think about actually giving the girls back to Michelle, but I had told Michelle to come and get them—so what if she actually showed up? Since before I met Michelle, I made all of the travel arrangements and carried the expense associated with seeing her. I wanted to be ready in case Michelle showed up on my doorstep.

Mandy was incredibly supportive! She assured me that there was nothing to support any purported kidnapping. "You've not required her to pay you for the care of the children, she has given you no financial support, and asking her to arrange to collect them, if she does, which I don't think she will, is reasonable. Beyond reasonable." I was glad for this news, and muttered that I wished I could file a harassment claim against Michelle. "You know…" Mandy tentatively began, "what Michelle is doing is not harassment. It's actually a nuisance. It is against the Telecommunications Act. It's just harder to prove."[1]

"What would you need to 'prove' a nuisance?" I asked. "You should see some of her texts." I read aloud some of the texts from Michelle.

"Yep, these are nuisance, not harassment," she said matter-of-factly. "But you could still file charges."

"Would that hurt us for the adoption?" I said, sparking back my fire to adopt the girls.

"Well, if you press charges against Michelle," replied Mandy, "You might be able to exhaust her with enough pressure that we could then say to her that you will drop the charges if admits she has the papers."

"I'm in," I said without hesitation. Mandy explained that in most cases, because a nuisance claim did not include threats of physical violence against me, and that her behaviour was not causing financial loss, it was not classified as harassment.

But because it wasn't a source of physical or financial danger, it was also less common for police to pursue it. "But I could call and speak with her about it," she added. "If you decided to file the charges, though, you'll have to be on top of the police to make sure they see it through."

"Really?" I gasped.

"Actual 'nuisance' charges would fall to the police in her local area," Mandy added. "And I could file a formal complaint, but as it would be a complaint from out of her area, it's even less likely that Michelle's local police would do anything."

"You would call her?" I ignored the impracticality of the complaint and focused on the fantasy that someone might tell Michelle to stop texting me such hatred.

"Yes, I could do that for you." she said with generosity. "But that isn't my area of police work at the moment. If you filed a nuisance complaint, another department would do the official call and the paperwork."

"Okay," I said. "So should I even bother? Who would I call?"

"I can make the phone call," she said. "And I'll make a record of the text messages. Depending on her response to the call, we can decide if it is worth it to file a nuisance complaint. I can do it from your place. I'm not working today; do you want to do it now?"

Within the hour, Mandy arrived with her daughter. I had dinner ready, and as soon as the girls were happily engaged, Mandy collected herself, sat up straight and transformed right in front of me. No longer was she the chatty mother who shared favourite TV shows and family meal ideas with me; she was a seasoned police professional. Her taut back was strong and her eyes seemed to narrow, invoking an invisible cloak of expertise that wrapped her and the entire room in power. I was in awe. She dialled the number, her phone on speaker. "Is this Michelle?"

"Yes?"

"This is senior constable Mandy Katene from the Queensland Police Service. I am calling you regarding a nuisance claim for text messages you have sent to Sherrie Gavin." She was a crackerjack cop in absolute charge of this phone call, and I loved it!

"Yes," said Michelle in a meek voice I had never heard her use before.

"I've seen some of the texts you've sent to Sherrie. Can you tell me about that?"

I slipped in and out of the room as we had agreed. In the living room, I was serving seedless watermelon slices and thinly peeled and sliced carrot sticks. In the office nook, I was cheering for Mandy in anxious silence. "Have you received the court documents from the Gavins?" Mandy asked, and after a pause, "I can e-mail them to you; would that be acceptable?"

As Mandy's conversation progressed, I heard Michelle crying off and on. She asked Mandy to explain what the documents meant. She asked if she was going to be arrested for giving the children away. She asked if she had to go to the U.S. for the court date to remove her from guardianship. This response surprised me! I had guessed that Michelle had no actual legal expertise, but being so emotionally beat up by her threats and derision, I neglected to understand how terrified she was about getting into trouble. Of how frightened she was about having to go to court in the U.S. and how alarmed at thinking she might have to pay for travel to the U.S. and back.

Mandy took her time with Michelle, explaining to her that she did not have to go to court in person. She explained that the documents were relieving Michelle and Trent of guardianship and thereby their financial responsibility for the girls, and that doing this would cost her nothing. Mandy suggested some free legal services if Michelle needed help to understand the documents. She then asked if Michelle had received the court documents. Michelle said, "Yes." Michelle asked Mandy if she would e-mail the documents *again* "to make sure they were the same ones the lawyer sent."

It was a solid thirty minute phone call, but as Mandy finished the call, she had a huge grin on her face. I stood in shock, amazed and so grateful for Mandy that I could not form words. Unbelievably, better than a nuisance claim, we had an admission that Michelle had received the documents. Mandy was a miracle!

CHAPTER NOTES

1. Telecommunications Act 1997, Australian Federal Register of Legislation, No. 47, 1997. https://www.legislation.gov.au/C2004A05145/latest/text

33

COURT DATE

Our first court date to remove guardianship from Trent and Michelle inched closer. Thankfully, since Mandy's call to Michelle a month earlier, Michelle was no longer texting me hateful threats. I did not want to cease all communication with her, so sent short, kind texts on occasion. Sometimes she replied that she was too busy for me, but more often than not, there was no response.

By the time the court-appointed time rolled around, it had been a year since that fateful night when I first met the girls. David informed us that there was no need for us to attend since this first step was not a petition for adoption. However, Ginny completed her penal sentence and volunteered to appear and testify that the girls were no longer living with the guardians and that she had been denied communication with the girls when they were in the care of Michelle and Trent, things that were both in violation of the original guardianship order. We asked friends to pray or think good thoughts on behalf of our application. In many adoption cases, this step in the adoption process can sometimes be waived, but with our immigration situation, having the guardianship removed positioned us in a stronger place to apply for visas. Many people wished us well in texts and messages, but one dear *Exponent* sister, Alisa, was especially in tune to my state of mind:

> *Sherrie, I have been and will be keeping you and the girls in my prayers. I am 150% on your side and hoping that you will prevail. I also think that yes, you need to do what is right for you, to fight for what is best for you and the girls, but not to run a triple marathon at a sprinter's pace—which is impossible. I hope/feel that this will work out for you, but no matter the outcome, I will be here for you.*

> *I feel I need to give you this blessing: May the guardian angels for you and for these girls ease the path and make the way for this adoption. May you be aided by unseen forces for good, for clarity, for love. May you be blessed with strength, and love, and support during these next few weeks especially. May you find some peace and rest in the eye of the hurricane. May the Spirit be able to take these obstacles and clear them out of your path. May you be blessed*

in every way. May you know of your worthiness of love and belonging. Sending my love, all day and always.

I burst into tears reading Alisa's words, overwhelmed by her words of love. I had many messages of love and support, which I carried with me as we awaited the first court ruling.

The e-mail from David with the ruling was short and sweet. He confirmed that Kyle, who had been recently paroled, was informed of this in-person court hearing in the U.S. state where the guardianship was awarded, but he did not attend. Ginny was there. Miraculously, the guardianship was removed! Michelle and Trent were no longer legally responsible for the girls. But this also meant that the girls' custody was somewhat ambiguous; Ginny and Kyle are the biological parents, so custody would traditionally fall to them in the state where the guardianship was first put in place upon the biological parents' incarceration in that state. However, as neither Kyle nor Ginny were allowed to leave this same U.S. state where they were both parolled, and since the girls were in Australia and no longer had passports, no one was in a position to travel. Thus, the girls would simply be remaining with me and Bruce as friends. However, our "friendship" with the girls was recorded in the court, and on a very positive note, Ginny confirmed on record that she was in favour of Bruce and me adopting the girls. Step one was accomplished.

Soon after this hearing, a separate court date was set for the adoption. I was sorely disappointed to learn that it was six months away. It felt like a lifetime! That meant that for six months, we simply had the girls living with us without any kind of legal security. Without any legally recognised relationship to the girls, this meant we also could not get new passports issued for them, nor could I enrol Cheyenne in preschool. We were facing six months of purgatory.

The *Exponent* bloggers responded with words of support, but I particularly appreciated the note from Holly, which read, "This is one of those things where the best option for everyone is just. so. obvious. that any sort of delay feels like torture even for someone just watching the process from afar." Holly's words were testament of the support we had, which I seemed to more frequently forget in my depressed haze. But I was not alone in carrying this burden. With her words, and the words of so many others, I felt more hopeful in the days following. We were on track and in a good position for adoption, and we could start working directly with immigration rather than anonymously.

Still, one cannot apply for a visa for two children who are in no way related to them. In many ways, we were still treading in unknown waters, hoping not to drown.

34

THE LAND OF THE LONG
WHITE CLOUD

"Why don't you go on a trip?" suggested Bruce one weekend when he was home.

"Me?" I asked. "Where?"

"Anywhere. Without the kids. Spoil yourself."

"I'll think about it." I felt guilty indulging myself with a trip. Usually spoiling myself meant stealing away for an hour once a month for a pedicure, sometimes girls in tow, where I read stories from a children's book to the entire salon. I was thankful that no one ever complained and even seemed to listen while I read. I surmised they wanted to hear my American accent more than they wanted to hear stories about baby animals, which were the girls' favourites. Bruce and I spoiled ourselves every now and again by walking a few blocks, with the girls in a double pram that we had been given, to Baskin-Robbins for ice cream. The girls quickly learned that they liked the look of the pink gelato, but they preferred the taste of plain vanilla or chocolate. And even though they liked ice cream cones the best, I always ordered a bowl for myself so I could take the pink plastic spoon home and wash it, adding it to our increasingly colourful cutlery collection.

But mostly, the girls had become my life. The idea of going away without them was uncomfortable, and I worried. Lately, I would sometimes wake in the middle of the night and discover that Cheyenne was not on her fully made mattress in my bedroom. I would find her sitting at the top of the stairs, seemingly wide awake, staring at the front door. In gathering her and putting her back in bed, she would call for me, and I would rock her, telling her I was there and that I loved her. She would eventually fall into a deep sleep, releasing whatever demons had been clinging to her. The following mornings, she never remembered what had happened.

Bruce headed out for work that week, and I was alone again with the girls, trying to keep life in routine. But I was tired, and, if I admitted it, I was burned out. One night, I fell asleep between the girls' mattresses on the floor, only to wake thirty minutes later completely alone. The girls had waited for me to fall asleep, then slipped downstairs to the living room to play. I was not happy. I was irate. "Get up to bed!" I bellowed.

At first, the girls giggled to each other like they were caught in a game. This made me even angrier! How dare they? Didn't they know how hard I was trying to protect them? Didn't they understand how poorly I had been caring for myself? I was suddenly out of control, trying to assign the ability to reason to them. "*Why* are you up?" I growled.

"We wanted to play," came Cheyenne's teary response.

"Play? *Play*? It's bedtime! What about *you*?" I jeered at Reesey.

"I don't want to sleep," she said. Her voice was frightened. I was disengaged from what was really going on: I was a mess of exhaustion, stress and declining health. My mind was racing; I wanted to scream at the court judge for making us wait for six more months, and I wanted to punch Michelle for everything she had put me through.

I wanted to hurt someone as much as I was hurting—and there, right in front of me, were two little children. Two little misbehaving children. Thoughts of spanking them came to my mind. I wanted to use them as the scapegoats for all of the hurt I was feeling. I knew this was irrational, and yet there I was, pulsing with anger, exhaustion, and vehemence. How dare they rob me of more sleep? How dare they sneak downstairs? Those two cherubs stood shaking in fear. *Fear of me.* I knew that hitting a child was selfish and wrong, and yet that was all I could think to do at that moment.

I did not want to hit the children. But I did not know what else to do! My mother hit first, sometimes asked questions later, leaving me resentful, hurt, and angry for years because of what I felt was unjust. Yet in my raw state, this was all I could process, the same childhood violence I had endured. "Get upstairs *now!*" I shouted. They quickly obeyed, tears of fear running down their faces.

I followed them to the front of the bedroom we shared. "*Stay here,*" I barked, turning away, not sure where I was going. I marched back down the stairs, desperate for an answer. *Redirect, redirect, redirect*, I kept chanting to myself. Was I supposed to redirect my own thoughts? How? Redirect them from playing? Well, that was done, they aren't even thinking of playing, they are terrified. *Of me.* I walked into the kitchen and began opening cupboards, searching for something, but I didn't know what! I was searching, searching, searching, trying to redirect my own mind. Trying to redirect me and my terrible behaviour.

I felt crazy, and I hated it. I hated myself for wanting to spank them. I hated myself for being so angry over something that twelve months earlier I might have thought was funny. I didn't know what to do, so I continued opening and closing cupboards, again and again, my mind racing, trying to find something that would "fix" this situation. I finally opened a high cupboard over the fridge and spied a family size bag of M&Ms. Grabbing it, I walked out of the kitchen and slowly paced up the stairs. I still didn't know what I was doing, but it seemed that on some level, whatever was going to happen would involve M&Ms.

The girls were still standing there, shivering in fear. *Help me, God*, I prayed in my heart. *Help me stop this, help, please, please… help… help me stop me…* I was afraid of my feelings, afraid of what I might do, and at a loss. Thoughts of *don't reward them for bad behaviour* raced through my mind, but I was beyond parenting. I was in survival mode. The girls stood shaking in fear, giving themselves to me. They were ready for me to grab them and start swinging my open fist on their behinds. They had been at the mercy of other adults who were not resistant to hitting. They knew that look in an adult's eye; they knew that frustrated anger in an adult voice typically meant violence. *I hated that they could see it in me.*

I looked at the bag of M&Ms. I ripped open a corner of the bag. This confused them; they stood, still vulnerable, mouths gaping. I poured some M&Ms in my hand. "Close your eyes," I commanded. Reesey was too afraid, but Cheyenne obeyed. I had believed for a while now that she likely took Michelle's punches on behalf of her baby sister. "Open your mouth," I spoke. She obeyed. I showed an M&M to Reesey, then placed it in Cheyenne's mouth. "Okay, what colour M&M is that?"

Cheyenne opened her eyes. A tiny smile began to creep across her face. Reesey looked at Cheyenne like they had just won the lottery. They began hugging each other and jumping. They were so very cute in their jammies. "C'mon," I said, my voice starting to return to normal. "What colour?"

"Red?"

"Nope. Orange. Try again."

She laughed, closed her eyes and opened her mouth. This time it was green.

"Brown?"

"Nope!" I said.

Reesey giggled. "It was green," she squealed. "Green one!"

"Reesey, you try!" Cheyenne giggled.

We moved back into the bedroom and pushed the mattresses on the floor together. The mattresses were fully made, with sheet protectors, bed wetting protectors, cartoon sheets, pillows and blankets. It was comfortable—comfortable enough for me to fall asleep. We all laid front down, leaning on our elbows. For the next twenty minutes, we took turns trying to guess the colours of the M&Ms based on how they tasted. "There used to be an ad on TV when I was little that said, 'M&Ms make friends,'" I shared. "Can we be friends even after I yell, even when you should be in bed?"

"You're my mummy, not my friend," said Reesey.

"You can be both," said Cheyenne.

"Okay," I said, "I'll be both. But I think I'll mostly be the mummy."

"'Cause you *are* the mummy," agreed Cheyenne.

"You can be a little girl sometimes," said Reesey. "But only in games." I smiled. Later than I preferred, after a few bonus hugs and kisses, but with a significantly happier feeling, the girls settled and went to sleep. I went downstairs and turned off all the lights. I checked my blood sugar, took a dose of insulin to combat the sugar in the M&Ms, and returned to the bedroom. I knelt down and silently prayed with all my heart, thanking God for intervening. Thanking God for M&Ms. Thanking God for the girls. Praying to be their mother, but ending my prayer by giving myself to God's will, whatever that might be.

As soon as the game started, the mood changed. It took a millisecond. But that millisecond was a miracle. A miracle that I needed. I needed to be reminded that this was all for the girls, and they deserved it. I needed to redirect my thoughts. The next morning, I searched for the least expensive flights I could find, to anywhere. Self care was on the menu! I did not trust myself to drive based on my ongoing fatigue. To my surprise, I quickly found that the best bargain priced flights were to New Zealand. Obviously New Zealand is another country, but because of its proximity to Australia, and the super friendly border, flights there were often classed as "local" on bargain travel websites. I had never been to Wellington, the federal capital of New Zealand, located on the southwestern tip of the North Island. I booked the flight and a shuttle service to a small hotel that included breakfast in the price. It was within walking distance of the Te Papa National Museum, and why not see a giant squid as a part of self-care?

Bruce arranged to work locally and hired a babysitter the girls knew to help him over the weekend and all day on Monday. Within a handful of days, I found myself in a 19th-century building that was converted into a hotel. The entry level consisted of a check-in area and a pub that promised to provide scrambled eggs in the morning. I found a tiny elevator that was just large enough for me and my carry-on suitcase and a narrow, zig-zag stairwell that consisted of creaky, unevenly spaced steps. I surmised that the building was heritage-listed, allowing for the narrow, "rabbit warren" floor plan that led to my tiny room.

Each step in this hotel seemed shrouded in a history that was unknown to me and yet connected me to generations of those who had been here before. Aged, colourless photos of the building from years past graced the hallways, reminding me that I was just one of hundreds of people who had passed through these hallways. Everything inside and out of my room was framed in dark wood, with high ceilings and single-paned windows that needed to be hand-wound to be opened. The room itself was small and simple, barely large enough for the full-sized bed. There was a bar fridge positioned like a bedside table and a desk with a TV. The bathroom had no room for a towel rack but a tightly placed chair solved the problem.

I felt like I was disappearing into another time, perfectly squirrelling myself away from thoughts of Michelle, bed-wetting and court. I visited the local grocery store for some of New Zealand's brilliant apples, plus some yoghurt, salads and disposable utensils, then went back to my room and slept.

I suddenly woke up around 2AM. It was about that time most nights when I was roused awake, sometimes for the second or third time. It felt strange to not be answering the call of a child. But within moments, I was asleep again, even deeper than before. Rising very late, I had breakfast when it was nearly time for lunch, then walked to Te Papa. I lost myself in looking at enormous Māori wood carvings, intricate weavings and passionate sculptures. I loved examining the quilts of early British migrant women and the woodcraft of the early British migrant men. The squid and other marine life exhibitions were a little creepy to me, but cool. And the whole time, I was thinking of how much more fun it would be if I was sharing this with Reesey, Cheyenne, and Bruce.

The second night, I video-called Bruce and the girls. The conversation was light and cheery, and they offered giggly conversation. The babysitter, Fiona, was helping Bruce and doing a magnificent job. Cheyenne and Reesey were wearing fancy pink dresses, and Fiona had French-braided their short locks, something I was not skilled enough to do. "You look beautiful," I gushed at Cheyenne. "I know!" she surged back, watching her image on the screen rather than mine. The adults in the background giggled.

A day later, I arrived home. I craved time with Bruce and missed him dearly. I didn't realise how much I missed him until I was well rested enough to process the fact. There wasn't much I could do but to be grateful for the much needed rest and change of scenery. Especially since Bruce left for the airport for work just minutes after I walked in the front door.

35

TURNING PINK

The weekend following my return, Mandy was scheduled to work especially late, so she asked if we could look after Mali for her. I jumped at the opportunity, grateful to have a chance to try to repay all of her generosity, plus Mali was a delight. The girls played together well, which took some of the entertainment pressure off of me. After a busy afternoon of playing every game imaginable, Mali, Cheyenne and Reesey were fast asleep by the time Mandy finished her shift. She silently scooped Mali in her arms without awakening any of the girls, returning to her own home.

The next morning, both Reesey and Cheyenne noticed that Mali had forgotten a doll. It was a baby Cinderella. "Mali forgot her baby," whispered Cheyenne in reverence when she found the doll. Reesey looked on in appreciative awe.

"I don't think Mali meant to forget her baby," I said, sensing Cheyenne was processing something.

"Can I hold her?" Reesey asked.

"Very gently," Cheyenne said, delicately passing the doll to Reesey.

"Oh, we'll return her to Mali, don't worry," I assured, curious about the way they were acting. They played for the entire day with the doll, taking turns in a way that was new. I began to notice that they both were especially tender and spoke very gently to this doll. And everytime we prayed, either to bless the food or at bedtime, both Cheyenne and Reesey thanked God for having the opportunity to look after "Mali's baby." These were not simple additions to the prayers, but heartfelt, clearly whispered words of sincere gratitude.

Mandy and I communicated about the doll, and because it was one of Mali's favourites, we planned to get it back to her. "I don't want to give her back," Cheyenne said.

"But Mali is her mummy. We can get you a Cinderella baby."

"No," said Reesey. "She forgot her. I want to be her real mummy." Suddenly I understood a part of what they were processing. But I did not know what to do other than to "redirect."

"Well, maybe the Easter Bunny will bring you a baby Cinderella…" I suggested, but the girls ignored me, playing and looking after the doll until Mandy came. They were gentle, playing very well together and talking to each other about what the doll would like best.

That night as I tucked the girls in bed, Reesey asked, "If Mali loves her baby, why did she forget her?" I knew right then that Reesey was not asking about the doll. Cheyenne was also listening intently.

"I think Mali is a very good mummy," I started, trying to formulate an idea. "And Mandy took Mali home when Mali was asleep, so she could not check to make sure that Cinderella baby was with her. So she didn't forget her. She loves her. And she trusts you! She trusted you to look after her!"

"But mummies who don't want their babies can't get them back," said Cheyenne firmly.

"Well," I paused, speaking in a peaceful and loving tone. "Mali wanted her baby. And she is a good mummy." I took a breath. "Sometimes mummies have babies that they can't look after for a day, or a week, or longer. But they learn to, and they get them back. Sometimes mummies have babies, but they know someone can better look after the baby than they can. Even though there are different kinds of mummies, the thing they all have in common is how much they love their babies."

"Really?" asked Reesey.

"Uh-huh. There are other Cinderella babies out there who don't have mummies who want them. We can adopt those babies and bring them home." Then I added, "I think the Easter Bunny knows who they are."

Cheyenne still wasn't convinced. "Real mummies don't leave babies even when they are asleep," she said. I did not know how to respond but shushed her to sleep, telling her I loved her. As I rocked her, I revelled in the natural fragrance of her gorgeous hair. I loved her honest smile, and the way she smeared food she liked all over her face. I loved that she called me "mummy" and that she called out for me when she was afraid. I loved her and Reesey in a way I had never before experienced love.

As I sat in the quiet of the dining room folding laundry that night, I tried to figure out what was going on inside my head. Why did I not believe the voice that I had heard on that first night that I met the girls? Why was I still so uncertain and so… full of doubt about parenting? I thought about all of the times we had submitted ourselves to IVF, where I allowed myself to imagine being a mother.

I came to the conclusion that somewhere, deep inside of me, I believed I would be a bad mother. Perhaps that is why I was never able to succeed at IVF? Because I believed I would be a bad mother? I knew better than this, but the months of disparaging texts from Michelle had made me question myself, my worth, and my ability. The question for that moment was, did I still believe this about myself? I was always praying to be "a good mother," but nothing seemed to be changing or answering that prayer. Unless… maybe, just maybe, I was a good mother? And maybe being a "good mother," wasn't the best goal, or even the best prayer. Maybe I should pray to be a *better mother*. Better than I am. Maybe I had the "good mother" part down, but I could become an ever better mother. Before I slipped in bed that night, I prayed exactly for that. To be a *better mother.* To do a better job parenting. To be a better wife, a better person, a better human being.

I held this concept in my heart for the next day, giving myself permission to be a *good mother,* with the goal of being an even better mother. I wanted to be *the* mother of Cheyenne and Reesey.

By the end of yet another busy day, I was too tired to make dinner, so packed the girls in the car and headed to a local drive thru. As we drove back, kid's meals in hand, I offered a question: "Cheyenne and Reesey, is there anything I can do to be a better mother to you?"

"No," said Cheyenne plainly and immediately.

"Are you sure?" I asked, glancing at them in the baby view mirror that was clipped under the rearview in the car. "Because if there is something I could do better, to be a better mummy for you, I want to try. I might not do it, but I want to try."

There was a pause. "You could wear more pink," said Cheyenne. Her response startled me. The simplicity of her answer was brilliant, and I loved it.

"Yeah, pink!" agreed Reesey.

"You don't wear pink very much," concluded Cheyenne. "More pink clothes and you'll be a better mummy."

"Okay," I said. I knew I could do this.

That night, I posted this "pink" conversation on Facebook, adding a quick question at the end asking where I could purchase pink clothes. I had been wearing dark blues and blacks for so long, with the occasional tan or khaki slacks, and as of late, having been in only the toddler section of clothes stores, I couldn't say if and where adult-sized pink clothes could be found.

"You need to make this girl's dream come true!" commented a friend from high school. "Get your pink on!"

"I saw some lovely things at Chermside," commented another.

"How do you not have anything pink?" added another, finishing with "LOL."

A few days later, I dropped the girls at daycare and headed to the mall, spoiling myself with a modest budget for new clothes. I came home with pink trousers, several pink t-shirts, pink nail polish, and pink pyjamas. But mostly, I came home with a pink heart. My heart had begun to blacken with hardness from stress, hurt, resentment and anger. I decided, again, on that day that I was in. *All in.* Every cell in my body, every hair on my head, and every thread on my figure—especially the pink ones—were all committed:

These girls were going to be my daughters. Even if it killed me.

36

MOTHER'S DAY FOR NON-MOTHERS

After a short lull following Mandy's phone call
and the court hearing, Michelle began texting me
again with as much vengeance as ever. Her messages
caused my phone to buzz wildly at all hours with
hateful messages that warped me into an ongoing
state of depression. We also heard through Ginny's
extended family that Kyle was making claims about
how he would confront Bruce and me at the next
court appearance to stop us from adopting the girls.
His reports were punctuated with additional threats
of physical violence, matching Michelle's threats of
calling the police on me if I did not text her back
quickly enough.

Increasingly weary, I kept restricting and
blocking social media accounts while bracing myself
for a long absence of Bruce. His work needed him
to be in Canada for six weeks, maybe more, and
Canada was just too far for him to come home on
weekends. This meant he would also be away on
Mother's Day.

Even at the best of times, Mother's Day was a depressive trigger for me, so I worked to concoct a plan for my emotional survival. Bruce's mother was newly diagnosed as being in the early stages of dementia, so rather than sit at home alone, I decided to make the day all about her. Within a day, I organised a budget trip to Sydney. I never planned to tell Michelle and decided months ago I would never send her anything again, especially not a Mother's Day gift like I did the year before. Besides her obsession with cyberbullying, I was not sure of her latest address. Though she had restricted me on Facebook, I caught a public post from someone else on her page, inviting others to help her move. I could not help but wonder if she was being kicked out for not paying rent again or if this was a rational choice. She remained tight-lipped in regard to anything really going on with her, Trent and their children but generously continued to deliver coldhearted texting tirades to me in what felt like a never-ending cycle.

Being now more familiar with road trips with kids, I planned stops along the ten hour drive. The first stop was at The Macadamia Castle, where there was a petting zoo, children's play equipment, and a copious variety of macadamia products. The girls loved everything but the macadamias and played hard, exhausting their energy. After another drive and a night at a motel, we stopped at Coff's Harbour, a marine park complete with penguins, dolphins, whales and other sea animals. Spaced throughout the day were shows involving the animals where we hand-fed fairy penguins, learned about crabs and whales and played on statues of dolphins. Because I chose to drive on a weekday, mid school term, there were no lines and ample seating everywhere. We even enjoyed a kiss from a dolphin.

The next day, we drove the rest of the way to Sydney. The girls seemed okay, but knowing we were headed for Sydney may have triggered them, and they were unsettled. This disturbed my father-in-law, who was worried about my mother-in-law and not interested in managing rambunctious toddlers. Sensing everyone's anxiety, including my own, I took the girls on a day trip to Canberra, the capital city of Australia. It was here where they nearly ran free within the safety of the National Museum through numerous interactive displays that perfectly entertained and engaged toddlers. Returning to Sydney that evening and through the following days, I kept busy with shopping, cooking and cleaning up after all meals, well aware that as my mother-in-law declined, my father-in-law had to take on all of the cooking and shopping—things he had never done regularly before. Hard work helped to fend off my internal Mother's Day demons, but Cheyenne had been unsteady and animated in dealing with her own Sydney triggers. She was having night terrors about seeing "Old Mummy," which deprived her of real sleep and made her even more cranky and disagreeable.

On the Saturday morning before Mother's Day, an old friend of my father-in-law's who had stopped in to say hello stated that he had no patience for Cheyenne. In a glowering voice, he added his own parenting advice, aimed at me. "You know, a swift…" he made a hitting motion, "would set her right."

"Well, that's not my thing," I said, brushing off his suggestion.

"Just once will do the trick," he said, his scowl steady. I wondered if he was reflecting my father-in-law's feelings. After all, the house had been sterile, tidy, and quiet before we arrived. It was most certainly not that way now, though I had tried to keep up with everything. The stress about my mother-in-law's declining health was palpable, so I could not help but wonder if he was holding a grudge or had shared with his friend about when Cheyenne told him, "I hope you drive off in a car and crash and die."

"I am not a fan of corporal punishment," I said, feeling a little cornered.

"A decent mother would make sure they are disciplined." He was beginning to raise his voice.

"I'm not their mother," I said. This was true, and I was in no position to fight with him while managing my Mother's Day issues and trying to support Cheyenne as she battled her own abandonment triggers. "And I don't hit children, mine or not." He looked at me, shocked, but left me alone. I was glad to see him depart shortly thereafter

and moved quickly to lay the dinner table with food
that I hoped everyone would like, and I earnestly
hoped might change the mood of the house. The
evening passed, and by the time the girls were in
bed, everyone seemed more at ease.

The next morning was Mother's Day. I rose
and fed the girls, then dressed them for church. My
in-laws were not members of the Church of Jesus
Christ of Latter-day Saints, so they stayed at home
while I went to my beloved and familiar Sydney
congregation. In many ways, the ward I attended
here felt like my "home" ward. But, as with most
wards, the membership changes, so in addition to
familiar friends, there were new and unfamiliar
faces as well. One of those was the new bishop, who
had taken the Mother's Day dominant speaking
position. As he began speaking, I found his talk
to be everything that made me uncomfortable
about Mother's Day in church. To my mind, this
was a disaster! He seemed to beam as he recited
vintage ideologies of womanhood equalling
motherhood, and of women being incomplete
without motherhood. He sobbed as he professed his
wife's miraculousness during childbirth and bore
his witness to the greatness of biological mothers.
It sickened me, and I regretted choosing to attend
church at all. My attempt at running away from
Mother's Day seemed to land me in a fiery pit! In
my mind, the bishop's words were constructed
with sharp, verbal toothpicks which, though weak,
still sparked and burned with a kind of clichéd

kindling that combined into a smouldering mess of presumptive fertility gaudiness, steadily puffing poisonous, privileged smoke directly at me.

As I began to allow this bishop's words to pull me into an abyss of self-hate and an internal sense of worthlessness, I sharply reminded myself that this day was about my mother-in-law, not me. Was it me doing this reminding, or was it the Spirit? I could not tell, but I was grateful for the redirection, which lightened me. But the meeting still had a chunk of time to go. To endure, I chose to shroud myself in a tightly woven cocoon of apathy. In this emotional swaddling, my heart refused to hear anything but the voices of the girls who I wanted as my daughters, who were playing quietly beside me in the church pew. Nothing else mattered. Nothing! As I relaxed, the words of Elder David A. Bednar popped into my mind:

> Sometimes in a sacrament meeting talk or testimony, we hear a statement like this: "I know I do not tell my spouse often enough how much I love her. Today I want her, my children, and all of you to know that I love her." Such an expression of love may be appropriate. But when I hear a statement like this, I squirm and silently exclaim that the spouse and children should not be hearing this apparently rare and private communication in public at church![l]

Thinking of this bishop's message as a private communication to his wife, for whom he was righteously grateful, I tuned his words out completely and engaged in my own academic thoughts. I recalled researching the history of Mother's Day years earlier, where I discovered that the 1907 founder, Anna Jarvis, publicly tried to rescind the holiday because of its falsely prescribed religiosity and commercialization.[2] I wondered when the Church of Jesus Christ of Latter-day Saints first started including Mother's Day in Sunday chapel services and made a mental note to "look that up some day." I further wondered if second-wave feminism in the United States had somehow timed and partnered with Mother's Day as a means to bolster motherhood theology as an anti-suffrage alternative. I mused at the silliness of a non-religious holiday being so wholly embraced by the church, possibly as an attempt by the patriarchy to placate women into a specific mould. After all, the commercialised world of mass-produced cards and flower shops brought Mother's Day to church, not the other way around.

With no academic research stockpile on hand in that chapel pew, I could only continue to muse, comparing it to Father's Day in Australia, which fell on the first Sunday in September. This meant that fast-and-testimony meetings always occurred in preference to Father's Day unless local ecclesiastical leaders gave permission otherwise. "Australian men are so lucky to not have to sit through Father's Day church services," I thought to myself. The girls were beginning to squirm, so I opened the "Mother's Day" gifted candy package that had been handed to me upon entering the chapel. I gave the candy to the girls, holding a finger to my lips to symbolise "quiet." They smiled and happily ate.

During the closing hymn, I suggested to the girls that we should go shopping and pick out a movie for the upcoming long drive home. They agreed. As soon as "Amen" was breathed, we were moving out of the pew before the first note of parting music was struck. I did not introduce myself to the bishop. I didn't even say hello to old friends. I had partaken of the sacrament, and that was more than enough on such a difficult day.

While shopping on Sundays isn't my preference, on that day, it was the best way to fill my mind with bright cartoon colours, songs of joy and happy endings. We also bought donuts.

That evening, I presented Madelene's favourite dinner of baked beef and vegetables with a homemade cake for dessert. When the time came, Mother's Day gifts were laid in front of my mother-in-law. It was all about her, and this made me happy. Amongst the gifts were hand-made cards from the girls, a set of DVDs that Bruce noted his father wanted, and a bracelet I had engraved "with love from your granddaughters." It was a risky gift, but with dementia, I decided that it would not matter if the girls were not permanent. Her eyes welled with tears as she read the engraving on the bracelet. She clasped her hands over mine. "Thank you," she said, clearly and with much emotion. Then deliberately, to me, and enunciating each word, she said "You can do it."

Her words were a deeply inspired gift, one that I had not expected or known how much I needed. I treasured them, and her. The very long drive and painful sacrament meeting had been completely worth it for that moment.

CHAPTER NOTES

1.   Bednar, David A. 2009. "More Diligent and
       Concerned at Home." General Conference of
       the Church of Jesus Christ of Latter-day Saints,
       October 2009.

2.   Anatolini, Katherine Lane (2009). Memorializing
       Motherhood: Anna Jarvis and the Struggle for
       Control of Mother's Day (PhD Diss). West Virginia
       University.

37

RECONNECTING

We returned from Sydney fairly unscathed, after a long-haul drive with plenty of stops at play areas and the new cartoon DVD. By mid- June, Bruce returned from Canada, faring worse than normal due to an ankle injury he sustained when running. I had not opposed his going overseas, but subconsciously, I was jealous. This manifested in my being impatient with Bruce as I worked to have him reconnect with the girls. I increasingly rolled my eyes at his attempts to parent and even shot an occasional stinging verbal dart. He was still working at a very difficult, pressure-filled job strictly for the paycheck that supported this crazy situation we were in, and he was just as stressed about everything going on as I was, yet I was unkind towards him. Before I knew it, he was travelling again for work, away for the entire work week. But at least he was in the same country and state.

"I'd like to go see Zoia with you next time you go," he said one Sunday afternoon between trips away. I had an appointment with her the following Tuesday, so after some phone calls, he arranged to not travel for work until Wednesday. When the time came, we drove in silence to the appointment, pretending that the music in the car was superior to our own conversation. In the meeting with Zoia, she began asking patient questions. But almost anytime Bruce spoke, I cut him off and reminded him that I was again taking all of the hits from Michelle and keeping communication open with Ginny, David and Thomas. Fifteen minutes into the session, Zoia cut me off. "What you are saying isn't fair," she said, holding her finger up the same way I did when reminding the girls to be reverent in church. "This is hard on both of you. It has not been easy for Bruce."

"But he is dragging his feet! Does he even want to adopt the girls?" I was exasperated but finally glanced at Bruce to see tears in his eyes. I was surprised, and then I was ashamed. Following that was a discussion about the futility of maintaining a close relationship with Michelle where she was allowed to attack me in texts and words. "After any of the times you have given into Michelle and Trent, and done exactly as they asked, have they ever made good on anything they have said or promised?" asked Zoia, looking directly into Bruce's eyes.

Bruce looked shocked for a moment. "No."

"Do you think that will change?"

There was a pause, then quietly, "No."

"Why do you think the guardians are going to change?" pressed Zoia.

"They won't," said Bruce with resignation.

"Bruce," said Zoia with the most strength and compassion I've ever comprehended in another human's voice, "I know you are scared. I know you don't want to lose the girls, so you are trying to make everyone happy, including Michelle and Trent. But there are a mountain of people on your side. And they are the *right* people." She spoke of trusting and supporting the courts. About not fearing and having faith.

This was not just a counselling session where we left feeling introspective relief; every word was a tightly wound strand of an invincibly strong rope that tethered Bruce and me together as one. We are a team. And Bruce and I are a family, with or without kids. We left with our marriage in a position to heal, our hearts filled with things to ponder, and an intense connection. "I miss you," I said to Bruce at dinner, above the ruckus of a meal shared with toddlers. With tears in his eyes, he responded, "I miss you, too."

With this fresh start, time started to feel like it was passing a little more quickly. It was nearly Cheyenne's birthday when I received a text from Michelle that wasn't aimed at insulting and berating me. "When is a good time for us to Skype tomorrow for Cheyenne's birthday?" she asked.

Bruce and I had prepared for this moment with the help of Zoia. "Right after we receive the signed papers stating the girls do not live with you anymore," I texted, exactly as we had all planned. I felt powerful in sending that message. It was great! Even though she was no longer their legal guardian, our adoption application and the associated visa applications would all look cleaner if we could fully remove Trent and Michelle's names from everything.

Rather than the instant insulting response I was used to, a more measured response came minutes later. "You are *so perfect,*" it read. "You're a *perfect* mother, sitting on your high horse, being *perfect.*"

We heard nothing from her on Cheyenne's birthday. For the first time since meeting the girls, we enjoyed a stress-free, small family birthday party with just the four of us at home. It was a magical way for Cheyenne to embrace being five years old, and we all basked in her happiness.

38

ADDRESSING AND ADDRESSES

"I have the documents ready to send off for giving notice to Trent and Michelle," David e-mailed six weeks later, asking for verification of address. Because Trent and Michelle had at one time been the girls' legal guardians, they could contest the adoption based on emotional connection. We needed to send them a joiner and waiver. The "joiner" was stating that they wanted the same thing we did, which was to see the girls adopted. The "waiver" means that they did not want to attend the court. If Michelle and Trent disagreed with the documents, there was also an enclosed document for them to sign and return, which signalled their protest to our application. We needed evidence that these documents had been supplied to them, showing in good faith that we were not trying to leave them out of the adoption proceedings.

I did not doubt that they had an emotional connection with the girls. They were, after all, the girls' aunt and uncle. Originally, I loved the idea of having an ongoing friendship, especially with Michelle. But working for more than a year to try to heal the emotional and physical scars of the children, and dealing with Michelle's impetuous text attacks, I simply did not want such negativity in my life. I also did not know what to do to repair my relationship with Michelle and wondered if, had I pushed back on her negativity sooner, she might not have spiralled out of control.

I texted Michelle, asking for her address, noting that it was so the court could contact her. She did not respond. I sent her an e-mail, and a Facebook message, but there was no reply. Looking again at her Facebook page, I saw a public comment from someone asking if she needed help with moving. It had been posted just a day earlier. I relayed this to David, "Do I need to phone her, just for the record, in case I need to sign a statement that I tried to get the new address?"

"This could all work to our advantage," David wrote back. "If we can show that we made a diligent search and inquiry as to their whereabouts, and cannot find them, you can sign an affidavit to that effect and we publish their names in the paper and send a summons to their last known address. In essence, they need to be hiding from us to avoid getting the court papers."

My mind was filled with dozens of guesses as to why Michelle and Trent might have been "hiding from us," though it wasn't until I read the words from David that it really meant something. From the start, Robin suggested that Michelle might be using the girls for government concessions and payments. Was she possibly trying to hide where she was living so she could keep collecting this government-provided dependent income? Or was she hiding from us, trying to stall the adoption? Or both? The only idea that came to my mind was that the Immigration Department might have her address. Knowing that it was unlikely for them to share her address with me, I still thought it was worth it to ask, so I typed a quick e-mail.

> *Dear Thomas,*
>
> *We have received information that the Jones family (current sponsors) are moving, or have moved. We have a U.S. court date this month for our taking guardianship and adopting Cheyenne and Reesey. Would you be able to provide the U.S. court with Michelle and Trent's address, presuming you have it? We hope to be in communication soon regarding that change so we can get residency sorted. We still have not found or received passports or Medicare cards for the girls.*

Almost immediately, Thomas called me to assure me that there was no way for him to share the address, and he asked me to remain in communication regarding our upcoming court proceedings. Though it was not the answer I wanted, I had the feeling that the immigration team was cheering for us.

What else could I do to get Michelle's address or a confirmation that she had received the documents? A thought came to mind… a crazy thought. Steadying myself, I decided to phone Angela, who had joined us at Costco on my first meeting with Michelle. Though Anglea was a much closer friend to Michelle than I was, I hoped she might be willing to share Michelle's new address with me. I had only briefly communicated with Angela since seeing her in Sydney when I first brought the girls home with me, but I asked her if she was willing to speak with me and get an update about what was going on. As a woman of integrity and not wanting to gossip, she agreed but wanted to speak with Michelle first.

After about fifteen minutes, she called me back. "Okaaaaaaaay," she began drawing out the term as if this was the beginning of a conversation as an independent moderator. "When two families are raising children together, they need to work together," she continued, seeming to settle in for a lengthy discussion.

"Yes!" I enthusiastically responded. "That is what we want!" My response seemed to confuse Angela and she abruptly went silent.

"We just need Michelle's address so the court documents can be sent to her. She won't give me her address, so I don't know what to do, but if you are comfortable…"

"What do you mean?"

"Michelle told me to never call her but that if I did not answer when she called me, she would accuse me of kidnapping the girls. So she is angry that I called her," I explained. I then related that we had been unable to provide the court with Michelle's address, and that the girls were on shaky visa grounds, adding that Ginny was out of jail, was in support of us adopting, but that Michelle refused to interact with anyone.

Then, I told Angela, "If Michelle opposes the adoption, that's fine. The court can even appoint a lawyer for her. But she needs to let the court supply the documents to her so she can legally do so. She refuses to send me or our attorney her address."

"She told me she wanted the girls to be adopted…" Angela said, sounding confused.

"Well, she's kinda doing everything that will make that NOT happen," I said. "We are working with lawyers, we are working with courts, we are trying to do everything legally. But right now…" I sighed. "She won't even allow us to enrol Cheyenne in school."

I did not want to speak ill of Michelle at all, and especially not to Angela. All I wanted was Michelle's address.

"Angela," I said, venturing. "It looks like some of the immigration paperwork for the girls… isn't… as honest… as it could be… and maybe…" I sighed again. "I dunno. We just want to be honest with… all of the governments. Right now, the U.S. court needs her address, and I know she has moved again, but she won't give her address to me." As I spoke this, I tried to quash my own frustration and anger, as well as control my emotions. So, with only slightly more strength, I concluded, "I am not perfect. And I am not angry with Michelle. But I am trying my best to do everything for the girls so they can be here legally."

"I'll see what I can do," Angela said with quiet firmness.

"If you wanted to, I could send you our attorney's e-mail and you can send him Michelle's address," I suggested. "That way, I'll never know what Michelle's address is."

"No," she said softly but firmly. "I'll talk to Michelle."

With that, the call ended, and all felt suddenly silent. I had tried everything. After a week, David confirmed that he had not heard from Michelle or Trent. So we decided to move forward under the umbrella that they did not want to be found. "Affidavit for you to sign is attached," David wrote. "Let me know if there are any changes. I'll need the original for filing. Please sign, notarize and send to me." We did this and sent the original statement to David.

ADDRESSING AND ADDRESSES

David placed legal ads in the newspapers, requesting for those who opposed the adoption to come forward. He also went to the judge and asked for permission to not have us attend court, in person, explaining that because we did not have passports or even birth certificates for the girls, there was no way we could leave Australia or enter the U.S. with the girls. The judge agreed, and we were given permission to attend court via video. Things were moving. It still felt slow, but it also felt, possibly—just maybe—like a quickening.

39

NAME CALLING

"Our office had a call from Michelle," said Zoia as I entered the reception area for our regular counselling appointment. Her voice was slightly louder and more business-like than usual. "She's called up and is demanding I speak with her." I was not expecting Michelle to contact anyone, especially not LDS Family Services. "She knows about the upcoming adoption date," confirmed Zoia. "And she knows that I signed the information stating that attachment had occurred between you and the girls, endorsing you as parents."

"Okay," I stammered. "What do I need to do?"

"I don't need to release anything to her about you, not even that I am seeing you," Zoia continued. It was clear that Michelle had shaken her. "She's being a bully," Zoia said frankly. "Demanding information and threatening the office with lawyers."

"Should we… do we…" I stammered.

"I didn't even know who she was," continued Zoia. "But she was asking for records of the girls by name. That's how I figured out who she was and what she was after." Zoia seemed rattled and angry, yet firm and protective. Settling down, any hint of ruffle was ironed within seconds. "She called up and gave an earful to Maddie," she said with compassion, gesturing to the trusted receptionist.

"I'm so sorry…" I said with all my heart to Maddie. She was one of the kindest people I'd ever met in my life.

"But I am *not* taking her calls," continued Zoia. "She's been told that we release no information and to stop calling." I wondered how many times she had called but dared not ask.

"Are you okay?" I felt terrible for her.

"Yes, I'm fine. Those are bullying tactics; I don't respond to bullies." It was not Zoia's normal voice, but within moments, we settled into a discussion regarding how to prepare ourselves if this did not work out.

"Am I a bad person if I can't do this anymore?" I asked her. "Because… Bruce and I…" I wasn't sure how to word it, because I desperately wanted to be the girls' mother. But I did not have it in me to keep climbing this eternal mountain. "…we decided that after the court date, if we can't adopt the girls, that we want out. We'll pay for the girls to fly back to the U.S. or whatever, but…" I paused. "I need to be done. We need to be done."

"It takes a strong person to recognise when they have had enough," assured Zoia. In our following discussion, I learned that she had known when I feeling the most suicidal. She knew I wanted to be a mother, but we discussed that maybe motherhood was not meant to be in my life. We also discussed how that is okay. Not every woman needs to be a mother, and certainly not if it entails the insults and abuse I endured at the hands of Michelle or constantly sitting on the verge of suicide. I needed to hear from Zoia that it was okay for me to quit, and in that session, she gave me that gift.

Later that day, my phone buzzed. It was Trent!

"You did *not* call Angela," he said upon my answering.

"Michelle wasn't giving me your address," I responded with honesty, yet cowardice, neglecting to add that he had also not provided the address. "Who else could I call?"

"What were you telling the church counselling people about Michelle?"

"Nothing."

"Really?" he replied in a distrusting, even slightly mocking tone.

"I'm not kidding," I said honestly. "They did not even know Michelle's name. I only ever called her and you 'the aunt and uncle.' They didn't know your names until Michelle told them." This was all true. Trent was quiet for a moment.

"Can you send us the stuff from the adoption attorney?" he finally said.

"Um, yeah," I said, slightly shocked. "I have been e-mailing everything to Michelle, but I can e-mail it through again. To what e-mail address?" He gave me his work e-mail address, and the conversation was suddenly over.

A few days later, we spoke with David. "We need an attorney to represent the girls in the case," he explained in a scheduled phone call. "I'm representing you, the father may have a lawyer, the guardians may also bring counsel, but the girls need an attorney."

"Okay," said Bruce. "How do we do that?"

"I have someone I recommend and can arrange for," replied David, telling us a name. "He's worked these cases before; I've known him to be unbiased and fair. He might not agree with me, or our position, but that is not what he is there for. He is there to represent the best interest of the girls."

"Hire him," Bruce immediately responded. "The girls need a lawyer, and you recommend him. Just do it."

Things were moving, and my hopes were up. Though I had been sometimes overly communicative with Bruce, there was one area where I was not: names. Bruce and I had spoken about the girls' names, but it had not ended well. The surname was an issue. When I first came to Australia, I was adamant about keeping my name, as I felt like between our new marriage and my new country, I still needed something to make me feel like… me. So although I was often called by Bruce's last name at church, I legally retained my last name, even on my church records. Bruce wanted the girls to have his last name, and though I didn't oppose it, I didn't like feeling obligated, sensing that it felt like the erasure of me. "Sharing a name with your husband implies traditional values to adoption officials," explained a female family law attorney I had contacted before David. "Forget sexism. It can't be about that right now. It's about creating the image of a traditional family created in a non-traditional way." Having already heard that other feminist couples had done the same, I accepted this lawyer's advice and softened. Shortly thereafter, I began the process of changing my last name to Bruce's after a decade of marriage. "The girls are worth it." I told myself, "and besides, Gavin is easier to spell and pronounce."

Bruce and I both knew adopted individuals who chose to change their own first name when their adoptions were final. For them, adoption symbolised their rebirth into a new family and a new life, and a new name helped to bury the ghosts of what was sometimes a terribly abusive early life. I loved the idea of the girls choosing their own names, so one afternoon, I approached them with this in mind.

"Cheyenne, if you could change your name forever and forever and forever," I began, "what name would you like?"

"Me, too?" asked Reesey.

"Yes! You, too. What name would you choose if you could?"

"Rapunzel," said Reesey immediately.

"Belle," said Cheyenne. "I'll be Belle."

I was not anticipating this response. I imagined they would choose names that did not involve cartoons. "Um... okay," I said. "But this isn't for a game, this is forever. Like you don't have to be Cheyenne or Reesey. Everyone will call you... say... Abigail. Do you like that name?" I always loved the name, so I hoped to plant a seed.

"I like Belle," replied Cheyenne, and then with energy and an inspired grin, "Belle Buttercup! A fairy! Tinkerbell!"

"I'm still Rapunzel," said Reesey. This was not going to plan.

"Okay. Thank you," I said. "Good information."

I was not going to name my daughters Rapunzel, or Belle Buttercup, or even Tinkerbell, if for no other reason than I was pretty sure that the judge deciding the adoption would not take our application seriously if we put those names on the petition for a name change. I found myself in the strange position of making everyone, including myself, happy. I chose Bruce's last name for the forms. I then chose to keep the girls' given names while I added middle names of my choosing. These perfect names seemed to sparkle on the adoption forms, and I felt joyous.

40

COURTING

In the days before the adoption proceeding, Michelle informed us of a letter sent to the judge. She sent me a copy of the letter via text message in addition to a rambling message about Ginny's long list of sins, as well as a good dose of vitriol aimed at reminding me of what a heartless, foul, stupid and selfish person she believed I was.

The letter was typical of what we had come to know of Michelle; she rambled on for five full pages about how she was devoted to God, loved the girls, but could not financially provide for them. She wrote that she was aware that her offspring did not get along with the girls, and that was why the girls could not live with her. She wrote how I had tricked her into taking the children and had refused to communicate, and even claimed that I paid Ginny a huge sum of money to get her to sign the documents. Michelle further claimed that Ginny was sexually promiscuous in every way and was a drug addict, so she probably would not remember that I gave her money. So if the judge could see in his heart to give Michelle regular access to the children, entirely at Bruce's and my expense, that would be best for everyone, according to her.

It was exhausting to read, and I wondered what would happen with this in court. "Most judges ignore these letters," David said, as he related that writing a letter with the intent to influence a judge is illegal and classed as a misdemeanour. He further explained that when a lawyer makes your case on your behalf, they may ask someone to write a character reference letter for the judge, but this is all done through an attorney, never directly to a judge. "But they do have to make a record of the letter from Michelle for the court," David added.

"So what does that mean for us?" Bruce asked.

"Well, if the guardians surprise us and have an attorney, or the attorney we hired to represent the girls thinks there is merit to it, it could be a problem. I needed to make you aware of it." He was nonchalant as he spoke, which invited me to not worry about the letter. We thanked David and prepared ourselves.

It was morning on the east coast of the United States where David and Ginny were waiting for court to start. I was so glad Ginny was there again! For us in our distant time zone, it was night, but we were ready. Around 9PM, Bruce and I cleaned the kitchen in silence, partly not wanting to wake the girls, partly from the cortisol rushing through our systems, stressing us into silence. We silently moved our dining table, placing it in front of a wall that was decorated with drawings made by the girls. At 10PM, we dressed in our "Sunday best." I was in a skirt and even applied make-up. Bruce was wearing dress pants, a shirt, and tie.

We did not have a set court time but knew we were on the schedule. We hoped that we would not be sitting up all night and that David would not have to spend his entire day waiting. Around 11:30PM, David's Skype rang in.

"Just checking to see if the Wi-Fi at the courthouse works…" he said, his video connection coming to life.

"Okay," I said breathlessly.

"How's everything looking?" asked Bruce.

"Looks good," replied David. "Ginny is here, and there doesn't seem to be much on the docket, so I hope we'll get in without too much wait time. The attorney for the girls just arrived, as well," he said, looking off screen for a moment.

"Is Kyle there?" asked Bruce. My heart was racing.

"There's a warrant out for his arrest," replied David nonchalantly with his southern drawl (oh, how I loved that slow pronunciation!). "So if he shows up, he'll be arrested. If that happens, we'll go from there."

"Is that a good thing?" I asked. I felt dumb.

"Well, not for him…" replied David. Bruce and I nodded in agreement, chuckling. "Now, are you sure you want to adopt the girls?" he asked.

The question confused me, and I looked at Bruce, who was looking at me. "Yes," we replied in union.

"Okay, so if they have future dental problems, are you going to…"

My mouth gaped open, and I almost laughed.

"We'll pay for the dentist," said Bruce.

"You're sure?"

Both of us: "*Yes!*"

"Well, they're going to open the court now, but stay here in case I need you. I can't keep Skype open in the courtroom unless approved by the judge, but I'll try to keep you updated if things look like they're going to be a while."

And with that, our wait officially began.

"Let's say a prayer together," said Bruce.

About ten years before I met Bruce, I was a new student at Southern Utah University, trying to paddle my way through a wholly different experience. Having grown up in New York, not only was Utah strange, college was like nothing I'd ever experienced before. Among all that I was absorbing, I remembered an LDS speaker teaching us to pray for whatever our heart desired. Pray for everything, no matter how crazy, outlandish, even impossible. Pray. Because God listens, and it never hurts to ask.

Through this whole process, I felt like I had been praying for the impossible. This moment was no different. "Yes," I whispered. Bruce offered the prayer. It was simple and peaceful, asking for the judge to be able to see what was really going on and

have a compassionate heart. He also asked for us
to be at peace, no matter what the results might be.
My "Amen" was sound.

Then, Bruce and I sat.

And sat.

I began to play solitaire on my phone.

An hour passed.

We were still sitting.

Bruce began to play a podcast of a Canadian
radio show he had discovered. It was colloquial
and sweet with clean humour, something a family
would enjoy listening to on a road trip, I surmised.
I kept playing on my phone, wishing I felt at ease
enough to crochet. We kept sitting. The Canadian
guy was starting to bother me. It wasn't him, it was
the waiting, but still. I tried to crochet but was too
distracted. Crocheting felt painful. I put it away.

That Canadian guy was really bothering me
with his slow folksy talk. I tried to focus on another
game of solitaire, but I was struggling. I wasn't
tired in the least; I was anxious. Not in a sweaty,
clenched-fist kind of way. But in an impatient,
longing and heart-wrenching way. I really wanted
that Canadian guy to shut up. Every word he spoke
seemed to take a million years, even though what he
was saying was absolutely charming.

Still we sat. Then suddenly, the Skype
connection came to life. I jumped, my heart racing.
I shoved my phone out of the way, nearly knocking

it to the floor. Bruce silenced the Canadian. Adrenaline raced through me like an electric shock. We both sat, backs straight at high attention.

We were ready to face the judge.

41

PINK

Instantly at attention, our rehearsed words at the ready, all we saw was David. "Well, the case happened," started David slowly, "and the judge doesn't need to see you." We were dumbfounded, processing that information. Did Kyle show and bring an attorney? Did Ginny change her mind? Did Kyle gain custody? Was the court hearing rescheduled? Where was Ginny? I didn't know which question to ask first!

"Let me be the first..." spoke David in a manner that I was sure was slower than any human had ever spoken before. "...to congratulate you. You are parents. Everything is final."

"Thank you," Bruce choked, relief visibly washing over his entire body.

"Yes," I choked, in a way that was between a giggle and a sob, "thank you so much." And then, to check, "I'm a mother?"

"You are a mother, and Bruce is a father," spoke David. He was smiling, and I was sure he was one of the best people in the world. Shock began to wear off and my thoughts began to form more clearly. I am a mother! An intense sense of responsibility and parental concern then hit me: I'd better do a really good job! This is serious! I am a mother. *Me!* Miracles do happen! I need to step up my game!

"Where is Ginny?" asked Bruce. Oh, my sweet husband! He was anxious to thank Ginny—so was I, even if I was still dazed at the happy news.

"She's in with the judge; he wanted to speak to her for a moment," answered David. This worried me. In a kind of unison, Bruce and I asked why the judge wanted to see her. "He wanted to commend her for doing such great work to turn her life around," replied David almost casually. The judge was right. Ginny had worked saintfully hard to get her life on a good path for herself, her future and her future family. God bless her! She was a miracle!

"Well, I'll get the paperwork to you in the next day or so," continued David. "It should be a week or so before I have your daughters' birth certificates for you." I was rapidly and reactively nodding, tears welling up again at the phrase "*your daughters.*"

Just then, Ginny's face popped on screen. "Why y'all cryin'?" she said, seeing our faces. It wasn't until she said that that I was aware that Bruce was crying as well. "I told you it was gonna work out!" Then, in just the corner of the screen, popped the judge's face. In the background we heard Ginny and David offer thanks to him, and for a split second he glanced at us through the screen. In that breath, he saw how happy we were with our blubbering tears of joy. He nodded briefly at us as we thanked him before swiftly walking away. Without a word, he was gone. He was an angel dressed in a judge's black robe, and I swear I saw white angel's wings on his back as he floated out of sight.

"Thank you so much," was all I could think to say again and again.

"Okay, well, I'll get to that paperwork," said David, wrapping up the Skype conversation.

At that second, I heard tiny footsteps on the stairs. I looked and saw Reesey padding towards me. I went and gathered my daughter (!) in my arms. "What are you doing up?" I asked quietly.

"Something woke me up," she said, and then shielding her eyes from the brightly lit living room, she said, "It's bright here."

"What woke you up? Are you okay?"

"Love woke me up."

I gasped. "Love woke you up?"

"Uh-huh." I stood, cradling my daughter, rocking her with an intense emotion. This love felt different. I felt different. I felt even more love for her and Cheyenne than I had ever felt in my life. Trusting that I was her mother forever, and not just for that moment, every ounce of my soul was free to love. I loved her intensely with every cell in my body. "Come to bed wif me?" she asked.

"Of course. Let's go right now."

I nodded at Bruce and carried her upstairs as Bruce closed the call with David. I put her in my bed towards the centre. Quickly, I slipped my pyjamas on, not bothering to hang my clothes or wash the makeup off of my face. In the two minutes it took to do this, Reesey was fast asleep. I kissed her sleeping cheek, and looked at *my other daughter,* Cheyenne, who was sound asleep on the mattress on the floor. Both girls had rosy pink cheeks. Glancing briefly in the mirror on my bedside table, in the faintness of the hallway light, I saw that I did, too. Pink, rosy, happy cheeks. Pink Mummy. Me. I was a pink mummy. I looked beautiful.

I slipped back downstairs, where Bruce greeted me, arms wide open, a brilliant smile on his face. Wordlessly, we grasped each other. At that second, we connected more powerfully than I have ever connected with another human being. It was as if at the instant of that embrace, we were married again, bound together with every power known on Earth and Heaven. We remained entwined for quite a while, rocking and telling each other, "I love you," again and again and again.

42

WEDDING

Bruce took the day off from work. We had not told the girls we were staying up late the night before for fear that they would not want to go to sleep. They arose as usual, dressed, and made their way downstairs, surprised to see Bruce.

"Daddy is home today?" asked Cheyenne.

"Yes!" I said, with a huge grin. "Come, " I said. "Let's have a quick family chat." The girls obeyed, sitting on middle steps. I knelt on a step below the girls, my toes touching the floor beneath, then Bruce joined us, also with a ginormous grin.

"Do you remember how we said we were going to fight like dragons to get to be your Mummy and Daddy forever?" I asked. The girls' mouths were agape, possibly still surprised at seeing Bruce and then being asked that question.

"We won!" said Bruce, too impatient to let them guess.

"We won?" spoke Reesey.

"*Yes!*" I said. "You are adopted. I am your Mummy forever, and Daddy is your Daddy forever."

"Forever?" asked Cheyenne.

"Forever. We are *never* going to give you away," said Bruce.

"And you never have to see Old Mummy again," I added.

Reesey started bouncing. "Yay! I don't like Old Mummy."

"Do you need the toilet?" I asked. She nodded, and I shooed her towards the bathroom. Cheyenne walked with Bruce to the kitchen, where Bruce set up bowls, cereal, and milk. Reesey had always been verbal about her dislike of Michelle, but Cheyenne remained diplomatic, saying she "liked Old Mummy."

"Do we ever have to see Old Mummy again?" asked Cheyenne again when I returned with Reesey.

"Um…" I thought for a second, not wanting to cause any hurt to Cheyenne, but also because I was more than happy to never have anything to do with Michelle. "I don't want to see Old Mummy because she hasn't been very nice to me, which means I don't like the idea of you seeing her. We can talk to Zoia and see if it's a good idea. But right now, we're not going to see her." As soon as I said that, it was as if an ocean of relief passed over Cheyenne's tiny, five-year-old frame. "I don't like her," she said. "She hurt me. She gave me away. Old Daddy shaved Reesey's head. I don't want to see them again."

"Okay," I said. "I'll always protect you like a dragon, so you never have to see them."

"I never want to." She spoke firmly, with resolve. "I don't like Old Mummy."

"Are we married now?" asked Reesey, shoving handfuls of dry cereal in her mouth. She liked cereal and she liked milk, but not together. "Like Rapunzel and Flynn Ryder?"

"Well, kind of," I said.

"Do I get to wear a dress?"

"You can wear whatever you like today," I replied, not understanding her.

"No… a white dress. Like Cinderella at the end, and Ariel, at the wedding."

"Oh!" I said, cluing in. Bruce and I had discussed having some kind of party or celebration when the adoption was final. Bruce had been hesitant to plan anything in case the adoption did not go through. "Well, we could have a wedding," I said.

"Okay, but I need a dress," replied my little fashionista.

"Okay," I said, giggling. "What do you think, Cheyenne? Should we have an adoption wedding?"

"With a cake?"

I smiled. "Of course! Weddings always have cakes."

"Yeah," she said thoughtfully. "Sounds good." Then she added, "With chocolate. And marshmallows."

Throughout the rest of the day, Bruce and I called friends and family to let them know that the adoption was real and final. I sent an e-mail to the *Exponent* bloggers list and received every kind of loving, congratulatory response from the bloggers, many who shared that they were shedding tears of joy on our behalf. We added text across a photo of the four us that read, "The adoption is final" and posted it on Facebook. More well wishes and congratulations came in, filled with love, joy and support. I felt like I was walking on clouds. I also was filled with absolute gratitude and love for Ginny. Never in my life has another human being blessed me as much as she had. I was keenly aware of the miracle of my being able to be a mother with the blessing of another mother. It was a celestial feeling, and I thanked God for adoption.

Bruce contacted the Department of Immigration to update them and begin in earnest the process of obtaining visas for our daughters. Likewise, I informed Trent and Michelle in a simple text that the adoption was final, and that they had no legal obligation for immigration or anything else. A few hours after I sent the text, my phone rang. It was an unknown number, but I answered anyway. "Congratulations," came the voice on the other end of the phone. It was Trent! I was surprised. "You guys can now get sealed," he said, referencing the LDS temple ordinance of being "sealed for eternity." His voice was sincere, and I thanked him. The call was short, but I was grateful.

Within a few weeks, we made arrangements to use the church building, scheduling our "wedding" the day before we planned to have the girls blessed as children of record. I made a combination adoption announcement and wedding invitation, then bought tiny white shoes with just a hint of a heel and off cuts of wedding dress fabric that I used to sew two little gowns. Just like at our wedding more than a decade before, I made a red velvet cake, with cream cheese icing, from scratch. Then the girls helped me cut pink fondant hearts that we placed all over the cake, in all the right spots.

On the wedding day, my visiting teacher, a professional hairdresser, came to the house and did all of our hair as her gift to us. Her generosity, and knowing that she was happy for us, struck me. I had not anticipated gifts, and yet—an army of friends RSVP'd and arrived fully armed with gifts that were an expression of their love and congratulations.

As we walked between rows of folding chairs set up in the recreation room of the church, our daughters took our hands and shyly walked with us to the helper, "Becky Gecko," who was performing our "wedding." Becky spoke of the power of eternal families and the blessings of our Heavenly Parents, then had Bruce and I speak of our love for each other and our daughters. Becky then had us each choose a small container with coloured sand. Bruce's sand was blue, mine was magenta, Cheyenne had purple and Reesey's pink. Becky had us each take turns pouring the coloured sand in a single jar. "Each of you has your own personality and gift to bring into making a family." she said. "Each is beautiful. When you add your different colours of sand in layers in the jar, your colours are beautiful and unique, yet rippled together, you become even more exquisite and different from every other family in the world. Each of your differences work together in harmony to make life more beautiful than without the others." We agreed. As the ceremony concluded, we chatted with friends and cut the cake, while all the children ran circles around the building and engaged in activities and games that were set up by friends who had volunteered their time. Everything was perfect.

The next morning, we went to church early, ready for the girls to be blessed. Bruce asked me for blessing suggestions, so I had penned some words that I felt would be appropriate. Bruce invited many of our friends to the front of the chapel, where a chair was set out for me so I could hold each of my daughters in turn while Bruce pronounced a blessing upon them. As I sat, the men's hands were at eye level for me. I was able to watch their hands from a view I had never considered or seen before. I saw Bruce's hand shaking; he was nervous and wanted to do well. But I also saw the steady hands of his friends gathered in a halo over our childrens' heads, being vessels of God-filled power and support. As Bruce spoke, I realised that he was repeating what I had written for their blessings, word for word. It was one of the most powerful moments of my life, and I felt physically enveloped by God's love.

It was a new day.

43

ALL SMILES

Shortly after Bruce and I married, I found myself thinking about all of the improbabilities and impossibilities that came with adoption in Australia. It seemed hopeless. I chortled at the thought of the perfect adoption for our situation. But I recalled the admonition to pray for everything, and I recalled my father teaching me that God is perfect and therefore has a perfect sense of humour. So I knelt down and began my prayer. I started by explaining that I was following the advice to pray for things that seemed impossible, and then proceeded to ask for just that.

"Please bless that there might be an American child in Australia who Bruce and I can adopt. And a little child, like a toddler or younger, and because they are American, um… we can somehow adopt them, and they can have dual citizenship, and… um… children. Yes! Children. Not just one. More than one American child in Australia who we will be able to adopt." I smiled as I closed my prayer, thinking that God would have a good chuckle at that most ridiculous invocation. More than a decade on, I am so glad that I offered that crazy, impossible prayer. Because with God, all things are possible. I am a living witness to that.

Adoption finalised, children blessed, and visas hopefully on the horizon, there was but one thing left for me to do. I went to my desk and pulled out the top drawer. At first, I could not see it, so I pulled the drawer out as far as it would go. I began pulling out pens, pencils, a stapler and stacks of papers... and then, in the very back, I saw the small green box. Inside was the $0.99 magnet set that said, "New Mom." I had bought it years ago for a baby shower for someone else but found that something inside me would not let me give it away. Instead, I shoved it in the very back of my desk, hoping that one day, I would be a "new mom."

With a huge, joyful grin, I silently opened the box, took out each of the three magnets, and rolled them between my fingers. I lazily shoved everything back in the desk drawer and made my way to the kitchen. The magnets were tiny enough to be considered a choke risk for children, so I put them at the top of the refrigerator door, facing me. I stepped back and stared as a beam of sunshine splashed across my face.

A few days later, I was surprised to receive a text from Michelle. It was the first contact I had from her since she sent the copy of the letter she had sent to the judge, which included a list of everything she could think to find fault about me. It was also the first contact I had from her where I felt wholly at ease. I still chose to sit for a moment, pondering what I would do if she was still trying to use me as her punching bag. It read:

> *Hi. We had a family home evening lesson last night about forgiveness, and I decided that I could forgive you for all you've done, so I hope you can forgive me, too, and we can just be friends and start fresh. Our van needs some repairs, it is not safe and we are unable to drive it. The repairs cost about $3,000, so I was wondering if you could loan me the money. It'll take me a long time to pay back, but I don't want to stress Trent out, so let's keep this between us girls and not involve our husbands.*

I was dumbstruck. I paused for a moment, then I blocked Michelle's phone number. And her Facebook account, and her e-mail.

SHERRIE GAVIN

44

CRAZY PRAYERS ARE THE BEST PRAYERS

Bruce had been dilligently and passionately working on the girls' visas. I had contacted our local Member of Parliament (MP) to ask for advice, which is not uncommon in complicated visa cases. But the response from the MP's office was, "a story such as yours would not exist, so we therefore cannot help you." This did not fill me with hope. But now that Bruce and I were parents, and our children had legally entered the country, we needed to update and pursue new visas.

We called Thomas and officially identified ourselves as the petitioners for our daughters. He seemed relieved to know that the adoption had gone through, and that, finally, they could actually help us. "Your case has come to the attention of the offices in Canberra," he said, implying the federal Minister for Immigration. Knowing this buoyed me; our situation was strange, and the right people were in the game.

After detailing what forms and documents were needed to prove that our daughters were the same children as on the expired visas, Thomas instructed Bruce to go to the nearest immigration office to present official copies of all the paperwork. Bruce did this the following day. He later relayed to me that after standing in a short line, he greeted the immigration officer with, "You're not going to believe my story, but…" Before Bruce spoke any more, and with an intense look on his face, the officer said, "We had a meeting about you today. Wait here while I get the supervisor." Bruce was ushered into a private room where they poured through his documents, made copies, and instructed him on the next steps.

Nothing was guaranteed. We would need to submit the visa application and have it rejected, as there was literally no precedent for families in our situation. Our case was then subject to being heard by an immigration adjudicator who would presumably reject it in favour of the seven justices on the High Court of Australia to decide. This whole thing was a long shot, but I was hopeful of a miracle. Another miracle. So was Bruce. But as we had learned, miracles take work. Bruce had poured through an abundance of legislation and legal information in regard to unusual visa applications. "The argument for us to apply for the girls to have a visa granted," he explained, "is to prove compelling or compassionate circumstances. I think we can argue both 'compelling' and 'compassionate' for our situation."

"Compassionate, for sure," I said, thinking of all that the girls had experienced.

"But also compelling," said Bruce. "We did the right thing. We saw children in need, and we took them in. That is the Australian way, or at least it is supposed to be."

He had a point. A few weeks before, as I was chatting with a group of fellow mothers about how the girls came into our care, I rhetorically asked, "Who wouldn't take two children home if their carers were throwing all of their things in rubbish bags, had shaved their heads, had been giving them away and saying they didn't want them?"

"I wouldn't," quickly huffed one of the women. The others remained silent, looking at the ground. "Well, it sounds like a complicated situation..." moused another, shrugging. "I'd stay out of it." That's when I understood that even taking the girls home with me was extremely uncommon. Even within the ward we had attended for over a year by that time, many of our fellow parishioners had surmised that we were some kind of *Ensign* story when the girls first came to us, and that the adoption had just miraculously, instantly happened. When they learned of the complications, and that the girls were not adopted, many backed off, and some were even unkind, suggesting that we give the girls back to their "real" mother.

"The thing is," Bruce explained further, "there was no organisation or law in place to protect the children. But we still did it. That is compassionate."

"And the compelling?" I asked.

"Well, the girls could have ended up being sexually trafficked for the rest of their lives. Instead, we did everything we could, contacted every legal and government authority we could, and adopted the girls. No law existed to protect them in their position, which makes this a compelling situation. It is a situation that no one was able to foresee and create legislation for." I felt nauseous every time I dared think about what might have happened to the girls had I not taken them with me. Would Australian immigration authorities see this as well?

Our initial visa application was rejected, as we expected. Reading the visa denial afterwards, I could see why. The law firm we hired for immigration had not included compelling or compassionate arguments, reserving their energy for the High Court. Having just paid a small fortune in legal fees to see the adoption through, I was not happy with the idea of paying yet another law firm, especially one that did not seem to do anything unless it was to appear before the federal judges. The more we read about unusual immigration cases, the more we believed that the next visa application would also be denied. Statistically speaking, the immigration adjudication step was the least likely to have a positive outcome. "We can appear before the adjudicator if you want us to, but the adjudicator never approves visas at that stage," our immigration attorney told us. "We've never seen it. We'll come in when it is time to go to the High Court."

"They're not even trying!" I said privately to Bruce in exasperation.

"Maybe that's a good thing," Bruce replied. "We won't have to pay for an attorney if we argue this next step on our own." Over the next weeks, the adjudication appointment was set, and Bruce diligently prepared the legal paperwork mostly on his own, only occasionally calling our immigration attorneys with a few questions. We gathered letters of support from Zoia, Mandy, and other friends who swore our story was true. Finally, Bruce and I fasted on the Sunday before we were to present our argument. I felt confident, but not as hopeful as I would have liked.

It was a Thursday when we stepped into the stone building. The interior walls of the court were an enclave of what I guessed was dark ironbark wood, a classic Australian tree that invoked a sense of majesty. There were half a dozen courtrooms along a hall that trailed long, navy-cushioned benches for the length of the space. The carpet was dark, yet the waiting area was light as a result of the metres-high windows that flanked the hall. Bruce was dressed in a suit, and the girls and I were in Sunday dresses. My purse was stashed with snacks for the girls in preparation for a long wait, but for security reasons, we were allowed to bring in little else but our court papers. This legal chamber was nearly empty; it was set aside one day per week for visa applications only, and besides us, there was only one other woman with a child. When they were called into one of the courtrooms, we were alone in the hall.

Bruce, the girls and I huddled together for a quick prayer. I don't know that the girls knew what was entirely going on, but they liked being dressed up and playing in a space with such long benches. We would appear before the adjudicator independently and in turns. Bruce decided that he would go first and was confident enough that he believed I might not even need to appear. Within minutes, Bruce was called to the courtroom. As she motioned for Bruce to close the door, I breathed in, hoping for the best.

In what seemed like all of five minutes, the girls had played with and eaten all of the snacks, and I was completely out of entertainment. As the time began to pass, the girls became bored. There are only so many things one can do to entertain children with disposable hand towels from the ladies' room, especially when you are trying to not make a mess. Eventually, one of the girls discovered an insect! Both of the girls were soon engrossed with the insect, crawling along the floor to see where its home might be.

It felt like Bruce was taking a really long time. Was this a good sign or a bad sign? I did not know. I decided to start crawling on the floor along with the girls, trying to prolong the entertainment value of the insect. As soon as I was on the floor crawling, Bruce opened the courtroom door in full view of the adjudicator. I scrambled to my feet, straightening my dress. Bruce looked tired. "The adjudicator wants to see you," he said with a hint of annoyance. I also sensed that he was disappointed.

As I went in, the adjudicator barely glanced at me and motioned for me to sit in the chair beside her. It was a modest but very official looking room, and although it had all of the signage of a court, the smallness of the space made it feel almost cosy. The adjudicator kept her face on the papers in front of her, where she checked off points to questions she asked and made notes. I relayed how I connected with Michelle through Robin and how I intended to call the police on the night I met the girls. But on that night, standing with piles of rubbish bags filled with the girls' belongings and being told how much trouble these girls were to Michelle and Trent… before I could finish, I broke, and tears came. For a split second, the adjudicator looked at me, then returned to her furious writing. I felt stupid for crying in front of her, quickly collected myself, and continued. I told her how Mandy was staying with us then, and that she was a police officer. I told her how I called Child Protective Services in both states, and each told me to call the other. I told her how I reported everything to my local police station, but they said no immediate crime was at hand. Within twenty minutes, I was done, and the adjudicator excused me.

She explained to Bruce that she needed to meet the girls, so we ushered them in. She simply asked the girls their names. "Reesey," said Reesey, unable or unwilling to say the rest of her name. Cheyenne was shy and reluctant to speak, but eventually shared her whole name, the one I had chosen for her. Hearing her say that was music to my ears.

And then we were done. "I don't think it's gonna work," said Bruce. But I decided to say nothing, enjoying the car ride home. Christmas was coming and the sun was shining.

Over the next few weeks, we fell into a normal family routine. We travelled to the U.S. Consulate in Sydney to obtain American passports for the girls with their new names. The trip actually felt more like a vacation than anything else, with the girls happily swimming in Grandma and Granddad's pool, night terrors a thing of the past. I enroled the girls in school for the upcoming year, which was relatively simple since I had their birth certificates naming me as their mother. Life was moving on at a smooth and happy pace.

One sunny summer evening, Bruce came home, shaking his head. "I can't believe it," he said. He was holding an opened, white envelope, thick with papers.

"Can't believe what?" I asked, continuing to prepare a dinner of mashed potatoes, Australian sausages, and peeled, sliced, fresh, bright pink apples. The girls were on an anti-green food phase, but I still placed tiny stalks of bright green, topless broccoli on the girls' plates, gambling for a bite.

"Compassionate and compelling…" he read aloud, grabbing my attention. Then, with bright eyes, he looked at me. "We have the visas."

"Are you serious?"

"Yeah!" Bruce read through the papers, continuing to mutter, "I can't believe it!" and "No one makes it through that stage of the visa process!" But Bruce did! Our daughters were safe and legally residing in our home in Australia. Raising my eyes to Heaven, I whispered, "Thank you" to God. It was over. All of it was over. And yet, my new life was beginning. I had never been happier.

That night at bedtime, I told the girls a story I had crafted at Zoia's suggestion. I had told the girls the story many times before. Each time, they listened in rapture. I felt the same way…

> *Once upon a time, Heavenly Father and Heavenly Mother made two nearly perfect girls. These girls were loved dearly by everyone. Everyone just loved them! Everyone loved them so much that they all began to fight about who would get to be their mother and father on Earth!*

Heavenly Father and Heavenly Mother had a big problem! Who would get to be their earthly parents? They thought and They thought and They thought. And then, They thought some more.

After a really long time, They decided on two mummies and two daddies. Heavenly Father and Heavenly Mother picked Tummy Mummy to have the girls in her tummy. They picked Tummy Mummy because she was so beautiful and so strong. They knew that even though it would break her heart, Tummy Mummy would make a very hard decision to make sure the girls would find Forever Mummy and Forever Daddy.

But then, Heavenly Father and Heavenly Mother had another big problem! Forever Mummy and Forever Daddy lived in Australia, and Tummy Mummy lived in America! How was Tummy Mummy going to find Forever Mummy?

Heavenly Father and Heavenly Mother thought and They thought and They thought. Then Tummy Mummy said, "I know how! If I have the babies in my tummy, then I'll let the girls be adopted. We can find another Mummy to look after the girls for a short time, then Forever

Mummy will find the babies!" Heavenly Father and Heavenly Mother thought that was a great idea.

Tummy Mummy had the babies, and soon the babies were with the other Mummy. The other Mummy loved them, but she was not a very good Mummy for them. She was a good Mummy for other babies, but not for the special baby girls. The girls started to be sad and confused. Sometimes they looked for their forever parents but could not find them. They almost gave up hope and started to be afraid.

One day, the Forever Mummy showed up and met the girls. She did not know she was supposed to be their Forever Mummy until she saw them. Then she knew. She loved them from the first second she saw them. As soon as Forever Daddy saw them, he loved them, too. So they worked and they worked and they worked. And sometimes they made mistakes. But they kept working because they knew they were supposed to be the Forever Mummy and Daddy.

Heavenly Father and Heavenly Mother were so happy that the girls had finally found their Forever Mummy and Forever Daddy! They decided to change the laws and rules in all the lands—just for a split second—to help the girls be adopted in their forever home. All of the people loved the girls. And the girls both went to college. And they all lived happily ever after as an eternal family.

The End.

The t-shirt I was wearing as I tucked them in bed was pink. Pink suited me well. I wore it nearly every day. It was my new favourite colour.

AFTERWORD

"No matter what your circumstances are, whether you are in prosperity or adversity, you can learn from every person, transaction, and circumstance around you."

— Brigham Young[1]

The adoption was a learning process, to be sure! I learned so much about not judging those who may spend time in prison, about how loving and willing government officials are at helping families, about faith and hard work joining hands to witness the power and majesty of miracles created by our Heavenly Parents and beloved brother, Jesus Christ. I am still learning about this, about myself as I parent, and more. I am so very blessed to have had such a beautiful experience with such a powerful end result that I am positive that my cup truly runneth over.

About five years after the adoption was completed, I reached out to Michelle. It was nearing Christmas, and as usual, I had been listening to many of the First Presidency Christmas Devotionals from past years as I baked Christmas cookies to share with neighbours and fellow church members. In listening to Howard W. Hunter's invitation to "forgo a grudge," I decided to e-mail Michelle.[2] I was seeking closure, and I was tired of holding on to negative memories about that time period. It also felt strikingly like the right thing to do. Though I had been hurt by her words, and angry with the ways she interacted with me, the truth is, I would not have my daughters without her. For this alone, I am eternally grateful to her. In an e-mail, I wrote, "I just wanted to drop you a line and wish you a Merry Christmas. My feelings towards you have been uncharitable, as I had been so hurt by your words. But I no longer want to hold a grudge. I am freeing myself from those feelings and hope you feel forgiveness towards me. I sincerely hope you and your family are happy and well."

It was almost a month later that Michelle responded, to my surprise. "Hi," she wrote. "I don't have any hard feelings towards you. I was struggling during that time and was not mentally at my best. I am sorry if I ever said anything that hurt you—that was never my intention. Thank you for reaching out. I really appreciate it, because I know it's never an easy thing to do; I admire your courage. I hope the girls are well." Heartened by her response, and feeling at ease, I wondered if we could somehow build a relationship of some kind? However, additional messages I sent to her following this interaction remain unanswered.

Bruce and I keep an eye on Kyle from a distance. Using online search engines, we have watched him age exponentially through an ongoing series of mugshots, with a list of convicted criminal charges that increases over the years. A short while ago, I read in a newspaper article about what was possibly his most recent arrest. His bail had been set at one million dollars, and if convicted, he could be in prison for the rest of his life. I sometimes wonder if he will try to reach out to us or the girls one day, but to date, he has not.

Ginny, as always, is amazing. When I asked her what feelings or thoughts she had about the adoption, she wrote: "I always remember that you told me you prayed for a child and possibly if it was in His will, one that looked like you, and you got two! Your prayer stuck with me because I also prayed that whatever happened, God would provide and protect the girls from all that was going on. And then you showed up! So both our prayers had been answered. That was confirmation that I also did what I believed was best. It has proven to be the best choice over a hundred times. It was always God's will for them to be your daughters."

In striving to get her life on a new path, Ginny's exemplary behaviour earned her an expunged record. She has since built a new, beautiful life with a wonderful husband. She and her husband have worked hard to build a loving home with Christ in their lives. We still message and video call each other to chat about life, husbands, the girls, gardening and a slew of other things. She is truly a good person, and I am in awe of her summer okra harvests!

Cheyenne supplied this update on our family: "Right now, my favourite things are reading, writing, art, sleeping, and walking our dog, Luna. I am grateful my parents adopted me, and I am mostly happy, especially when I don't have homework. I am working on getting my driver's licence. I am not sure what I want to be when I grow up, but I feel like my parents will support me to choose whatever I like best. I am glad that Dad works from home now, and I look forward to every Friday because my Dad and I have lunch together (usually at a pizza place). At lunch, we talk about things, I try to forget about homework, and he reminds me about homework. My mom and I don't really have a "thing" we do, but we talk a lot, which I like best when she isn't telling me to clean my room. Reesey has a tradition where she gives my mum a snow globe every Christmas, and I like that we have family traditions. Reesey is working to find herself and has a large group of friends. We both go to counsellors sometimes, which I think is good and helps. If anyone is looking for advice about adoption, I say to stick with it because it is all worth it in the end. I want to adopt when I grow up. I love my family."

Not to be left out, Reesey added: "I like bouncing on the trampoline, and I can do some cool tricks. I just started high school, and it's pretty stressful, but I'm keeping up pretty well. I like hanging out with my friends and when dad takes me driving because I can't wait for my licence. I think adoption is cool, and when I'm old, I wanna adopt. My parents are really supportive of me, and I know that they will support me in my future with whatever I choose to do."

Truly, life is about learning. Learning to push ourselves, set lofty goals, pray for the impossible and work to make dreams come true. Every step must become a lesson to help us to become refined diamonds rather than a burned-out lump of coal. Feeling gratitude for the challenge is possibly the most difficult step, but even that can be accomplished, even if it takes time. I have always been grateful for my daughters. I am also deeply grateful for the refiner's fire that finally brought them to us.

It has been over a decade since I first felt impressed to write this book. It was not easy to write; I sometimes felt triggered from some of the memories, especially when reading through the hundreds of painful and disparaging text messages. But my daughters have always been worth it. Being their mother has been more than I ever dared to hope! In the years post-adoption, I have been to counselling to learn how to heal, process the stress, trauma and secondary trauma of that time period, and learn to forgive things I once thought were unforgivable. Bruce and I also attended couples counselling to help strengthen our marriage and get us on solid ground. With all of this, we continue to grow as a family, and I feel immensely blessed. I still feel not quite at ease in Relief Society, especially when the focus is on motherhood rather than womanhood. But I do my best to support women in the choices they make for themselves. Most importantly, in investing in myself, I am checking my blood sugars regularly, and I am finally fulfilling my dream of achieving a PhD.

Perhaps that has been the best lesson I have learned: Dreams really do come true.

CHAPTER NOTES

1. Brigham Young, Journal of Discourses, Vol 4, No 52. https://journalofdiscourses.com/4/52

2. Howard W. Hunter. "The Gifts of Christmas," First Presidency Christmas Devotional, December 1994. https://www.churchofjesuschrist.org/study/ensign/2002/12/the-gifts-of-christmas?lang=eng